MORE PRAISE
CONSCIOUS DREAMING

"This is more and better than just a book about how to remember and understand dreams, although it is that kind of book and as good as any such recently published. . . . [Moss's] book excels because he extends its purview to include shamanic dreaming, dreams of dead loved ones, healing dreams, angels, and spirit guides. [His] unusual approach to a perpetually intriguing subject is likely to appeal to a wide spectrum of readers."

Booklist

"In *Conscious Dreaming*, Robert Moss expands the horizons of dream-work, helping his readers to incubate their dreams, work with their nightmares, use their dreams for healing, and determine which dreams may contain telepathic or precognitive information. The influence of Native American shamanism is apparent, but—like shamanism—Moss's approach is practical and grounded in everyday life and daily experience. The writing style of *Conscious Dreaming* is engrossing, and once captivated by the information and suggestions, Moss's readers will find the book an invitation they can hardly refuse."

Stanley Krippner, coauthor of *Dreamworking, Personal Mythology,*
and *Dream Telepathy*

"*Conscious Dreaming* offers a provocative alternative to western beliefs about dreams. Each chapter presents illuminating lessons in the shaman's art drawn from intimate study of cultures as diverse as Native American to Aboriginal Australian. Robert Moss writes beautifully about the visionary intensity of his own dream life and recounts engrossing examples from participants in his workshops to illustrate the broad range of spiritual, sensuous, compelling, magical impact that dreams can have. I recommend *Conscious Dreaming* as fascinating reading for anyone interested in dreams."

Deirdre Barrett, Ph.D., editor of *Trauma and Dreams*

CONSCIOUS DREAMING

CONSCIOUS DREAMING

A Spiritual Path for Everyday Life

ROBERT MOSS

Crown Trade Paperbacks
New York

Published by Crown Trade Paperbacks, 201 East 50th Street, New York,
New York 10022. Member of the Crown Publishing Group.

Random House, Inc. New York, Toronto, London, Sydney, Auckland

CROWN TRADE PAPERBACKS and colophon are trademarks of
Crown Publishers, Inc.

Printed in the United States of America

Designed by Rebecca Aidlin

Library of Congress Cataloging-in-Publication Data is available
upon request.

ISBN 0-517-88710-X

10 9 8 7 6 5 4 3 2

For my teachers in the
Real World and the
Shadow World,
and for all dreamers.

CONTENTS

Part Two
DREAMS OF POWER

10. THE CREATIVE POWER OF DREAMS *306*

ACKNOWLEDGMENTS

You can't just sit down and write a book of this kind; you must live it. I learned in childhood that the dream world is a real world—possibly more "real" than much of waking life—and I've been working with my personal dream journals for more than three decades. Still, it has taken me a long time to find the simplicity (and maybe the courage) to write openly about these experiences. I could not have written this book without the guidance and encouragement of many teachers and friends. Here I can honor only a few.

Among the many fellow explorers in the Association for the Study of Dreams who have fed my passion for dreamwork and my understanding of alternative approaches, I am especially grateful to Rita Dwyer, Stanley Krippner, Jeremy Taylor, Patricia Garfield and Strephon Kaplan-Williams, all generous and inspiriting teachers. Aad van Ouwerkerk helped me to realize the importance of formulating dream mottoes. The late Jessica Allen—a luminous being—showed me the possibilities of dream theater. Michael Katz introduced me to techniques of Tibetan dream yoga. Joanne Rochon opened doorways into dreaming through her art and confirmed the benefits of doing dreamwork with the events of everyday life. John Hotchin lent his scientific precision to the task of logging and evaluating precognitive dreams.

In my understanding and practice of shamanic journeying techniques—and for important personal discoveries—I am greatly indebted to Michael Harner, who has led the shamanic revival in modern society, and to Sandra Ingerman, a true doctor of souls. Ginny Black Wolf, an intrepid shamanic stalker, helped me develop the methods of tracking inside the dreamscape described in this book.

I learn more about the gifts of dreaming every week from the many adventurous spirits who attend my workshops, and from members of my Active Dream circles. Wanda Burch, one of my soul sisters, has shared in many experiments over the past decade. Lonnie and Suzanne were dream allies when I most needed them.

Stuart Krichevsky has proved himself to be a dream agent, championing and shepherding this book from delivery to publication with humor, insight, and brio. Leslie Meredith and Sherri Rifkin brought me the joy of working with *real* editors who love their work and do it supremely well.

At my house, as in any dreaming culture, we start the day by asking, "What did you dream?" The best advice on handling nightmares I ever received came from my youngest daughter, when she was just four years old. My wife and daughters share in the adventure, and help me to walk the path of soul.

My deepest debt is to my teachers inside the dream world.

This is something all *dreamers* will understand.

If you bring forth what is within you
what you bring forth will save you.
If you do not bring forth what is within you
what you do not bring forth will destroy you.

The Gospel of Thomas

The dream world is the real world.

Seneca Indian healer

Sender of true oracles
while I sleep send me your unerring skill
to read what is and will be.

Greek Magical Papyri XVIIIb

CONSCIOUS
DREAMING

Introduction

SUMMONED BY DREAMS

I do not wish to hear about the moon from someone who
has not been there.

Mark Twain

Anyone who takes the sure road is as good as dead.

C. G. Jung

CALLED BY SEA EAGLE

*M*y fascination with dreams springs from my early childhood in Australia, and that is where my exploration of the dreamworld began.

I had a strange, solitary boyhood—blighted or blessed, according to your point of view. Between the ages of two and eleven, I suffered twelve bouts of double pneumonia. After the third of these attacks, a Melbourne physician with a memorable bedside manner told my parents, "You'd better give up on this one and think about having another baby. This one is never going to make it."

But somehow "this one" seemed to keep dying and coming back. The doctors could never quite figure out why, just as they could never find a treatment for the swarm of allergies that for years made it dangerous for me to breathe normal air and then vanished overnight. Drugs had dwindling effect. The doctors eased off prescribing penicillin toward the end of these ordeals for fear my body would become completely impervious to it.

To survive, I had to learn how to breathe, even when I was drowning inside my own lungs. I had to learn how to shift attention so I could shut out sensations of physical pain. I became so good at this that shutting out the pain became another of my vulnerabilities. When I was nine, I mentioned a mild discomfort in my lower right abdomen to my father. He ran to fetch a doctor who lived nearby, knowing that there could be a serious problem since I had long since ceased to complain about pain. When the doctor came, he had me rushed to the hospital. My appendix was about to burst. The surgeon told my family that if I had arrived an hour later, I would almost certainly have died. My resistance had been weakened by yet another bout of pneumonia; the doctors did not believe my body could have withstood the shock of a ruptured appendix. But I had become so inured to shifting my awareness away from physical pain that I failed to report a cry of alarm from my body until it was almost too late.

The reward for long weeks and months spent in the half-light of sick-rooms was an interior life that was wondrously active and exciting. In dreams and dreamlike states, I traveled to other places and times. I re-lived scenes from the life of a Royal Air Force pilot, a dashing fellow who was also a member of a secretive magical order. I saw him shot down over an occupied country in World War II and killed in captivity by Nazi collaborators. I felt this RAF pilot was intimately related to me. I have been dreaming about him, off and on, for much of my life.

Other dream visitors came to me in childhood. One was a radiant young man who called himself Philemon. He first appeared to me when I was about seven. He came from the edges of the Greek world, from a community on the Syrian or Phoenician coast where the tides of several world religions washed over each other in the first centuries of the Christian era. He belonged to a Mystery school and communicated with me in the precise but difficult vocabulary of the Neoplatonists, whom I discovered in libraries only many years later. He taught me that all true knowledge is *anamnesis:* the act of remembering what the soul already knows. He fed my passion for ancient history and comparative religion, which I briefly taught at university. I never thought of him as a dead person, still less an "imaginary companion." Philemon was wholly real to me. His guidance helped me make sense of my storms of illness and eventually showed me a path to healing. He explained the meaning of the caduceus of burning bronze I saw in the sky on the eve of my last childhood battle with pneumonia.

Years later, when I discovered Jung and immersed myself in his books, I was excited to find that the great psychologist also had a vision guide called Philemon. Jung perceived his Philemon differently, as an old man with the horns of a bull on his head and the wings of a king-fisher. Jung wrote that *his* Philemon convinced him of the objective re-ality of events in the psyche. One of the labors he set himself in his last years was to build a monument to Philemon with his own hands, at his home on the lake at Bollingen.[1]

But as a small boy, I could invoke neither Jung nor the Neoplatonists to persuade the concerned but skeptical people around me that my en-counters with Philemon and other spiritlike beings were more than fever dreams and hallucinations. The isolation imposed by my crises of illness was deepened by the fact that I was both an only child and an "Army brat," sent to eight different schools, on different sides of the Australian continent, before I arrived at university. In the small society I knew in those days—predominantly WASP, highly chauvinistic, and class-conscious—nobody spoke openly about dreams. On my father's side, my family was straitlaced Scots Presbyterian, wedded to the fierce Calvinist teaching that only the elect will be saved, a matter decided before birth, and that even the elect will be damned if they fail to justify themselves through works. All show of emotion was frowned upon. Talk of dreams and spirits was immediately suspect as "Irish superstition," a charge to which my mother was keenly sensitive since on her side, we were Irish and in no way alien to the Celtic affinity for spirits—in both senses of the word! My mother's aunt Violet was a well-known psychic medium as well as an opera singer, Dame Nellie Melba's understudy and frequent companion. But Aunt Violet lived in West Australia, with the rest of my Irish relations, and most of my boyhood was spent on the East Coast, where my mother felt obliged to crush all outward signs of "Irish unreliability" under the stern gaze of the elders of the kirk.

My family, my schools, and my church all told me that dreams do not matter, that communication with spirits is unhealthy or undesirable, and that the dead do not speak to the living. Yet my childhood dreams were often more real to me than anything that took place in the schoolyard or my home. They were as real as the thrilling walk I once took through the Queensland bush, under a sunshower, when I heard the she-oaks sing and saw a sea eagle drop from the sky in a blaze of white feathers and cry out in a language I knew I could understand if I could only change my hearing.

An aching loneliness came with my inability to find friends and teachers with whom I could share my dreams safely and confirm their validity. For a few precious months, during one of my brief remissions from illness, this wall of loneliness was breached.

We were living at this time in Fortitude Valley, an inner suburb of Brisbane that has since become Chinatown and a notorious red-light district. I was six years old. In the street, after school, I ran into a slightly older boy who seemed as out of place as myself. His name was Jacko and he was an Aboriginal. He came from a broken, uprooted family. His father was in jail, and his mother was often drunk. He spent his best times with his uncle Fred, a talented artist who made a fair living painting gum trees and koalas for the tourist trade when he was not drinking. My family had the reflexively racist attitudes toward "blackfellas" that was typical of middle-class Australians then, and perhaps now. They frowned on my association with Jacko. But I would still find a pretext to spend time with my new mate, get on a tram, and head off to hunt lizard and yabbies and talk. Our best talk was about dreams.

Jacko was the first person I knew who came from a *dreaming* culture: a tradition that prizes dreams as a valuable source of guidance, encourages dream-sharing, and respects those who "dream strong." As Aboriginals tell it, the ancestors dreamed this world—that hill, this river—into being. The Dreamtime is not a story of long ago. It is a sacred space, a hidden dimension of reality into which you can travel along the paths of dreaming, if you truly know how to dream. Jacko talked matter-of-factly about all of this. He might say, "My uncle Fred went into the Dreaming and he got the idea for a painting, the kind that's not for the tourists." Or: "I had a visit from my grandma last night. She's been gone ten years or so. She told me what Mum needs to take for her sciatica."

In this down-to-earth way, I heard things my own culture had not only failed to teach me but had actively denied. I learned that through dreams, we approach our deepest creative source. That in dreams, we receive messages from the dead, messages that may be vital to our health and well-being. That in dreaming, we can journey outside our bodies; we can travel into the future as well as the past and encounter spiritual guides in other dimensions of reality.

I have not seen Jacko in forty years, except in dreams. I do not remember what tribe he belonged to, if indeed he told me. But he lives in my heart and memory as the first dream teacher I encountered in ordinary reality. When my own community was telling me to forget about dreaming, in essence Jacko was saying: *Just do it!*

I have spent most of my adult life outside my native Australia, in Europe and North America, and have been on safaris to other places. Most of what little I know about Aboriginal dream practices comes from books, especially the work of two great Australian ethnographers, A. P. Elkin and R. M. Berndt, and the beautiful, evocative writings of James Cowan. Yet, if only by osmosis, something of the native Dreaming of

Australia seems to live in me. The possible depth of this influence came home to me, through a series of powerful dreams, as I was preparing to write this book.

In each of these dreams, a messenger came to me in the guise of a sea eagle. This magnificent aquatic raptor, native to the northern coast of Australia, has flown with me in dreams for as long as I can remember. I learned only recently that among the islanders of the Torres Straits, off the northern tip of Queensland, the sea eagle is often the companion spirit—the power animal—of the *zogo le,* or shaman.[2]

When I returned, after many false turnings, to my boyhood awareness of what dreaming can mean and began to practice and teach dreamwork and shamanic techniques, it seemed natural to me to paint a sea eagle on my first deerskin drum. In the image on my drum, the sea eagle lifts his wings in a splendid arc, white feathers shining over the black plumage below. His intent yellow eye dissolves distance. In his talons, he grasps a lively green-yellow snake, raising the serpent energy to a higher plane.

This is my favorite drum. It can pulse soft and gentle as a mother's heartbeat. It can roll like thunder. In my workshops, I use it to help people release their everyday inhibitions and journey in nonordinary reality in search of adventure and spiritual allies. We use drumming as a doorway into the Dreaming. Winged by the drum, dreamers reenter their dreamscapes or discover new ones. They bring back messages. They resolve conflicts. They see round the corner. And within the circle, riding the drum, they enter each other's dreamspace. The experiences that flow from this are powerful and moving. Sometimes they are life-transforming. They suggest that we are all related, and that our identity and consciousness are not bound to the physical body or to time and space.

In my dreams, I have often flown on sea eagle's wings. In my workshops, he helps to wing others.

Yet when sea eagle swooped down on me in a violent, disturbing dream in the fall of 1993, I did not know what he was trying to tell me.

This dream was vividly real. It was one of those experiences that are less "dreamlike" than hyperreal: in which colors seem brighter than in the daylight world, in which all the inner senses are aroused and intensely alive.

The dream began as a rehearsal for a situation in everyday life. In the first scene, I was trying to conduct a workshop in a lecture theater where the seats were bolted down and set in rows at a steep angle. I was frustrated because I like to arrange people informally, in a circle, so that everybody can spread out and nobody is set above the rest of the group.

Then the dream locale shifted abruptly. I entered a dream within the dream with an entirely different quality from the rather humdrum dream that framed it.

Now I was on a beach, wearing my Australian hat. I spotted a blur of white feathers against the sun. In the next instant, a huge bird dived straight at my head. He sank his talons into my hat, apparently bent on carrying it off. I saw the bird's yellow eye, close to my own, the black curve of his beak, and the gloss of his ruff, as we struggled together on the sand. He hooked his talons into my hand, and I felt a stab of pain. I got out my pocketknife, to defend myself. But I was anxious not to harm him, because I recognized him. He was a sea eagle and I knew, inside the dream, that we were intimately connected. Yet I refused to surrender my hat.

After this skirmish on the beach, I moved back into the earlier dream and reported on my struggle with the sea eagle to the people gathered in the lecture theater.

I woke excited but confused. I felt this dream contained an urgent message, but its most important content was obscure.

It was easy to deal with the rehearsal element. I guessed that the scene in the lecture theater might be a preview of a workshop I had been invited to conduct at the world conference of the Association for the Study of Dreams in Leiden. I called Rita Dwyer, a friend in ASD, and asked her to request a space where I could arrange workshop participants in a circle. As it turned out, this was a helpful precaution. The room originally assigned to my Leiden workshop was a forbidding space, a formal lecture theater very much like the one in the dream.

I remained puzzled by the struggle on the beach. Why did sea eagle want my Australian hat? Was he trying to strip me of some aspect of my identity—my Australian roots—or recall me to it?

I felt sure that if the message was truly important, sea eagle would come again.

He returned two weeks later, this time as an unambiguous ally. In a conscious dream, in the twilight zone between sleep and waking, I allowed him to place a metal circlet around my head. It looked like a simple band of iron. But once he had placed it on my head, it blazed with light, like a rayed crown. He perched on my left shoulder, and other birds joined us—a redtail hawk, a swarm of hummingbirds.

I felt an urgent tug and found myself airborne. I experienced momentary unease when I realized I was out of my body. I could see my inert form below me on the bed. I resolved to go with the flow. Soon I could see the great bends of the Mississippi, the sawtooth crests of the Rocky Mountains. The Pacific swells flickered and vanished, far below.

I was drawn down, into a coastal town where apartment blocks fronted a long white beach like upended ice-cube trays. I saw the bright spray of bougainvillea against red-brick walls and realized I was now entering the retirement community to which my mother had moved after my father's death. My mother and I had had a mixed relationship. Though we had shared powerful spiritual experiences after my father's death, we had recently had disagreements that reopened old wounds. Now, in the dream when I entered my mother's apartment, we enjoyed a loving reunion that laid our misunderstandings to rest.

At this point, still conscious I was dreaming, I wanted to come back to ordinary reality. I felt a strong desire to call my mother in Southport, Queensland, and check on her. I wanted to make our dream reunion come true.

But sea eagle was not yet finished with me. I experienced another peremptory tug and found myself journeying through rain forest, deep into the hinterland of Queensland's Gold Coast.

Another creature from my childhood dreams was waiting for me: a water buffalo. He brushed my face with his horns and guided me to a muddy creek. As I looked around, I saw I was standing among Aboriginal elders. They had painted themselves with circle designs for a sacred ceremony.

The mud below us was being churned by something enormous I could not identify. It seemed to be half-snake, half-fish.

I turned to the Aboriginal elder who stood closest to me, seeking guidance. He told me, "This is the way it began, with a struggle in the mud. This is the first of all creatures. This is the beginning of our world."

I woke with those beautifully cadenced, mysterious words echoing through my mind.

This new dream of sea eagle contained a mystery deeper than the first. The part I could understand clearly called for immediate action. I telephoned my mother and we had a long, loving conversation in which we were able to mend our fences, as in the dream. I soon had reason to be deeply grateful for the dream summons that brought about this reunion.

Three months after this dream, my mother died suddenly. It is a terrible thing when we part from close relatives without having had a chance to rise above the inevitable conflicts and resentments of family life and have a true meeting of hearts and souls. When that happens, unfinished business will haunt us, sometimes in the most literal sense. My summons from sea eagle ensured that though we were separated by great distance, my mother and I were not divided in spirit.

But a mystery remained in the shape of the thing "half-fish, half-snake" I had seen writhing in the muddy creek. It was a mystery I was unable to penetrate until events in waking life caught up with the dream.

I flew back to Australia for my mother's funeral, at which I spoke of dream messages from my father from which both of us had benefited greatly after his death seven years before. When I laid a beautiful white stone at my mother's resting place within a rose garden, I recognized a scene from another dream, now a year old.

After dealing with family business and some of the grieving, I decided to take a few days for myself and do something quintessentially Australian: to go walkabout and rediscover something of my native earth.

Through a series of seeming accidents and coincidences, I wound up in a dusty town in southeast Queensland called Beaudesert. Someone told me there was an Aboriginal housing co-op in the town, and I decided to drop in and see what evolved. I was received by a hearty rugby player who told me, as soon as I mentioned dreams, that I needed to talk to Frank, who was reputed to be a "spirit man." Where was Frank?

"Oh, he'll be out at his shack in the hills." It would take a couple of days of hard bush walking, I was told, to get up there.

But shamans are tricky people. Two minutes later, as if drawn by his name, Frank walked into the office. He was a heavy man, with strong, flattened features and dark eyes that turned amber with the light.

Frank was guarded at the start of our conversation. We spent an hour or two sniffing each other out, while he sipped orange juice in a pub and his boy worked the poker machines. Then I told him my dream about the thing in the mud and the painted elder who told me this was how the world began.

The atmosphere around the table was transformed. Frank's eyes glowed. He said with quiet intensity, "I reckon you've been sent to us for a reason. You've just told me the start of our secret Creation story. What you saw is the bull eel. In the Mununjalli tribe, we say it is the first of all creatures."

I learned some Aboriginal cosmology that day, because of my dream. I was also invited to sit with elders and spirit men of several Eastern tribes. I was led by a guide on a long trek, skirting quicksand, to a place Frank held sacred. He claimed he had once seen a bull eel the length of a telegraph pole in a waterhole along this creek. It was the place from my dream.

In Western society, one needs different credentials in different circumstances: a license to drive a car, a higher degree for academic tenure, certification to practice as a psychiatrist or social worker. In a dreaming culture, when the tradition is alive, the most important qualification is to have the right dream.

In this book, I'll help you to identify and work with your own "right dreams" and the worlds of possibility they can open for you. The gifts of dreaming may come through spontaneous sleep dreams, through creative incubation (when you ask for dream guidance on a theme), through conscious dreaming in the twilight zone between sleep and waking, or through shamanic soul journeys to other worlds or other times. All these doors are open to you *now*. The keys are offered in this book.

My methods have been influenced by teachers of many traditions, who have often introduced themselves in unexpected ways. Every time I have come in contact with indigenous peoples, in the course of my wide travels, I have found myself reawakening to ways of seeing and dreaming that were shared by all our ancestors. My encounters with the Iroquois Indians of northeast America have been especially important in my practice and teaching of dreamwork. I have found their ancient shamanic approach to dreaming a powerful tool for unlocking the energy and insight of dreams today.

FOLLOWING RIGHT DREAMS
AND BIG DREAMS

*A*mong Native Americans, whose cultures also value dreaming, a shaman is widely described as "one who dreams." In the Mohawk language, the word is *ratetshents,* which simply means "dreamer." The Kagwahiv, an Amazonian people, say that "anyone who dreams is a little bit shaman."[3]

I knew very little about American Indians and almost nothing about the Iroquois when I moved to a farm in upstate New York in the mid-1980s. I had spent ten years jumping on and off airplanes as a foreign correspondent based in London, and another five on the commercial fast track in New York, following the popular success of a thriller that was published by Crown in 1980. It was time to slow down, put down some roots, and discover where I was meant to be going, as a writer and a human being.

I foraged up the Hudson Valley and found a run-down farmhouse secluded from the outside world among rolling cow pastures and virgin woods. The graveyard of the original Dutch settlers was on the hill behind the barns. The borning room where they had delivered both calves and babies seemed like an auspicious place to labor on new books.

Then I started dreaming in the Mohawk language, and everything changed.

I dreamed of an elderly Indian woman who was both a clanmother and a powerful healer. In the first of these dreams—fully conscious I was dreaming—I found myself flying on the wings of a redtail hawk. The sensations of flight were intensely real. I reveled in the lift of a thermal and was shaken when a flight error made me scrape my side against a spruce on a hill near Lake George. I was drawn to a lodge where the clanmother spoke to me for what seemed like hours in a lilting, musical voice. As she talked, she displayed several strings of white and purple wampum beads, and later a large wampum belt with human and animal figures. I understood that this belt was a symbol of her authority. But I had only a general sense of her message, because she insisted on communicating in her own language.

The next morning, as I walked my dogs, a redtail hawk swooped over the brow of the hill and circled ten feet above my head, screeching insistently. I felt—as I had felt with the sea eagle that had come to me as a boy—that I could understand it if I could only change my hearing.

The old Indian woman returned in a succession of dreams. So did two other dream characters who seemed to be related to her. One was a warrior shaman who first showed himself in a wooden fright-mask with eyepieces of polished brass. He was an ambiguous, troubling figure, a sorcerer who could use his powers to kill as well as to heal, to steal souls as well as restore them.

The third of my new dream acquaintances intrigued me most of all. When he first appeared, I was uncertain whether I was watching myself, dressed up in eighteenth-century finery for a stage performance, or a separate personality from the colonial era. I had a notion who that other personality might be. Through a chance discovery in the Bryn Mawr bookstore in Albany, New York, I had just been introduced to one of the most colorful characters from the first American frontier: Sir William Johnson, an Irishman with a passion for life in all its aspects, who flourished in the 1700s as both King's Superintendent of Indians, an adopted Mohawk warchief, and a redoubtable ladies' man. Johnson's name was omitted from the history books I had studied in Australia and England. But as soon as I heard his voice, echoing through the dusty pages of one of the fat, blue-bound volumes of his collected papers, I sensed I had found a kindred spirit. My dreams deepened this sense. In later, conscious dreams—when I had embarked upon a fictional account of his exploits—Johnson appeared as a distinct personality and tutored me at length on his life, loves, and Indian intrigues.

My dreams at the farm had given me a new cast of characters. There was clearly a story to be told here, very different from the stories I had been telling in my previous books, and the storyteller in me leaped at the prospect. The Australian Aborigines say that the big stories lie in wait for the right people to tell them. I felt, in a similar way, that I had not found my new story; it had found me. I had no idea what the finished shape of this story would be. I did not know that it would radically rescript the story of my life.

I set off into Iroquois Indian country, to unlock the meaning of my dreams and locate my dream characters in their native settings. With the help of Mohawk speakers on the Six Nations reserve, near Brantford, Ontario, and at Kahnawake, near Montreal, I learned to decode some of the phrases from the old Indian woman that I had jotted down phonetically. Though Mohawks recognized some of her words, she used expressions they found archaic and obscure. A medicine man suggested that the mystery words might be Huron, and indeed I later found some of them in early Jesuit missionary reports from Huron country. I learned to call the old woman Aksotha—which means "grandmother" in Mohawk—and to describe her as a *ka'nistenhsera,* or clanmother, and an *arendiwanen,* or "woman of power." An Onondaga friend showed me an ancient wampum belt that depicted a she-wolf suckling human figures and told me that such belts were traditionally badges of authority for Iroquois clanmothers. This wampum belt was similar to the one I had seen in my first dream of the clanmother.

I described my recent dream encounters to a native elder, who said matter-of-factly, "I guess you had some visits." He counseled me not to talk in public about the names and details of some medicine rituals that are traditionally kept secret but had come to me in dreams. He told me, "Some of the great ones stay close to the earth, to defend the land and our people." He allowed that some of these beings might speak to outsiders in dreams and visions, "if you dream true."

I learned that the traditional Iroquois are a people of dreams. Long before the first European set foot on American soil, the Iroquois taught their children that dreams are the most important source of guidance, both practical and spiritual, that we can draw on in life. The first business of the day in an Iroquois village was dream-sharing. A strong dreamer—a *ratetshents*—would be consulted on the meaning of obscure or troubling dreams. The whole community would often become involved in dreamwork, especially if a dream seemed to contain a warning of death or disease. The Iroquois believed that important dreams call for *action.* If we can see the future in dreams, for example, we may be able to alter it. But this will require specific actions and rituals designed to avoid an unwanted dream event, or to fulfill a desirable one. In their dreamcraft, the Iroquois made a whole science of shamanic and ritual techniques to confirm precognitive dream messages and enact or avert their consequences.[4]

The traditional Iroquois approach to dreams is radically different from the one that has prevailed—at least until recently—in modern Western society. The Iroquois teach that "big" dreams come about in one of two ways. During sleep, the dreaming mind is released from the body and from the limitations of place and time. The dreamsoul can now range far and wide, into the future or the past, to places at a great distance from the sleeper's body, and into hidden dimensions of reality, where it may encounter spirit guides and ancestors. Alternatively, the dreamer may receive a visit from a spiritual being, who may assume almost any form—that of a departed relative, a bird or animal, a godlike being, or even an extraterrestrial.

In the Iroquois view, in other words, "big" dreams come about either because we have an out-of-body experience during sleep (which is seen as entirely natural, and likely to happen to almost anyone on any given night, whether or not they remember) or because we receive an interesting dream visitor, who may be another dreamer traveling outside the body or may come from dimensions of reality beyond the physical plane.[5]

A "big" dream is distinguished by its content as well as its origin. It may contain information of vital importance to the dreamer's health or physical survival. It may introduce spiritual guides and allies and recall the dreamer to his or her true life purpose.

For the Iroquois, dreams are central to healing. Dreams are "wishes of the soul." They put us in touch with our deepest spiritual source, and what it desires for us. If we refuse to honor this source, we will lose soul energy and our spiritual protectors may abandon us in disgust, leaving us vulnerable to illness and misfortune. Dreams provide insight into the causes of illness, which is often related to soul-loss or the intrusion of negative energies, including psychic attack and the influence of the unquiet dead. Dreams reveal the psychospiritual causes of disease before physical symptoms develop.

For a traditional healer, dreams are vital tools in diagnosis and treatment. I met an Iroquois healer who likes to take a personal item from his client—usually a piece of clothing—and place it under his pillow when he goes to bed. He says this helps him maintain his focus on his client during the night so he can dream the nature of the complaint and the necessary mode of treatment. In his dreams, he is often advised by his dead grandmother—once renowned as an herbalist—or by the Bear, the animal most strongly associated with healing among the Woodland Indians.

My researches were leading me in many unexpected directions, on and off Indian reservations. I acquired all seventy-three volumes of the *Jesuit Relations,* which contain remarkable accounts of the dream spirituality of the Iroquois at the time of first contact with Europeans; for more than a year, this was my favorite reading. I studied with Tom Porter, a Mohawk spiritual leader whose visions soon led him to lead a band of his people from the Akwesasne reservation back to the Mohawk Valley of their ancestors to live in a spiritual community and revive the old ways. A Cayuga medicine man shared his techniques for relocating lost souls. A Chippewa shaman painted maps for me of the paths and gateways she uses in journeying to the spirit worlds.

But my principal teachers—as at the beginning—were in the dream-world itself. My dreamlife was becoming extraordinarily active and profuse. In many dreams, I was not only fully conscious but aware that I seemed to be journeying outside my body. I received many more dream visitors, including departed members of my family. After my father's death in November 1987, he appeared to me repeatedly in dreams, often to relay specific messages to my mother containing information of great practical value that was previously unknown to either of us.

This rush of inner experience was almost overwhelming. It had long been my practice to start the day, at the family breakfast table, by sharing dreams, and I was fortunate to have a small circle of friends around the world with whom I had shared dreams informally for many years. New friends in upstate New York shared my resurgent passion for dreamwork and encouraged and steadied me in my explorations.

But there were storms blowing up within me that I was unable or unwilling to discuss with anyone. In dreamlike states, I battled with sorcerers—especially the fellow in the fright-mask—and malevolent ghosts and my own shadow self. In waking life, I was now deeply divided, profoundly disaffected from previous ambitions and definitions of success.

I read everything I could find that might give me a handle on what was happening to me, from Stan Grof's work on spiritual emergency to Robert Monroe's *Journeys out of the Body.* In Joan Halifax's splendid anthology, *Shamanic Voices,* and in Mircea Eliade's classic *Shamanism* I found accounts of shamanic initiation that seemed amazingly familiar. These reassured me that if I was going crazy, I was going in interesting company. I read Michael Harner's book, *The Way of the Shaman,* and found much of his territory familiar, too. Then I heard that Harner was leading a workshop in my neighborhood, on top of a quartz mountain at the edge of the Berkshires.

This was my first sustained exposure to the core techniques of shamanic journeying that Michael Harner has made accessible to thousands of contemporary Westerners. Michael is an anthropologist who "broke the glass" after doing fieldwork among the Jivaro Indians, becoming a shamanic practitioner and a vigorous leader of the current shamanic revival in our society. I knew that the use of monotonous shamanic drumming to facilitate a shift in consciousness was central to his approach. I had long been aware of the power of percussion to induce trancelike states; I first heard a Celtic bodhran when I was three years old, and Aboriginal clicksticks not long after, and I had danced all night to the *batá* drums in *candomble* and *umbanda* ceremonies during several visits to Brazil. However, I came to Michael's workshop with certain misgivings. I doubted whether techniques traditionally held secret within shamanic lineages and magical orders could or should be imparted to anyone with the time and loose change to spend a weekend at a holistic retreat. I felt such gifts should be reserved for those who have undergone initiatory trials and proven their calling, perhaps by dreaming the right dream.

The power of my personal experiences in Harner's workshop overwhelmed my resistance. One of these experiences—an Upper World journey, powered by the drum—marked a watershed in my sense of purpose and possibility, so I will share it briefly here.

Rising from the upper branches of a tree, I journeyed through cloudlike membranes to explore many successive dimensions of the Upper World. Some appeared to be deserted, or peopled with entities that had nothing to communicate to me. At several points, my passage was opposed by threatening gatekeepers I had to outflank, pacify, or overcome.

I saw many forms of the Goddess, and other figures familiar to me from dreams or mythology—which (as Joseph Campbell observed) is composed of collectivized dreams.

To rise beyond a certain level, I had to change form. I became the lightning. At the highest level, I came face-to-face with a whole pantheon of figures from many religious traditions. Beyond them, behind them, projecting them from its own center, was an immense being of Light. To look at it directly was like staring at the sun, into the darkness at the heart of Light.

I flew with winged beings over beautiful green valleys, resembling those of our world but completely unspoiled—landscapes fresh as the first dawn.

When Michael's drum sounded the recall, I did not want to come back. Finally, I saw my own body carried back—a lifeless corpse—in the talons of an immense eagle, a Storm Bird big enough to shadow mountains.

When I opened my eyes, I found a little group had gathered around me, looking worried. I was told I had been "gone" for twelve minutes longer than the other people in the circle. "We were getting worried you'd checked out," one woman reported. "You didn't seem to be breathing and we couldn't find a pulse. You looked like you were dead."

I tried to shrug this off, joking that I had been prone to "checking out" of ordinary reality since childhood. But that journey stayed with me and lives with me still. It gave me personal insight into the One behind the many masks of God, and a glimpse of paths and territories in nonordinary reality I might be able to visit again.

Despite my banter at the workshop, I felt I had died and come back in some quite literal sense, just as I had done in my childhood illnesses—with the vital difference that this time the experience was *intentional.* I reflected that if I had been a Native American, I might have changed my name at this time to honor an experience that had so profoundly affected my sense of identity.

With the ardor of a new convert, I rushed to put my discoveries in a book very different not only from my thrillers but from the historical novel with an "Indian side" that I had embarked on when I started dreaming about Sir William Johnson. This book was based on my encounters—through the dream-gate—with several people from an earlier time, including the Iroquois shaman who first appeared as an antagonist but became my ally after many inner battles. I had the odd feeling that this *dreamer* from long ago was tracking forward through time, seeking information that could help his people in a brutal struggle for survival. But I lacked the objectivity to present these visionary encounters en clair. I tried to mask my experiences as fiction; the result was a curious mélange of history, dream reports, and speculation about doppel-gängers, time travel, and parallel universes. One of my publishing friends commented, "Some people who read this will follow you to the moon. Others will think you've gone bananas."

I decided to put that manuscript in a drawer and forget it for a few years. There remained the small problem of earning a living. I had had the luxury of following my dreams for several years without collecting a regular paycheck; now the bills were piling up. My advisers in publishing urged me to go back to writing thrillers, and the side of me that worries about the mortgage and the school bills told me they were right. *Make good money now,* it hissed, *and you can follow the path of soul later on.*

The problem was that the new me wasn't interested in playing the old games. And my dream source kept tugging me in a very different direction. For example, I decided that one way to pay my bills might be to crank out another thriller with a Russian theme to cash in on the success of my previous best-seller *Moscow Rules.* But every time I tried to rough out a proposal, my creative juices seemed to dry up. So I decided to ask my dream source for some ideas. This is the dream that came:

The Master Chef Is on Strike

> *I am in a banquet hall. The tables are laid for hundreds of people, with opulent settings, bone china, and sterling silver. This looks quite promising. However, I am told there is a problem in the kitchen. The manager explains to me that the master chef walked out in disgust when he read my menu. The master chef refuses to cook any more Stroganoff. If I insist on serving this Russian dish, we will have to hire inferior cooks out in the street.*

This was not the dream I had asked for, but I am certain now that it was the dream I needed. I could not dismiss the message, since I had incubated this dream, even writing my request for guidance on the pad by my bedside table. And what exactly *was* the message? In my dreams, the kitchen—the place where things are "cooked up"—is often a metaphor for my creative center. I felt that the master chef, in my incubated dream, represented the most creative part of me. By rejecting my menu, my creative source was making it unambiguously plain that it refused to collaborate with my commercial plans.

I dropped my "Russian" project and immersed myself in new research into dreams and shamanism, wrote a few articles for adventurous journals, and devoted several hours a day to working with my personal journals and sharing dreams with others. But a publishable book still seemed a long way off, so I forced myself to write a forgettable thriller—with my dream source protesting every inch of the way—and sat down to produce yet another. This time, my dreams definitively called a halt to my foolishness and showed me the path I must take. I again asked for dream guidance and was again reminded that the dream source has a deeper agenda than that of the little everyday mind:

Requickening

I am trying to drive through chewed-up streets, partially blocked by construction work. I come to a chute like a storm drain, leading upward. I try to shinny up, but there are no handholds and I keep slipping down. A companion I hadn't noticed before flies up effortlessly and reaches back to help me up. He looks a lot like me, only fitter and stronger.

Now I am in a forest clearing. Through the trees, I see something up on stilts that looks a bit like a gigantic coffeepot. Maybe that's where I will get guidance for the new potboiler. Conscious I am dreaming, I start walking toward it.

But something pulls me, gently but firmly, in the opposite direction. I know I have the power to choose, but I submit to this force. I am drawn backward. I find myself in a circle of native people who live close to the earth. I am uneasy that I may appear to be intruding. But they welcome me as one they have long been expecting. They have a place prepared for me in their circle.

When the fire becomes friendly, I lie in the midst of the circle. The people lay burning coals on my eyes, my ears, my tongue, and over my heart. They explain they are doing this so I will be able to see, hear, and speak clearly. They tell me, "We are opening the passage from your heart to your mouth so that henceforth you will speak only from the heart."

I woke fired up with energy and excitement. The first part of the dream seemed clear to me. I should give up on the new potboiler—evoked by the glimpse of the giant coffeepot—and go in a completely different direction. The second part of the dream left an indelible impression of what that direction entailed. The word spoken over me resembled the "rare words of requickening" in an Iroquois Condolence Council.

Once again, I abandoned a narrowly conceived commercial project because of a dream.

But this time, the dream helped me to move decisively in a more creative direction. My novel *The Firekeeper,* which describes the shamanic dream practices of a lineage of Iroquois women healers as well as the life and passions of my dream character Sir William Johnson, flowed directly from this dream.

The dream of requickening had a larger influence on my life. I recognized the clogged and broken roads in the early scene; my life had been full of false turnings and detours and self-obstruction and fallings from the way. Walking in soft rain by a lake in the woods, still feeling the warmth of the glowing coal the dream people had placed over my heart, I knew the time had come to make a personal and unconditional commitment. I repeated their words to the lake and the trees and the hawk that came knifing through the clouds: "Henceforth, I will speak only from the heart." I felt a tingling sensation all over my body. Truth comes with goose bumps.

Since that time, dreams have assumed ever-increasing importance in my life. To me, they are an inner authority, a creative touchstone in all things, uniting seemingly disparate matters: from career choice to the most basic economic and financial decisions that life requires of us, from the most mundane questions of being and doing, getting and spending—which they enliven and vest with new significance—to the most spiritual questions of higher purpose and self-understanding. They have brought vitality and excitement into my inner and outer life, forging the two spheres into the truth of a path with heart, the only path to walk.

HOUSE OF DREAMS

*M*y change of heart was accompanied by a change of house, both literal and metaphorical. This, too, was steered by dreams.

The first time I heard of Troy, New York, was in a dream I did not immediately understand. In this dream, I was enjoying a lavish black-tie dinner in a rather English country house. An elderly woman—not one of the diners—kept bobbing up behind my seat, trying to get my attention. I was ignoring her because she was uneducated and seemed rather simple. She appealed to one of the male diners to intervene on her behalf. After this, I listened to her for a bit, but was put off by the way she expressed herself. For example, she told me, "When you were six years old, they sent a UFO just for you. They put a beam through your body." This sounded like supermarket tabloid stuff, and I indicated I was not interested. But the woman persisted. She told me I should check with a friend called Wanda. "Ask her about Millie." And she told me repeatedly, "Troy will be very important in your life."

Since I was reared on Homer and tales of the Trojan War, it never occurred to me that the woman in my dream might be talking about Troy, New York. I did remember to check with Wanda Burch, a fellow dream explorer who had become a close friend. She told me she had vivid memories of a psychic called Millie Coutant, a woman of limited education from the Saratoga area who had passed on several years before. Wanda had kept tapes of several psychic readings Millie had conducted, including one at the former home of my dream acquaintance Sir William Johnson. When I listened to these tapes, I realized I was hearing the voice of the woman in my dream. Though it was likely that a local woman like Millie would mean Troy, New York, instead of Homer's Ilion when she said "Troy," I only made the connection in the light of two subsequent events.

When my wife, Marcia, became pregnant the following spring, a friend's recommendation led her to a progressive clinic in Troy, where I later attended Lamaze classes. My daughter Sophie—who announced her name to my wife in a dream when she was five months pregnant—was born at Samaritan Hospital in Troy that December.

Before Sophie was born, I started dreaming of a house that was not my own. Dream houses are often richly symbolic, hinting at what may be buried in the basements of the psyche, offering treasure chambers of possibility, warning of possible problems with the dreamer's wiring or plumbing. But these particular house dreams were highly specific. I looked through French doors into a dining room with flowered wallpaper. I mended a stone wall behind the house and relaxed on a freestone terrace. I explored the creek on the border of the property. These images—coming in a dozen recorded dreams—made me intensely curious, and somewhat restless. They coincided with the feeling that, after spending several years in relative isolation at the farm, it was time to come back into a community and contribute to other people something of what I had learned.

The house dreams were paralleled by a second series of dreams that I found more troubling. In one of these dreams, I watched surveyors drawing a line across the farm. I was relaxed when I woke, but I became uneasy as I tried to figure out what was going on in the dream. Was it possible the government would try to seize some of my land, citing eminent domain, in order to widen the highway? Did the apparent division of property herald divorce? My unease increased when I dreamed our family attorney was representing the other side in a legal matter, sitting across the table from me with his female client.

As so often happens with dreams that foreshadow future events, I had limited understanding of these two series of dreams before they started to be enacted in waking life.

Driving along Route 2 through the outskirts of Troy, I noticed a beautiful house set high on a hill. I did not know it was my dream house when I glimpsed it from the road, and there was no indication that the house might be available. But I was sufficiently intrigued to call a realtor. I told him that he should phone me if the house ever came on the market. Nine months later—the term of an average pregnancy—the realtor called to tell me the house was now for sale. As soon as I drove up behind the house and saw the freestone terrace and the stone wall behind, I knew I had found my dream house.

The purchase and the sale of the farm both came together in a dream-like way in the space of forty-eight hours that same week. I was determined not to sell the farm to a developer who might subdivide it, disrupting the natural wildlife sanctuary we had created. I was blessed to find an immediate buyer who loved the land and the oak; she planned to breed Arabians. There was one complication. She would need considerable time to find a buyer for her own place in Westchester County. The realtor came up with a solution. Why not make a paper subdivision of the property, allowing the purchaser to buy half the land now, the rest later?

The upshot was another case of dream fulfillment. Driving south along Route 66, on the edge of my property, I noticed surveyors plotting a line across the farm—and realized I had entered a scene from a dream that had come before I had even contemplated selling the farm. Then my local realtor, Frances Schools, called with an unusual request. "You're leaving the immediate neighborhood," Frances reminded me. "And you know plenty of lawyers. Pat's new to the area and could use a friendly lawyer she can trust. Why don't you let her have your attorney?" So I parted with my family attorney—and walked into another dream when I arrived for the closing to find my family attorney seated across the table from me with his new client.

There were complications with bankers and financiers along the way, and further dreams counseled me, quite specifically, on whom to trust and where to go for the critical loan. The cumulative effect of all these correspondences between dreams and waking events during the house move was a strong sense that this was "meant" to be. As I watched the synchronicities multiply, I often had the sense of a friendly hand on my shoulder, nudging me to go straight ahead or bear left.

Now I recalled Millie's insistence that Troy would be important in my life. My downstate friends, already puzzled by my withdrawal to a rural farm, were utterly perplexed by my move to Troy. At the turn of the century, Troy was the most affluent city, per capita, in the United States. But its iron foundries and shirt factories were long gone, along with the fortunes of the merchant princes who had put up its splendid public buildings, elegant row houses, and stately manses up on the hill.

Troy could still boast three colleges, a world-renowned music hall, and some of the best restaurants north of Manhattan, but its reputation was not that of a leafy college town. The older generation remembered the painted ladies in its long-gone battery of bordellos and honky-tonks, guarded by off-duty cops. Downtown was languishing, the library was threatened with closure, city hall was mortgaged, and the Democratic machine boss who had once ruled the roost was on his way to jail for graft.

Why had my dreams brought me here? Surely not just for the beautiful house on the hill. A new dream suggested the answer:

Patricia Garfield Moves to Troy

I read in the paper that Patricia Garfield has moved to my neighborhood and is conducting a series of dream workshops. There is tremendous excitement over these workshops. People are surprised and flattered that a famous author is doing this work in Troy. The most interesting thing about her workshops is that she is helping ordinary people to bring dreamwork to where they live.

At that time, I had not yet met Patricia Garfield. But I had read her wonderful book *Creative Dreaming* back in the 1970s, when it was first published, and I had been enormously impressed by how she managed to make techniques from many cultures accessible to ordinary people. I recounted my dream to a friend over lunch. "The dream is about you," she told me point-blank. "You're the famous author who moved to Troy. You're the one who's going to hold these dream workshops."

By dreamwork standards, this was of course a breach of etiquette, which demands—as Jeremy Taylor and Montague Ullman wisely insist—that if you are going to comment on another person's dream, you must begin by saying, "If it were my dream . . ." That way, you avoid the appearance of passing judgment, or of setting yourself up as any kind of expert.

But we did not stand on ceremony over lunch. I knew my friend, a prolific dreamer and a highly intuitive woman, was absolutely right. Maybe I had been drawn to Troy to do what Patricia Garfield was doing in my dream: to meet the challenge of adapting what I had practiced and shared in in private gatherings to the lives of mainstream people trying to hold on to the job, find the right partner, pay the rent, and get their kids through school. There had been moments, in previous years, when I had considered transplanting myself to San Francisco or Santa Fe, both cities I love that are full of adventurers in consciousness. I was thrilled by the challenge that now presented itself at my new front door, in a gritty rust-belt community: to bring dreamwork and shamanism to where most people live.

Synchronistically, that same week I received a call from an acquaintance at RCCA, a regional arts center located in downtown Troy. She wanted to know if I would be interested in teaching some programs at the center. "Sure," I told her. "I'll teach people what I've learned about dreams."

Though I now conduct programs for active dreamers all over the world, I still cherish the opportunity to work on an ongoing basis with people from all walks of life in my immediate neighborhood. At various centers in upstate New York, including the Omega Institute, the consultation center at the Catholic diocese, Blue White Rainbow—my favorite New Age store—and the arts center in Troy, I lead workshops for programmers and visual artists, business executives and therapists, Goddess followers and Catholic nuns.

This book flows from what I have learned from the dream explorers who come to these workshops. Often they are drawn to these classes by a numinous dream of shamanic quality. They come with the big questions: Who am I? Where am I going? Is there a deeper purpose to my life? What would be the consequences of changing my job, my partner, my attitudes? What happens when I die? Can I heal myself? Am I ready to be healed?

Dreams give us the answers if we attend to them, because they come from a source that is deeper and wiser than the everyday waking mind. To attend means more than to listen; to attend, literally, is to "stretch" yourself. To work fully with our dream source, we are required to stretch our understanding, to go beyond familiar maps. The best guide in these territories is likely to be a seasoned traveler, a frequent flier.

THE ONLY DREAM EXPERT

*T*here are many approaches to dreams, and all have some validity since dreams are multilayered and people dream in many different ways.

In working with dreams, it is experience, not theory, that matters. Whenever a theory ossifies into a set of rules and prescriptions that denies fresh experience or tries to make it conform to old ideas, it is time for that theory to be cast aside.

In this respect, the story of Freud and his school is a cautionary tale. At the beginning of this century, Sigmund Freud performed an immense service by insisting on the importance of dreams—"the royal road to the unconscious"—in a society that generally denigrated dreams and dreamwork. But Freud and the Freudians came to elevate hypotheses about the functions and meaning of dreams into dogmas. The Freudian approach associated dreams with illness rather than wellness, denied soul, and reserved dream interpretation for a well-paid clerisy who alone were held competent to decode the "latent content" of dreams. This approach is inherently authoritarian. It usurps the dreamer's authority over his or her experience. It says, in effect: You are not the expert on your own dreams. Freud and his school actually presumed to tell us what to look for and what *not* to look for in our dreams. Freud's attachment to his own theory became so self-blinding that he burned his personal journals when he found that his dreams dared to challenge his opinions about what dreams mean.

I like what Carl Jung said about dream theories: "I have no theory about dreams. I do not know how dreams arise. On the other hand, I know that if we meditate on a dream sufficiently long and thoroughly— if we take it about with us and turn it over and over—something almost always comes out of it."[6]

You will not find a theory of dreams in this book. Instead, you will find exercises and travel reports designed to help and encourage you to explore your dreams and to manifest the energy and insight of your dreams in daily life. The travel reports are culled from the many thousands of dreams I have recorded in my personal logs, and from thousands more that have been shared with me in workshops and private sessions. The exercises are those I have found most effective in working with my own dreams and in leading dream workshops. These exercises combine recognized modern dreamwork techniques with ancient shamanic practices, such as the use of drumming to put the dreamer back inside the dreamscape to explore its meaning, dialogue with a dream teacher, and resolve unfinished business.

Dreamwork is no more a province of psychology than an annex of theology or anthropology. Your dreams are your property, and you are the final authority on what they mean. This does not deny the fact that the meaning of many dreams is obscure. Although my impression (contrary to Freud) is that the dream source seeks to communicate with us as clearly as possible, dreams take us beyond the limited understanding of the everyday waking mind, and so they must often resort to a symbolic language. We also miss dream messages because we remember only a fragmentary or garbled version of the fuller dream experience, or we are simply unwilling to face what the dream may be telling us.

For these reasons, it is often helpful to share dreams with a partner or a whole circle of fellow explorers. I am awed by the discoveries that are made every week, in this way, in my Active Dreaming workshops. After all my years of working with dreams, I find that a complete stranger can still help me to unlock an important dream message that had remained hidden from me.

In dreaming cultures—to which all of our ancestors belonged—everyone was presumed to be a dreamer. Someone who was not in touch with his or her dreams was regarded as less than human, a spiritual and emotional cripple. Dream-sharing was seen as fundamental to the identity, as well as the health and security, of the family and the community.

Among indigenous peoples, it is widely recognized that some individuals are specially qualified to function as dream counselors. But these are not "experts" in the modern sense. They are people who catch many dreams and have a special relationship with the dreamworld and its inhabitants. They have developed the ability to enter conscious dreams in which they can scout out the future, communicate with the spirits, or enter *your* dream and clarify its meaning. They are versed in procedures that may help you to fulfill the promise of a happy dream or avoid the enactment of an evil one. These are the "strong dreamers," or shamans. They are the first dream counselors in the evolution of our species. They are also the first doctors, therapists, storytellers, artists, and priests. But first and last, they are dreamers, called to their vocation by numinous dreams, trained and initiated inside the dreaming.

"The dream world is the real world," says a Seneca Indian healer.[7] Dreams are real experiences, and the meaning of the dream lies inside the dreamscape itself. Because our memories of dreams are so often clouded or partial, and because the waking mind tries to edit these memories into forms that serve our waking assumptions, the remembered dream is often different from the fuller dream experience. To recapture that experience requires a technique for cutting through the fog and going back inside the dreamscape. This may be required to check whether a dream message relates to a future event, to resume communication with a dream guide, or to resolve unfinished business. Dream reentry is one of the key shamanic techniques I use in my workshops and explain in this book.

Another is the method of running a "reality check" on all dream material to establish whether the dreamer has received a warning about a possible future event, or something happening at a distance. Dreams are constantly rehearsing us for challenges that lie ahead, and the dreaming mind is not confined to the conventional limits of space and time. In early societies, "strong dreamers" were prized for their ability to scout ahead in dreams and bring back accurate information on where game animals were to be found, or where the enemy lay in ambush along a trail. My personal experience—confirmed by my work with many other active dreamers—is that once you get into the habit of recording your dreams and checking their content against later events, you will realize that you routinely glimpse many things before they happen in waking life. This is an entirely natural and quite frequent phenomenon. Once you learn that you have the natural ability to see into the future in dreams, you can start to experiment with your ability to change that future—a central preoccupation for shamanic dreamers.

The travelers' tales in this book come from my personal dream journals, from my dream partners, and from fellow explorers who have shared their experiences with me. The exercises and visualizations have evolved through constant experiments with the many adventurous spirits who have attended my workshops. Part one starts at the beginning, with guidance on how to improve your dream recall, work with a dream journal, incubate dream solutions for problems, and overcome nightmare blocks. I then describe the nine basic techniques I find most helpful in exploring dreams. Since dreams are multilayered, any or all of these techniques may be relevant to *your* dreams. We move on to the exciting process of sharing dreams with partners. I try to give you something of the experience of working with a circle of active dreamers, from the initial relaxation and energy-raising exercises to our games of dream theater. Chapter 4 invites you to become a *conscious* dreamer, embarking on dream adventures from a waking state. We now move deeper into the dreaming of the shamans. Chapter 5 introduces the core techniques of shamanic dreaming—including journeywork, shape-shifting, and rituals of dream enactment and avoidance—that I have incorporated into my practice and teaching in ways that may encourage you to experiment for yourself.

The stories and exercises in part two are designed to help you apply the techniques of Active Dreaming to the challenges of everyday life, and to help you discover the deeper story you may be living. You will learn how to use your natural ability to "see round the corner" in dreams as a navigational system that can help guide you through the hazards of daily life. You will read many accounts of how our departed loved ones return in dreams with vital and life-affirming messages; you will also learn to screen and discriminate among communications from the spirit world. You will discover many ways—both familiar and unexpected—in which spiritual guides present themselves in dreams. You will learn to work with your "dream doctor," who often warns about possible problems long before physical symptoms develop and shows you what may be wrong with you in a way that helps you to get well. You will read powerful and moving accounts that suggest that dreams, in themselves, may be healing experiences. Finally, we will explore the ways in which dreaming and dreamwork can help you to get in touch with your creative source, live more spontaneously and generously, and follow the path of heart. The dream source is also the source of creativity, intuition, and our deepest personal truth.

We stand on the shoulders of those who came before us. I could not have written this book without the guidance and example of many teachers, including my teachers inside the dreamworld. If I lay any claim to originality for this book, it rests on only two things: that I have brought together techniques from many traditions and adapted them to the needs of people living in today's society; and that *Conscious Dreaming* springs from a life lived in passionate engagement with its theme.

At the start of each workshop series, I issue this caution: "I cannot tell you anything you do not already know, at some level of your self." The problem is that, in what Yeats called "the daily trivial mind," you may have *forgotten* who you are and why you entered into this life experience. Plato held that we forget what the soul knew before it came into the body, and I believe he is right. The Makiritare, a shamanic people of Venezuela, say that people had forgotten even that they possessed human souls until the first shaman, Medatia, started to dream. His dream carried him whirling up through the roof of his house into many dimensions of the Upper World, where he found his spiritual teachers. Armed with their knowledge, he returned to earth. At night, while they slept, he called the dreamsouls of his people to him, one by one, and reminded them that they were human. So they left the filthy burrows where they had been living with wild pigs and snakes—not knowing what they were—and became people again.[8]

Dreaming, we remember who we are and what we may become. Active dreaming is soul remembering, a return to the source. As we become active dreamers, we can bring more of its wisdom into the circumstances of our waking lives, to empower and heal ourselves and others.

You are fully prepared for this adventure if you are willing to catch your dreams, if you can allow yourself to be open-minded about what they may be telling you, and if you can agree *never* to tell another person what her dreams mean or permit her to do that to you. Others can help you to unlock the meaning and power of your dreams. But in the final analysis, it is your own intuition that will confirm what the dream is telling you and guide you on where to go with that. The only expert on your dreams is you.

Part One

ACTIVE DREAMING

Dreams are the facts from which we must proceed.
C. G. Jung

1

BECOMING A DREAM CATCHER

All would be well could we but give us wholly to the dreams and get into their world that to the sense is shadow, and not linger wretchedly among substantial things; for it is dreams that lift us to the flowing, changing world that the heart longs for.

W. B. Yeats

There is one elementary truth, the ignorance of which kills countless ideas and splendid plans: that the moment one definitely commits oneself, then Providence moves too.

W. H. Murray, The Scottish Himalayan Expedition

REAL MEN ARE DREAMERS, TOO

If someone tells you, "I don't dream," what he or she is really telling you is, "I don't remember." Sleep laboratory research has confirmed that the average person dreams for between ninety minutes and two hours every night, in no less than four to seven cycles. And these numbers only account for the dreams associated with rapid eye movement (REM), when the researchers in white coats can watch a sleeper's eyeballs moving under his lids as if he were following a tennis game. Dreams and dreamlike activity are also associated with other phases of sleep. The lab research tells us little about the *big* dreams associated with out-of-body experiences, when the dreamer may appear to be completely inert, even comatose—or may, at the other extreme, be snoring the roof off in the style of the character Jack Nicholson plays in *The Witches of Eastwick,* a style that is quite unconnected with sleep apnea or other routine disorders. There are also the dreamlike experiences that come in the twilight zone between sleep and waking, which is the scene of many important visitations.

By the most conservative computation, if you add up all the time in your life you will spend dreaming, it will total at least six to seven years. Once again, the figures do not do justice to the real situation, because in dreams we are not confined to linear time: you may find that experiences that seem to occupy days, months, or even years in the dreamworld transpired in a moment of ordinary time. In the Muslim hadith there is the wonderful story of how the prophet Muhammad journeyed through all the heavens on his mystical steed, guided by Gabriel, the archangel of dreams, recorded all of the Koran—and returned to find that the glass of water he had knocked over in the moment he fell into his ecstatic trance had not finished emptying.[1]

You will dream tonight, whether or not you remember. You will have four to seven dreams (or whole series of dreams). You may also have a spontaneous out-of-body experience in the dream state. If you dream in

REM sleep for markedly less than the average ninety minutes, something is interfering with you. The interference may come from drugs, including widely prescribed sedatives and sleeping pills, alcohol, caffeine, a bad conscience, serious depression, or psychic disorders for which shamans have other names. Recent scientific research indicates that people with serious depression dream considerably *less* than average and have very limited dream recall. Depressives often deny dreaming at all. Significantly, when a depressed patient starts dreaming more profusely (as measured from REM sleep) and reporting more dreams, this is usually a sign that he or she is out of the trough of despair and is starting to get well.[2] This is only one of many indicators that dreaming is fundamental to our health and well-being. Serious alcoholics sometimes succeed in virtually suppressing REM-state dreams through their persistent self-abuse. The result is brain lesions and waking dementia. The dreams they have sought to drown pursue them in daylight as nightmarish hallucinations.

For the Stone Age primates from whom we are descended, sleep must have been a rather dangerous activity, with saber-toothed tigers and leathery raptors on the prowl. Dreams were the guardians of their sleep, but not in Freud's shriveled and inverted sense. Our ancestors used their dream radar to scan their external environment for dangers, while their bodies slept. I do not mean merely that through dreams they were able to process signals from the outer world—the feral scent of a night hunter, a distant footfall—while sleeping. Their dream radar allowed them to see and sense over great distances, farther than they could have done with their physical eyes and ears. They needed this advantage in order to compensate for their physical inferiority in relation to superbly efficient predators. Through dreams, they kept vigil. Through dreams, they were prepared for crises and challenges that lay in their future.[3]

Human biology has probably not altered much in the past ten thousand years, for all our genetic tinkering and spare-parts surgery. We still have the equipment our ancestors used to operate dream radar and communications systems that were in no way less "advanced" than the gee-whiz guidance systems that won the Gulf War, and that are a great deal more useful and versatile in everyday life.

So why do so many adults in Western society deny that they dream or insist that dreams do not matter?

These attitudes are partly the work of societal pressures.

To begin with, men have a special problem. For generations, boys have been taught that "real men" do not show their inner selves. I once spoke about dreams at a city Rotary Club. The luncheon was attended by three hundred businesspeople, mostly white, middle-aged, prosperous—and male. My talk was well received, but most of the questions came from the handful of women in the room. As I was leaving, however, I was cornered by a bank president, a pillar of the local community, who seemed anxious to confide in me.

"I have a friend who keeps having the same dream. Does it mean something if you keep dreaming the same thing?"

I was gentle in responding. A man of a certain age and upbringing is as shy as a fawn when it comes to talking about his dreams.

"If it were my dream," I told the bank president, "it might mean the dream source was hammering me on the head to get my attention. Of course, it depends on whether it is truly the same dream. Often what we call a recurring dream is really a serial dream, that delivers the story in installments."

"Like a TV miniseries?"

"Exactly."

Things looked promising. The bank president appeared to be trembling on the brink of a revelation. Then he saw a couple of familiar suits approaching. He cleared his throat and said loudly, "Very interesting, Robert. You know, *my wife dreams.*"

He plainly felt that his patriarchal image, and maybe his basic machismo, would suffer if he were caught talking about his dreams.

Ironically, *dreamers* were venerated in hunter-warrior cultures, where they operated (among other things) as military-intelligence and psychological-warfare specialists, and even as grand strategists. Actually, our greatest warriors, the ones who do not spend an instant worrying about their macho credentials, have always known this. Gen. Norman Schwarzkopf was reportedly guided by his dreams, as well as his state-of-the-art technology, in making tactical decisions during the Gulf War. He was in a grand tradition that includes Julius Caesar, who crossed the Rubicon because of a dream.

The hardheads who deprecate dreams or profess not to dream at all, in truth, are not our warriors, but men who feel threatened in their masculinity—most often by women, most of all by the unacknowledged feminine spirit, which inhabits us all, inside them.

Other social factors have militated against dream-sharing and dream-work in Western societies, at least until recently. For centuries, the church applied crushing weight to deny the validity of personal experience in the worlds of spirit. Personal revelation is always perceived as a threat by religious monopolies. "Dreamwork is real church," enthuses Jeremy Taylor, a Unitarian minister as well as an inspiriting teacher, one of the founding fathers of the modern dreamwork movement. Real church sidelines the middleman or clergy and opens a path to a direct experience of the sacred. It is not surprising that this does not appeal to religious authoritarians.

The story of organized religion, in this regard, is thuddingly familiar: A solitary prophet or avatar, heralded and guided by dreams, brings his vision to the people, shaking the temples of established belief. He skips over all conventions. He heals like a shaman; he works with energy fields, casts out evil spirits, breathes lost soul-stuff into the places where it belongs. He is reviled, exiled, and sometimes murdered by the powers that be, by the priests and the pious. Long after his death, when he has won a big enough posthumous following, his cult is hijacked by the lineal successors of the people who damned him when he was shaking things up. They proceed to circulate an edited and bowdlerized version of his teachings, depriving women (for a start) of any significant role in the story. Then they shut the book and say the time of revelation is over.

The process is chillingly described in Dostoyevsky's parable of the Grand Inquisitor in *The Brothers Karamazov*. It would be nice if we could read this as a period piece, but in a time when fundamentalist intolerance is again on the rampage, it has a disturbingly contemporary feel. The brand of the Grand Inquisitor has burned deep. Journalists, as an occupational group, are as hard-boiled as any bunch you are likely to encounter. But I recall a conversation with a senior editor I'll call George that produced the following exchange:

George: "You keep talking about something you call the dream source. What exactly is the dream source?"

RM: "You might call it the Self, as Jung did. You might call it the Atman. It's enough for me to say that my dreams come from a source that is infinitely deeper and wiser than I am."

George: "You're saying the dream source might be something like God?"

RM: "You could say that."

George (looking worried): "But what if"—his lip trembled—"what if it's *the devil?*"

RM: "You're kidding."

George wasn't. He shunted the conversation on briskly to the latest bullpen gossip about hanky-panky at the White House. But for an instant, his seen-it-all mask had dropped, exposing a raw, pulsating fear. My hunch is that fear stemmed from scary dreams George had tried to keep in the closet, dreams that showed him things about himself he preferred to leave in the dark. But the name George gave to his fear has a pedigree.

To impose its control over bodies and souls, the medieval church not only demonized half the cosmos; it demonized the dream source and the personal unconscious—a poor name for what is also our channel to higher consciousness. Though George counted himself a cheerful agnostic, at that moment, in that clubby watering hole on the Upper East Side of Manhattan, the breath of the Grand Inquisitor was on his neck.

Carl Jung, the son of a Protestant minister who had lost his faith, observed that organized religion exists to protect people from a personal experience of the divine. Hopefully, we and our churches will evolve beyond the need for such defenses. In these things, there is simply no substitute for personal experience.

If fear of dreams breeds witchfinders, it also spawns reductionists, who are perhaps more deadly (or at least more deadening) because they invoke scientific jargon in a society where "science" is widely presumed to have all the answers. Turn a certain kind of scientist loose on the dreaming mind and you will soon be informed that dreams are hallucinations spawned by the wash of chemicals, or nonsensical clutter triggered by random neural firing. Such findings are usually reported without a single reference to the researcher's personal experience of dreaming, which speaks eloquently about their value.

There is all the difference in the world between a genuinely scientific approach and *scientism,* the dull ideology that denies the authenticity of what cannot be quantified and replicated under laboratory conditions. It is scientism, not genuine science, that is the enemy of dreaming. True science is hungry for fresh data and new experiments, ready to jettison theories that our understanding has outgrown, ever alive to the possibility that the universe (like the dream source) is putting bigger questions to us than our best brains can put to it. It is no accident that the pathfinders of modern science—Einstein and Pauli, Kekulé and Bohr, even Sir Isaac Newton in his day—have been dreamers and practical mystics.

There are no "experts" on dreams. You are the final authority on your own dreams. If you need guidance, seek it from frequent fliers, not academics who put plate glass between their experiments and their experience. If you are going on vacation and want some restaurant tips, you wouldn't want to take advice from a guidebook whose author had not sampled the fare for himself. You would rather consult a seasoned traveler who has been to your vacation spot. This is the way you should approach advice on dreams.

For the best counsel, consult a child who is young enough (or sufficiently free-spirited) not to have been corralled into thinking that dreams are "only" dreams. I will never forget the first time I conducted a dream workshop for elementary schoolchildren. They were "talented and gifted kids" from grades four to six in a school district in upstate New York.

I asked at the start of each session, "How many of you remember your dreams?"

They all did. They all thought dreams were important, too. Most of them said they had dreamed something before it happened.

A boy who looked like a miniature Marine with his fierce brush cut and precocious muscles jumped up and told us how he got mad with his dad when the family got lost in the station wagon on the way to a golf vacation in Myrtle Beach. "I kept telling Dad what turns to make, because I had dreamed the whole thing and I knew the way. Dad wouldn't listen to me, because he doesn't believe in dreams. We wasted a whole hour finding the motel because Dad says real men don't dream."

Dad was dead wrong.

CATCHING YOUR DREAMS

*B*efore you can work with your dreams, you have to catch them. Dream catching is an exciting sport, the most thrilling and rewarding game I know. Like skiing or sailing, it demands practice and familiarity with the terrain and the weather conditions.

You don't need to buy any equipment more costly than a notebook and a ballpoint pen.

You begin by deciding this is something you want to try. Your motive may be curiosity or adventure or the feeling you need a new entry point to approach your problems. Perhaps you are already on a spiritual quest. Maybe you need a better way to distinguish what you truly think and feel from the clutter of other people's feelings and opinions. Maybe you just want to have fun.

Susan Novotny, an attractive but overworked bookstore owner I know, became a dedicated dreamer after she woke from a magic-carpet ride. For the third or fourth year in a row, she had promised herself a midwinter getaway from the snowbelt to an island in the sun, but had failed to find the time or money to take her vacation. Then she had this dream:

> I was at a beach resort on St. John. Everything was vividly real. I can still feel the sun and salt air on my skin, the warmth of the sand between my toes. I can still smell the fish broiling on the outdoor grill. I had the pleasure and romance of a two-week vacation, all in one night. It didn't cost me $2,000 and I didn't have to wait for my bags at the airport.

She made it to St. John the following winter and found herself inside the scenes from this dream. Shamans say that in dreams, we are already choosing the paths we will follow in waking life.

If you are ready to become a dream catcher, you will make room in your life for your dreams. Here are some basic tips on improving your dream recall:

1. Clearly state your intention to yourself. For example: "I want to re-member my dreams tonight." Or: "I ask for the guidance of my dream source." Reaffirm your intention when you lie down to sleep. You may want to write this down as a statement or request and put the piece of paper on your bedside table or under your pillow. If you have fairly good dream recall already, or if there is a major concern you need to explore, you may wish to formulate a more specific request. For example: "How can I be healed?" Or: "How can I best handle the job interview?"

2. Have your tools ready. Put a notepad and pen (or a tape recorder, if you prefer) on your bedside table where you can reach them easily with-out having to grope around or turn on the light.

3. Give yourself time to bring your dreams back. Allow yourself some ex-tra time in the morning to laze in bed and let your dreams come back to you. It's best if you can wake spontaneously, without an alarm. If you must use an alarm clock, set it to a buzzer rather than the radio, so you don't get caught up in the clutter of the outside world as soon as you wake. If you are new to dreamwork, you may want to start your experiments over a weekend or a vacation break when you can set your own schedule.

4. Give yourself space. Try to record your dreams before getting out of bed. Try using a penlight if you find you can't write in the dark and do not wish to disturb your partner. If necessary, creep into the bathroom to jot down your notes; a lot of good dreamwork begins in the bathroom.

5. Write your dreams down at once. This may seem like cruel and un-usual punishment when you wake from a dream at 4 A.M., but dreams are fleeting, often gone within minutes if you release your attention. Furthermore, the most powerful and urgent dreams often come at in-convenient times. If you tell yourself you can go back to sleep and catch them later, you'll probably find you are wrong.

6. Start with a few trigger words. You can use these later to produce a fuller report. The dream scene you remember most clearly is probably the one from which you have just woken. Summarize it in a few words. Make sure you include any names and phrases you recall. You may find yourself triggering memories of earlier scenes. Write these down, too. Your notes will often give you a dream sequence in reverse order, like a movie run backwards. You can correct this when you write a finished report in your journal.

7. *Don't censor your dreams!* The dream source can be brutally frank about aspects of your personality, behavior, and desires you prefer to ignore or repress. Let it speak! It knows you better than you know yourself in your everyday mind.

8. *Don't interpret!* Concentrate on capturing your dream experience *raw* before you start worrying about what it means. Don't reject dream material as "weird" or "trivial." A dream that seems bizarre may be dramatizing an issue in order to grab your attention, or guiding you beyond your normal level of awareness. A mundane-seeming dream may contain important precognitive material; much of waking life is also ho-hum.

9. *Pay attention to your feelings.* Your feelings about your dream are often your best guide to its meaning and urgency. The storyline may seem banal, but if you have strong feelings about the dream, there is something here you need to work on. Pay attention to your physical sensations as well. Dreams are bodytalk as well as soultalk.

10. *If you wake with no dream memories, relax.* Roll around gently in bed. Sometimes dreams are coaxed back when you get your body back to the position you were in when they originally came to you.

11. *Put out a welcome mat.* If you still have no dream recall, take a moment to write down what you are thinking and feeling. Your thoughts and sensations may be part of your dream hangover, even if you have lost the dream. By writing *something* down, you are putting out a welcome mat for tomorrow's dreams. You are signaling that you are at home and ready to receive. You may notice, as you get into the swing, that there are cycles to your dream recall. For example, some women report heightened dream activity during their periods and around the full moon; others experience a blackout effect.

12. Always do something with your dreams. Keeping a journal is a first step. Sharing with a partner is great home entertainment and will help sustain your commitment to catching and working with dreams.

YOUR OWN BOOK OF DREAMS

$\mathcal{T}$he most important book on dreams you will ever read is your own dream journal. You will be astonished by how much you will gain by keeping a dream journal and consulting it regularly. I have been working with my personal dream journals for more than thirty years, and I am still discovering the wealth of resources they can unlock.

For a start, once you start working with a dream journal you will become very clearly aware that many dreams do not deliver their story in a single episode. The plot is often developed through installments. Some of these dream series are concluded the following night; some run for as long as a TV soap opera.

The meaning of many dreams is obscure because they depict events that have not yet taken place in ordinary reality. In such dreams, we encounter people and situations from the future. If you are keeping a dream journal, you will soon find it easy to log the correspondence between your dreams and subsequent events. This will help you to hone your ability to recognize and work with precognitive material in your dreams. It will also enable you to check your dreams for guidance on the best way to behave or respond in a developing situation. In dreams, we often scout far beyond current circumstances, bringing back glimpses of what lies ahead on the various paths that are open to us in waking life. When waking events catch up with such dreams, it can be very useful to go back to the original report for confirmation or cautionary advice.

For example, I once asked my dreams for guidance on how to get the business side of my life in order—an example of *dream incubation,* which we will review as a technique later in this chapter. In the dream that came to me, I was hurrying to catch a ferry. In order to get to the ferry, I had to scramble over tables loaded up with packages and cartons of books. The location was the bank of a wide river, close to the sea.

I woke feeling cheerful and confident. I knew I had got to the ferry on time, though I was puzzled that I had no recollection of the boat itself, or my fellow passengers. The theme of needing to speed up in order to get on board the boat (or the train or plane) was very familiar, and I took it as an advisory to deal with some long-neglected paperwork. But I was stumped by the significance of the ferry and all those packages of books, until an event took place in waking life that was highly relevant to "the business side of my life."

Eighteen months later, my agent, Stuart Krichevsky, called me over a weekend to tell me that he had decided to set up his own literary agency and hoped I would join him. I asked for details. He told me his main office, for the time being, would be located in Dobbs Ferry, New York. He would be sharing space with a friend in the book-packaging business. Stuart had just mentioned the two key elements from my dream: the ferry and the book packages. I hurried to pull an old dream journal from the shelf to confirm the details. The overlap between my old dream and a later event brought me a strong sense of *confirmation* that Stuart was the right person to handle the business side of my literary career, and I did not hesitate to join him in his move to Dobbs Ferry. When I drove down to the old Hudson River port (where there is no longer a ferry) to lunch with him a few weeks later, I found myself inside the landscape from my dream.

You will find yourself using your dream journal in other exciting ways. Dreams offer nightly readouts on your physical, emotional, and spiritual health. By tracking and comparing these reports you can monitor the state of your health, your relationships, and your progress toward (or away from) your larger goals.

Journaling is creative play, richly rewarding for its own sake. It will build your talents as a storyteller. You will find yourself writing effortlessly and may discover you have far greater literary abilities than you previously expected. You may discover similar artistic gifts if you choose to draw your dreams and map your dream journeys.

Journaling helps to mobilize intuition. Working with night dreams, you become more alive to the dreamlike symbols and synchronicities of waking life.

Your dream journal will become a personal treasury of images, charms, and teaching stories, the vocabulary of soul. As you work with dream symbols, you will discover that they resonate with the great mythic themes of humankind, which is natural, since (as Joseph Campbell observed) myths are collective dreams. You will see that your life is part of a larger story.

If you are not already keeping a dream journal, you should consider starting one tomorrow, with your take from tonight's dreams. Here is how to begin:

1. Choose the right book. Members of my dream groups work with everything from handmade paper and morocco bindings with fancy clasps to spiral-bound steno pads. I use thick, college-ruled notebooks, "neatbound" for tidy stacking. I leave the left-hand pages blank, so I can add comments later on, and I reserve a section at the back for an index.

2. Keep your journal private. Keep it in a safe place, under lock and key if necessary. Nobody has the right to read your journal without permission, and you should be guarded about granting such permission. Your journal is a place where you must be absolutely honest with yourself and your dream source. If your partner is a snoop who refuses to honor your need for privacy, maybe you need a new partner.

3. Make a date with your journal. Ideally, you should write up your rough notes in your journal each morning, while your memories are fresh. If you can't manage this, try to set aside time in the evening. Don't leave it too long, or you may find you can't make sense of your notes.

4. Date your reports. The exact time when you woke from a dream is sometimes highly significant; you may find that it corresponds to an outer event, or to another person's dream activity. You may also notice that certain types of dreams cluster around the anniversaries of big events in your life.

5. Give your dreams titles. Think of each dream as a story and give it a title, even if the dream is only a fragment. Don't agonize over this; you are not competing for a literary award. Put down the first phrase that comes to mind. Sometimes this phrase will bring out a dream message you may have overlooked or undervalued. Here's a sampling from recent workshops. How many of these titles resonate with you? "Watching Movies in Church." "Meeting My Younger Self." "Spilled Juice." "Naked in Public." "My Shoes Don't Fit." "Stranger in the Mirror." "My Dead Grandmother Comes to Visit." "Selling House." "Back in School." "Flying." "Cutting Up Snakes with a Butterknife."

6. Note your feelings and immediate associations. If your mother does not figure in your dream report, but you have a hunch the dream relates to her, write that down, too. Notice your physical sensations when you came out of the dream. You might want to mention what was on your mind the previous day. Little dreams are often full of day residue. However, big dreams are more closely related to what lies in our future than what is behind us.

7. Index your dreams. A running index of dream titles will help you locate dream material quickly and track recurring themes.

8. Note recurring themes and locales. Is your dream self constantly changing trains or clothes? Are you being pursued? Do you often get telephone calls in your dreams? Do you frequently find yourself naked in public? Are you drawn again and again in dreams to places you do not know in waking life?

9. Log correspondences between dreams and waking events. Go back to your journal at regular intervals and check the dreams that seem to foreshadow external events. Where appropriate, insert a newspaper clipping, a letter, or some other memento.

10. Note overlaps between your dreams and those of other people. If you share dreams frequently with one or more partners, you will notice interesting parallels. Sometimes one person's dream seems to hold the key to another's. You may be able to identify *interactive dreams* in which you and another dreamer share the same dreamscape.

Above all, have fun! Decorate your journal with sketches, snapshots, or postcards that evoke your dreams or simply reflect your moods. Track your dream images through a good dictionary of symbols. Try recasting some of your dream reports as poems, and don't listen to your inner critic (the only critic with whom you need share this exercise) as you do this.

DREAM INCUBATION

*S*ocieties that value dreams evolve recognized techniques for approaching the dream source for guidance and healing. These may involve journeying to a sacred place, purification, invocation, and sacrifice. Pilgrims traveled from all over the ancient Hellenic world to the sanctuaries of Asklepios, the god of healing. They came bearing gifts of wheat cakes and honey, to camp out under the stars and hope for an initiatory dream that would satisfy the priests that they were worthy to be admitted to the *abaton*—the "forbidden dormitory" of the god— where they might receive a *big* dream that would heal their ailments. The Greek magical papyri, prepared by pagan and gnostic practitioners in the first centuries of the Christian era, describe all sorts of rituals intended to bring about prophetic or healing dreams:

> Take a linen strip, and on it you write with myrrh ink on the matter, and wrap an olive branch and place it beside your head, and go to sleep, pure, on a rush mat on the ground, saying the spell seven times to the lamp: "Hermes, lord of the world, who are in the heart . . . who send forth oracles by day or night . . . Reveal a sign and send me your true gift of prophecy."[4]

If the issue is serious enough, the authors of the papyri recommend sweetening the pot with the blood of a dove or a crow.

If you are into ritual, you may prefer this less sanguinary suggestion from Cornelius Agrippa, the sixteenth-century German magus:

Let there be made an image of dreams, which being put under the head of him that dreams, makes him dream true dreams concerning anything that he hath formerly deliberated of: and let the figure be that of a man sleeping in the bosom of an angel. . . . Thou shalt write upon the breast of the man the name of the effect desired, and in the hand of the angel the name of the intelligence of the Sun.[5]

In all inner work, however, it is intention, not ritual, that matters. If you have a question you truly need answered, or a problem you truly need to solve, you can take it to your dream source. In all likelihood, you will get the guidance you need from the dreams that will come to you—if not on the first night, then within a fairly short period. All that is required is that you (a) formulate your question or request clearly; (b) clear your channels—for example, by laying off alcohol, drugs, and caffeine and by not overeating before going to bed; and (c) that you agree to accept and work with the dreams that are given to you.

Here's how it works:

⟶ EXERCISE: PILLOW TALK

1. State your intention clearly. You may express it either as a question or a request. For example: "How should I handle the job interview?" Or: "Help me to be healed." A good place to start is by asking to improve your dream recall or to have better communication with your dream teachers. Whatever your question, it should relate to something of real importance to you. In my experience, dream incubation works best if your intention is positive, life-affirming, and open-ended. One of my favorite requests for my dream source is "Help me to unlock my full creative energy."

2. Write down your question or request. Remind yourself of it throughout the day. When you go to bed, place the piece of paper or the index card with your question under your pillow. (This really does help!)

3. Record your dreams and explore how they might answer your question. At first glance, you may not see a connection. Keep looking: it's probably there. If you have failed to catch any dreams, jot down the first thing that comes into your head—and be alert for any unexpected or striking incidents in waking life that may also have a bearing on your question.

4. Remember that the dream source is wiser than the ego! When you put a question to your dreams, you are inviting your greater Self to comment on your affairs or help you to straighten them out. But your deeper Self wants more for you than your ego agenda. You may be asking for help to fulfill your present goals—only to be told by your dreams that your present goals are all wrong, and you should take a completely different direction.

WORKING THROUGH NIGHTMARES

> The wheeling of the stars is not infinite
> And the tiger is one of the forms that return.
> *Jorge Luis Borges*

*O*ne reason infrequent dream recallers may be uneasy about working with dreams is that the ones they tend to remember are the scary ones. If the dream source is trying to convey a message, and we persist in refusing to listen, it will resort to shock techniques to get our attention.

A nightmare is actually an aborted dream, one we fled before its full message was delivered. Remarkable discoveries await us when we develop the pluck and the skill to return to nightmare scenes to unveil their fuller meaning by the reentry techniques described in chapter 4.

Consider, for example, the kind of nightmare in which you find menacing intruders inside your house. This could be a warning about the invasive sources of illness, or a literal caution about the risk of a burglary or break-in. Alternatively, the intruders could be helpful messengers you have been trying not to heed. Jeremy Taylor tells a hilarious story about a nightmare messenger who broke into a man's dream home and pursued him in the fearsome guise of a fire-breathing dragon. The dreamer kept waking in a cold sweat, heart banging against his ribs, until he resolved—with Taylor's encouragement—to face his adversary and demand to know why it kept coming after him. When he was able to do this, he noticed that the nightmare dragon was no longer so scary. It was more cartoonish, but quite disgusting, since it was slimed over with a thick coating of black tar. The dreamer demanded to know why the dragon was after him. He was told that his pursuer was his nicotine addiction, and that it was time to get out from under it. As a result, the dreamer quit smoking.[6]

Being chased is one of the most familiar nightmare themes. The question to ask is, *What am I running away from?* In dreams, we often run away from things that we can't control. These may be closely related to habits or attitudes we can't control in waking life either, like that nicotine dragon. A useful question to ask about nightmares of this type, after waking, is "What part of myself am I running away from?" But it is better still to go back into the unfinished dream and put that question to the adversary himself.

Trying to escape dream challenges by fleeing back into ordinary reality (or still worse, by trying to bolt the door shut against the dream source in general) is a poor life choice. The issues we confront, or fail to confront, in dreams are issues we need to deal with *now*. In an even larger sense, the dream state is an arena in which we are trained and tested in choice and courage and our ability to grow. Flee the arena, duck the training, and you will find yourself obliged to take the same tests in waking life. Where will you flee then? Back to the dreams you wouldn't face? Into a fog of addiction?

The ways we sometimes try to escape from challenges in waking life are similar to the ways we try to get out of disturbing dreams.

My Jeep was totaled a few years ago by a woman who ran a red light. She alighted briefly from her car, which had suffered only minor damage. She moved her hand over her eyes, blocking out the scene. "I don't have time for this," she said in a drowsy monotone. "This isn't happening."

She climbed back into her car and made as if to drive off.

I had to reach through her window and turn off her ignition to persuade her that we needed to trade insurance information and wait for the police. When the cops arrived, she had moved to a different phase of denial. She told them she had had the green light. Fortunately, several witnesses were available to give the cops the facts.

The woman driver's initial response to a nasty situation was to flee the scene and tell herself nothing had happened. This is precisely what we do when we run away from a dream challenge and dismiss it as "only a dream."

The woman's second response was to rewrite her experience in an inauthentic way: "I had the green light." We do this when we try to manipulate dream images in ways that distort the authentic dream experience to suit the ego's fantasies of control.

We need to confront our issues on the ground on which they are presented and work forward toward genuine resolution. The first and all-important step is to *stay with the dream.*

What are the shapes of your deepest fears and insecurities? You can count on your dreams to show them to you, over and over, until you have grown beyond them. Thus nightmares often present recurring themes. You are falling—maybe because you don't yet realize you can fly. (In dreams, flying is perfectly natural.) You are being swamped. Your teeth fall out. Your toilet keeps flooding. Monstrous attackers—tigers, serpents, hulking brutes—are out to eat you alive. Or you are scared by something more nebulous: by what may lie behind that closed door, or at the top of that stairway to the attic.

What you think you can't face, in all probability, is exactly what you need to face. How do you develop the resolve and resources to do that? By working with dreams the old-fashioned way, the shaman's way. This means coaching your dream self to stay with the dream until you have confronted and integrated your fears.

Here are a few tips on how you can prepare yourself to do this:

⏵ WORKING YOUR WAY THROUGH NIGHTMARES

1. Dialogue with your fears. Ask yourself: What is blocking me? What am I running away from? Why am I afraid to finish this dream?

2. Dialogue with your dream adversary. Ask whatever is menacing you: Who are you? What are you doing in my dream? What are you trying to tell me?

3. Rescript the role of your dream self. Ask yourself what would happen if you changed your attitudes and actions in the dream you left unresolved.

4. Dream the dream onward. Imagine the dream unfolding beyond the point at which you woke up. If you don't like what seems to be happening, see if you can create a happier outcome, maybe by calling up help. But don't be content with a cute solution that seems less real than the original dream. You may find that resolving this dream requires action from you in outer reality as well as inside the dreamscape.

5. Invoke allies. It's okay to ask for help! You may even be about to discover that your dream adversaries are allies in disguise. We can learn a lot from shamans about this, as in the case of dream tigers, who figure with surprising frequency even in the dreams of modern Westerners who have never seen a tiger outside a zoo or a circus.

➤ DREAM TYGERS

> Tyger, Tyger, burning bright
> In the forests of the night,
> What immortal hand or eye
> Could frame thy fearful symmetry?
> *William Blake*

Among the indigenous peoples of Southeast Asia, the tiger or clouded leopard is frequently the animal guardian and soul companion of the most powerful shamans. Such shamans are believed to be able to shapeshift into tiger form not only to fight enemies but also to heal and to test and initiate shamans-to-be. In Sarawak, a shaman might seek to scare away the evil spirits that bring disease by eating fire and blowing smoke over his patient and then by transforming into a clouded leopard (*Neofelis nebulosa*). In the Malay states of Perak and Selangor, according to Richard Winstedt, an early anthropologist:

> A magician at a séance will growl and sniff and crawl under mats and lick the naked body of a patient, his growls and move-

ments showing that he has been transformed and so far from being possessed by his spirit helper has obtained control of it. During a séance, it is alleged, a tiger appears at least once, though experts debate whether it is the real animal or only a were-tiger.[7]

The Malay shaman's affinity with the tiger survives physical death. One of his souls is believed to transfer to a tiger, which becomes a source of magical knowledge to his successors. The decisive initiation test for a shamanic apprentice—the shamanic equivalent of taking your bar exams—is a fearful confrontation with a tiger spirit who will grant him the power to communicate with spirits and enter the spirit worlds at will only after he has demonstrated his courage. The would-be shaman may see himself torn limb from limb, so he can be made new, in a new dream body.

The Senoi, a forest people of the Malay Peninsula, also believe that the tiger is the shaman's most powerful spirit helper. The Senoi are said to teach their children that nightmare adversaries are hostile spirits *(mara)* that become spirit helpers *(gunik)* when they are confronted and overcome. When a dreamer develops the courage to confront and accept a tiger that challenges him in dreams, he becomes a shaman.

Though popular accounts of Senoi dream practices have been discounted by recent scholars as overly idealized,[8] they have inspired an approach to dreamwork that is essentially shamanic and *works*. In dealing with the dream tigers, its key insights are these:

- We need to confront dream adversaries, not run away from them.
- If we flee from a scary dream, we need to learn how to go back inside it and face up to our fears.
- It's okay to call for help in order to do this.
- When we overcome dream adversaries, they become friends and helpers.

Small children sometimes seem to know intuitively how to do these things. At four, my daughter, Sophie, told me she had had a scary dream in which she was chased by "hairy monsters." She seemed remarkably composed about this at the breakfast table. I asked what she had done about the hairy monsters. She told me, "I put on a dragon costume and chased them back."

2

NINE KEYS TO YOUR DREAMS

It is a capital mistake to theorize before one has data.

Sherlock Holmes

If you do not do something with your dreams, you will not dream well.

Huichol shaman

➤ A TRAVEL KIT

A recurring theme in my dreams, and probably in yours, is of changing my clothes and accessories. When I started studying shamanism, for example, I dreamed I was in a fancy men's clothing store, looking at the kind of "power suits" I used to affect when I was a magazine editor in London, trying to fit in at the gentlemen's clubs of St. James's. In the dream, I started stroking the fabric of a blue, double-breasted pinstripe—very Savile Row—when suddenly it changed into a coat of animal skins, trimmed with fur. I looked for the maker's name. The tag read "Shamanic." As life went on, I realized that this dream not only reflected the profound change that was taking place in my values and preoccupations, but the change I would eventually make in the way I presented myself in public. Dreams of changing clothes—like the equally common dream in which you see yourself naked or only partially dressed in a public situation—are often about how we present ourselves to other people, and how we are seen (or think we are seen) by them.

A frequent variation on this theme, in my dreams, is of getting kitted out for an expedition: putting on bush clothes for an African safari or an Australian walkabout, donning an insulated suit for a trek across Antarctic ice floes, or a deep-sea diver's gear, or a space suit for intergalactic travel. These changes of costume and accoutrements are often the prelude to thrilling dream adventures.

This chapter is designed to offer you a travel kit for your own dream explorations. The techniques outlined here are those I have found most useful in working with dreams. Because dreams can have many layers of meaning, many or all of these techniques may be relevant in exploring a single dream. The first two steps will become almost automatic once you have gotten into the habit of working with your dream journal, and they require less detailed explanation than those that follow.

1. TRUST YOUR FEELINGS

*A*lways pay attention to how you feel when you wake from a dream. Your feelings and bodily sensations may be your best guide to the relative urgency and importance of a dream, and its positive or negative implications.

A young woman called Lisa brought the following dream report to one of my classes:

> *I am in the bathtub. I seem to be trancing out. I come to my senses when I realize the tub is overflowing. Now I'm trying to reach the faucet to shut off the flow of water so I won't make a mess.*
>
> *Next I'm in the kitchen, throwing up. I keep vomiting up red liquid. It keeps flowing and flowing. I'm scrambling around to get cups and containers to hold it so it won't make a mess on the floor.*

In many people's minds, the image of upchucking huge quantities of "red liquid" might sound a medical alarm. But Lisa was serene, almost radiant, as she recounted this dream. I asked how she felt when she woke up. She told us modestly, "I was happy I finally had such an interesting dream to share with the group."

These certainly did not sound like the reactions of a person who might have seen herself spitting up blood. Asked to describe the "red stuff," she said it reminded her of Kool-Aid. She recalled—during further discussion—that one of the containers she picked up was a plastic mug with cartoon figures on it, the kind of mug some of us associated with feeding a baby. The earlier image of the overflowing tub made me think of the bag of waters breaking before childbirth. "If it were my dream," someone suggested, "I'd take a pregnancy test."

Lisa flushed to her ears. She had spent many years trying to conceive a baby, without success. After that workshop, she took a pregnancy test. At the next class, she told us with a dreamy smile that she was going to have her first baby. It was the quality of her feelings that had provided the key.

On the other side of the scales, the warning contained in a somewhat humdrum dream report of a country drive (described in a later section) was trumpeted by the fact that the dreamer kept clutching at her stomach as she shared it.

Your "felt sense" of the dream—to borrow Eugene Gendlin's phrase—is not only your first clue to its character and importance, but is likely to be your final assurance that you have unlocked its meaning. Take your sense of the dream into your body and see if you notice any changes as you call back the images. As a young woman relived the dream sensations of sitting in a swing in an unknown amusement park, she felt a sexual charge as she gripped and released, gripped and released. A Freudian might have made this connection reflexively—and might, on this occasion, have been right. But the meaning of dreams cannot be determined solely on the head level, and the dream might have meant something altogether different. In working with your dreams, you will find that the rush of discovery brings physical sensations. You may feel suddenly hot or cold. You may get shivers.

2. FIRST ASSOCIATIONS

*I*n keeping a dream journal, you will want to get into the habit of jotting down your first associations with the dreams you record. What floats to the surface of your consciousness in the first minutes after waking may come from layers of the dream that have eluded you, or from deeper levels of dreaming.

You can make a game out of highlighting key words in your dream report and jotting down the associations they bring to mind. Maybe you find (as I do) that you quite often dream about *shoes;* maybe you've lost your shoes or left them somewhere or are shopping for new shoes or find your new shoes pinch. After a dream in which I swapped shoes with someone else, I made the following list of my associations with shoes: "Shoes enable me to walk on the ground without hurting myself or picking up dirt and trash. Shoes have soles. They sometimes come with strings. 'You can't understand a person until you've walked in his shoes.' 'If the shoe fits . . .' I can put them on or off. Shoes are what ground me." Several of these quick associations gave me insight on that dream, and a recurring dream motif. Your personal list will tell you far more.

My first impressions might extend to a guess at the overall message of a dream. For example, I dreamed that I visited a clinic where people seemed to be getting ready for a brain surgery operation. I became concerned because packages of chopped meat were on the same table as the brain matter that was going to be used in the transplant. My first hunch, on waking, was that my dream was an animated commentary on the kind of scientist who reduces the mind to "a computer made of meat." The following day, a reporter called me out of the blue and asked me to comment on the theory that dreams are the meaningless side effects of "random neuronal firing" in the brain.

Your first associations with a dream may surface material that is not in your remembered dream, and this may be especially valuable.[1]

You might record a dream that seems to have nothing to do with Duluth, but find that the word *Duluth* springs to mind shortly after you wake, in those precious minutes when you are still lightly connected to the dreamstate. Maybe your dream involves someone who has a connection with Duluth. Maybe it involves a future visit to Duluth you do not yet know—in your waking mind—that you will one day take. Maybe Duluth is a fragment from another dream you have wholly forgotten. Or maybe you picked up something just now, in the twilight state between sleep and waking, when your natural telepathic ability is least inhibited.

I woke the other morning, after a thunderstorm, with bits and pieces of many dreams, including scenes of a lush green valley with waterfalls.* The word *Ailill* came into my head. I knew its spelling, but also heard its unusual pronunciation: "Ah-*lill*," with the stress on the second sylla-

---

* Electrical-storm activity seems to heighten psychic receptivity and increase the number of dreams we recall. However, individual dreams on such nights are often interrupted, and dream reports may be fragmentary, possibly the effect of multiple awakenings.

ble. It sounded Celtic, and subsequent research turned up some interesting information about the legendary King Ailill of Connaught, spouse of the formidable and insatiable Queen Madb. In one account, Ailill was credited with the ability to project dream doubles that were perceived by other people as fully physical.[2]

I had fun following this prompt into the world of Celtic heroes and shape-shifters. Then at my dream workshop that night, a woman just back from Hawaii started enthusing about a magical store on Maui called Ailill, which she pronounced as I had heard it in my dream; she explained that the store owner, an Irishman, had taught her to do this. She showed me travel brochures of Hawaii that contained a picture of waterfalls that reminded me of the scene in my dreams. The next day, I received an invitation to conduct a workshop in Hawaii. My first impression—the Irish name plucked from the air—put me on the track of an almost-buried dream that may have been preparing me for a trip to Hawaii.

3. REALITY CHECK

*T*hough dreams are inner experiences, they often contain accurate information about external reality. In both subtle and unsubtle ways, dreams incorporate signals from the outside environment—the barking dog, the lightning flash, the sound track of the late-night show your partner is watching on the TV next door, or the phases of the moon. Your dreams are equally likely to reflect your body's reactions to whatever you ate or drank the night before, and your mental attempts to process the events and emotions of the day.

However, dream material is not restricted to what is available to the dreamer in the past or present. In dreams, we are constantly scanning ahead, preparing for future challenges. Many dreams contain accurate and helpful information from the future, and from places the dreamer may never have visited in waking life, although this information is often scrambled in transmission and garbled in transcription. In working with dreams, I have never wasted more time—or seen others waste so much time—as when I have ignored messages of this kind in favor of symbolic interpretations.

Before I do anything else with a dream, I ask, *Could this dream mean exactly what it says?*

If my dream takes me into an unfamiliar but realistic locale, I will ask myself, Is this a place I will visit in the future, or a place where something relevant to me is happening right now?

Even for dream enthusiasts, it is possible to do extensive work on only a limited number of dreams. But I try to run this kind of "reality check" on *all* my dreams, including the most trivial-seeming, bizarre, or fragmentary.

To run an effective reality check on dream material, it is necessary to record your dreams as completely and faithfully as possible, without editing. I confess that I still miss some of my dream messages by letting my internal editor interfere.

On the morning of December 13, 1994, I made the following entry in my dream journal:

Journey to the East

I am taking trains across Holland. At one stop I ask other passengers if we have arrived at Nijmegen. They are anxious to help. They tell me we are not yet at Nijmegen; I will know the town by a certain church steeple. I have been to the east, to the sea. I have been in the water fully dressed. My clothes are still drenched, and water is pooling around my feet.

I was not surprised to find myself in the Netherlands in this dream. I had recently returned from conducting some Active Dreaming workshops at Oibibio, an adventurous holistic center in the old Mercury Building in Amsterdam, and was planning to return there two months later. I had never been to Nijmegen, but the name of the town rang a few bells. My friend Aad van Ouwerkerk, an intrepid dream explorer, had recently moved there and had invited me to visit him. Nijmegen is also the "twin city" of Albany, New York, near my home.

But I was confused by one oddity in my dream report. It stated that

I had been "to the east, to the sea." I am no expert on Dutch geography, but I needed no atlas to tell me that the seacoast of Holland is to the *west*. How could I have been swimming in the sea if I was in the east of the country? It made no sense.

I proceeded to flout my own rules by editing my dream report to fit my waking mind's notion of geography, instead of going back inside the dream to clarify the facts or simply leaving the question open. I inserted the word "also" into the key sentence in my dream report, so it now read: "I have been to the east, *also* to the sea."

Why so much ado about the geography of Holland? Six weeks later, at the end of January, Holland suffered the worst flooding in forty years, as the swollen Rhine spewed its waters into the Maas and smaller rivers running through Holland, causing them to burst their banks. While the Dutch labored to shore up the dikes, hundreds of thousands of people were evacuated from their homes. The area that was subject to the worst flooding was around Nijmegen, in the east of the country.

I now realized my dream had given me clear warning of an impending natural disaster in a country on the other side of the Atlantic. Interestingly, when I reported this story to a Dutch businessman on my return trip to Holland, he became very excited at the mention of a church steeple in Nijmegen. He showed me a set of color photographs of a former monastery in the town, complete with church steeple. The buildings had just come on the market; he was considering buying them and converting them into an international conference center.

This little story contains an object lesson. Whatever else we intend to do with a dream, we should try to honor these principles:

• *Let the dream speak for itself.* The dream may not make sense immediately to the waking mind because it is telling you more than you already know, in your ordinary consciousness.

• *Remember that dreams involve the future as well as the past.* For this reason, you may not be able to grasp the full meaning of a dream until waking events catch up with it.

Finding a correspondence between a dream and a possible future event or another situation in external reality does not exhaust its meaning. The dream may contain symbolic messages beyond its literal content. For example, Paul came to me in high excitement with what he regarded as a fine example of dream precognition:

> *I dreamed I was at a big train station, maybe in New York City. A stern man tells me I must help a lost child. I have fifteen minutes to help her find her parents. I rush around asking people if they are her parents. I haven't found them when my train comes and I feel terrible, like I'm going to be punished. But when I board the train, a friendly conductor tells me I'll have a second chance to find the child's parents. Next time I'll have four hours to find them.*

At the time of the dream, Paul had no plans to make a train trip. But that same week, he received a call from his ex-wife, inviting him to visit. He took Amtrak to New York City. He explained that his train was delayed fifteen minutes going down, and four hours coming back. "Isn't that neat?" he said, smiling.

I was obliged to tell him that, if this were my dream, the correspondence between the time intervals in the dream and the delays in waking life might serve to keep it fresh in my mind—and underscore a possible connection with my visit to my ex-wife—but seemed unlikely to constitute the primary meaning. I asked Paul how he felt when he woke from the dream. He admitted that he had felt consuming guilt and pain, only slightly offset by the friendly words from the conductor. I asked him to describe the characters in the dream as completely as possible. The "stern man" was dressed in black, "like an undertaker." The child was a girl of four or five, with braids in her hair, dressed up "like she was going to church." Did Paul know a child who resembled her? Paul eventually conceded she might have been his own daughter, now twenty-six, when she was that age. Had anything happened in her life at that time that might have caused her to "lose her parents"—and perhaps a vital part of herself? It took a great deal of courage for Paul to follow this line of exploration to its natural conclusion. His daughter's mother had died in a horrifying accident—the kind that might result in deep trauma and soul-loss—when his daughter was a small child. Paul now recognized that his dream might be asking him to acknowledge that he was one of the "lost parents," and to help to bring home the missing part of his child.

In Paul's case, the overlap between a dream and a subsequent waking event led to an exploration that opened deeper layers of meaning.

We must not mistake the possible literal fulfillment of a dream for its sole meaning. But it is no less shortsighted—and sometimes quite dangerous—to neglect the possibility that a dream may contain an entirely literal warning about developments in outer reality.

We tend to remember only bits and pieces from dreams and often jumble together elements from several dreams into a single confused story. It is also difficult for our waking minds to receive accurate impressions of people and situations encountered in dreams that we have not yet come across in waking life. So it is often hard to decipher a message about future events until those events catch up with the dream.

Eva dreamed that a plump woman with frizzy hair came into her office with two dogs, a black Lab and a golden retriever. The frizzy-haired woman sat down opposite the desk and launched into an angry tirade against her neighbor. As she talked, the golden retriever dwindled in size until it became a toylike miniature and was carried out in a box. After waking, Eva spent a few minutes trying to analyze her dream. She considered the possibility that her "light side" (the golden retriever) was losing out to her "dark side" (the black Lab) because she was letting the "angry part of herself" (the frizzy-haired woman) take charge. Then she went to the office. A couple of hours later, the frizzy-haired woman she had seen in her dream entered the room, sat down opposite her desk, and launched into a tirade against her neighbor, whom she accused of poisoning her dogs. She had two dogs, a black Lab and a golden retriever. The golden retriever had died. Apart from the fact that the dogs were not physically present, Eva's dream was played out exactly as she had recorded it.

In one of my dreams, I seemed to be in the home of a friend called Phil, who lives near Indianapolis. I entered a series of man-made caverns, expensively furnished and climate-controlled, in which a huge quantity of human bones was stored. Phil was absent for most of the dream, performing some personal rite in a cavern that seemed to be framed by a colossal rib cage. When he appeared, he looked like an American Indian, naked apart from the bone necklace that hung over his heart. I was intrigued by this dream and wondered what Phil had been up to. Then my wife received a call from the wife of an American

Indian friend, Ray Gonyea, who had been working for the Smithsonian. She had called to tell us that her husband had recently undergone heart surgery, which she attributed to the tremendous stress he had suffered while working to repatriate human remains—the bones of Native Americans—from the Smithsonian collections over the previous two years. He had quit his job and they had moved to Indianapolis.

Even if we cannot complete a reality check on a dream until subsequent events are played out, we should leave open the possibility that it may contain a message of this kind. However, occasionally our felt sense of a dream indicates greater urgency. When the need to get the message straight carries this kind of urgency, the most effective technique I know is dream reentry, which is at the heart of shamanic dreamwork.

4. DREAM REENTRY

*D*reams are real experiences, and a fully remembered dream is its own interpretation. The meaning of a dream is inside the dream itself. We release it by learning to go back inside our dreams in a relaxed state. By learning how to reenter dreams, you will develop the ability to clarify messages about future events, resume contact with inner teachers, and resolve unfinished business. Through this method, you will put yourself in closer attunement with the creative source from which dream images flow. As a natural side benefit, you will probably also find that you are increasingly able to embark on conscious dream journeys from a waking state, and retain awareness that you are dreaming as you move deeper into the dreamscape.

To understand the process, we need to get one thing clear: *The dream you remember is not the dream itself.* By the time you are fully awake, you have forgotten 90 percent, if not more, of your nocturnal adventures. A partner's love bite, a ruckus in the street, a child tickling your toes, can shoo away most of your remaining memories. By the time the editor in your waking mind has finished processing and tagging the scraps that are left, your dream memories may be quite remote from the dreams themselves. At best, to quote Ann Faraday, remembered dreams are merely "postcards from a journey."[3]

Suppose you fly down to Rio and bring home a few snapshots of Sugarloaf Mountain and bathers in string bikinis on Copacabana beach. How much of your adventure is contained in the photos? Do they carry the smell of palm oil, the bittersweet tang of *batida limão,* the slap of a tropical rainshower? Or the drama at Customs, the rippling laughter of the girls at the samba school, the dance of your nerve endings when you entered (or renewed) a romance that woke up all your senses? Of course not. However, as you study the pictures, you may find yourself sliding back into the fuller experience.

Dream memories are like this. Even as snapshots, they are often unsatisfactory: out of focus, with key characters missing their faces, subject to multiple exposure and mess-ups in the darkroom. But with practice, you can learn to use these blurred images as windows through which you can reenter your dreams, relive the adventure, and bring back important gifts.

Dream reentry requires two things: your ability to focus clearly on a remembered scene from your dream, and your ability to relax and allow your consciousness to flow back inside that scene. If there are scary things inside the dream you are nervous about confronting, or if you have difficulty relaxing, you may find dream reentry easier if you have a partner to talk you through the process, or the support of a whole circle. Shamanic drumming is an especially powerful tool for dream reentry and opens the possibility of taking a partner with you into your dreamspace to act as your ally and search for information you may have missed.

At this stage, I will simply share several examples of successful dream reentries that illustrate both the method and its applications, followed by an exercise you can practice on your own.

━ CASE #1: THE MEMPHIS MUGGERS

Wanda dreamed she was in a darkened parking lot in a downtown neighborhood. She watched a couple walking toward their car and realized she knew the man. He was a former lover, someone she had not seen in more than ten years. She assumed the woman was his wife or girlfriend.

Suddenly, more figures loomed up out of the shadows. Wanda saw a couple of tough-looking men, darting between the cars. They closed in on her ex-boyfriend as he was fishing around for his car keys. There was a brief scuffle. A knife flashed, and Wanda saw her former lover fall to the ground, gouting blood. His female companion had also been stabbed.

Wanda woke feeling awful. She felt certain that one or both of the mugging victims had been killed.

She called me at an unsociable hour of the morning to ask for advice. She was now in a state of guilt and confusion. Was it possible that in some part of herself she wished her ex-lover dead?

I had shared dreams with Wanda for many years and had observed that she often seemed to pick up messages for other people, including accurate glimpses of future events. I asked her a few questions about the dream, focusing on the location. Where had the mugging taken place?

She was not sure. She felt the dream location was somewhere in the South, maybe in Memphis, where she had gone to school and her former lover still lived.

I suggested to Wanda that she try to get relaxed and go back inside the dream. I offered only two specific pieces of advice: "Try to identify exactly where this is happening. Then you might try to give the dream a different ending and see if that feels natural."

Wanda did the reentry on her own. She simply snuggled down in bed into a comfortable position and let her consciousness float back to the parking lot.

She now saw that the parking lot belonged to a grand public building with Grecian columns, maybe a courthouse or city hall. She noticed a trashed apartment block, a vacant lot, and billboards and street signs nearby. She took a closer look at the muggers and was able to describe them in sufficient detail for a police Identikit artist to make up their pictures for a wanted poster.

She made a valiant attempt to change the ending of the dream. She tried to picture her ex-boyfriend coming out of the marbled building earlier or later, so he would not run into the muggers. She tried to bring the cops into the scene. These devices seemed artificial. Her dream was not a movie script that could be rewritten in some cute or arbitrary fashion; it was *real*.

"I couldn't change the ending," she reported back.

I took this quite seriously. I often go back inside my own dreams when I am not satisfied with the message or the outcome. When I find I cannot change events in the original dream in a way that seems natural, I take this as a message that the dream is an accurate reflection of events that are taking place in ordinary reality—or *will* take place unless I take appropriate action in waking life.

I asked Wanda if she was still in touch with her old flame.

She had not seen him for years, since she moved to New York. She knew only that he was married and was working for a Memphis law firm; his secretary had sent her a change-of-address card within the past year.

"How would you feel about calling him up and telling him the dream?"

"He's a trial attorney, a real left-brain type," Wanda demurred. "And, jeez, he'll probably think I want him dead because he married the other woman. On the other hand, he knows I'm a nut."

She agreed to call the ex-boyfriend and report her dream without commentary.

After she told the dream, there was a long silence on the Memphis end of the line. Then the lawyer said, "Thank you."

He told her he was grateful for the warning. It seemed that Wanda had described the precise location where he parked his car outside the legislative building in Memphis. Unknown to Wanda, the lawyer had been doing a lot of work in that building for one of the committees. He had also fallen into the habit of meeting his wife there at 7 P.M. on Friday evenings, prior to going to a restaurant for dinner. He was aware that the downtown neighborhood was increasingly unsafe at night, but had not focused on a possible danger to himself or his wife—until Wanda called with her dream. Because of her call, the lawyer decided to change his routine and meet his wife at a restaurant in a safer part of town.

Did Wanda dream a possible future she was able to help the probable victims to avoid? The question cannot be answered with certainty, since there is no way of proving that the stabbings she dreamed would have taken place if she had failed to make her phone call. What does seem evident is that, by using the technique of dream reentry, Wanda was able to provide practical and helpful guidance for another person, drawing on information that was not available to her in waking life.

— CASE #2: AMY'S ROOM

In dreams and in dreamlike states, Amy reported, she kept returning to a place she did not know in waking life. She described the scene as follows:

I am in a room with bare, whitewashed walls, near the ocean. The room is sparsely furnished, with a dark table against the wall and a pair of armchairs in front of the fireplace. I am sitting in one of these chairs. I am much younger, maybe four years old. In the chair opposite me is an elderly man who reminds me of a college professor who was brilliant but could be a royal pain in the ass. He died eight years ago. In this room, I am comfortable with him. The windows have no curtains. Beyond them is sea and sky.

When I heard Amy describe this recurring dream scene, two possibilities leaped to mind. The first was that she might have lost part of herself at an early age, because of childhood illness or abuse. This four-year-old Amy was inhabiting a separate space, as in the dream. However, the fact that the adult Amy kept being drawn to that place might suggest that her lost child was ready to come back to her. My second thought was that Amy's room by the sea might be a special place—a stable locale in the dreamscape to which the dreamer could return, whenever she liked, to seek instruction from her now-friendly professor.

These two possibilities did not seem to be mutually exclusive. But I kept both to myself. I was eager to know what Amy would discover for herself, once she made the conscious decision to reenter her dream. After some breathing exercises, she felt she still needed help to get over her left-brain inhibitions, so her reentry was conducted with the help of monotonous shamanic drumming. I gave her two basic guidelines: to explore her dream location as thoroughly as possible, and to seek information from one or both of her dream characters.

With the aid of the drumming, Amy had no difficulty putting herself back inside her dream room. She now realized that she was in Greece. The place had the feel of an earlier time, perhaps the fifteenth century. She sat down at the table and started writing with a quill pen.

She noticed that her four-year-old self was still sitting in the big chair by the fire.

"Why aren't you with me?" Amy asked the child.

"I had to go away because of the pain," her four-year-old told her.

Moved to tears, filled with returning memories of childhood grief and loneliness, Amy opened her arms to her younger self.

Then something wonderful happened. "We came together. We sort of joined up. Suddenly there weren't two of us anymore."

Still inside the dream, feeling larger and stronger, Amy plied her professor with questions. "What are trying to tell me?"

"When are you going to pay attention?" he chided her. "I've been sending you messages since I died and you've kept on ignoring them. *You have to dance while you can.*"

The last phrase struck Amy on a very deep level. She loved to dance but had been under a lot of pressure at work and had been denying herself this outlet for her energies.

"I'll dance!" she promised, feeling the surge of four-year-old playfulness.

As her teacher proceeded to counsel her on many aspects of her life, she realized he was immensely wiser and more powerful than the short-tempered academic she had once known. She wondered if he was really the same man. "When he moved in the room, his shadow swooped and soared like an enormous bird."

The walls of the whitewashed room fell away, revealing an ocean of possibility.

When Amy came back from that dream reentry, she was different, lighter and brighter. I whispered to her, "Welcome home." I believe a spontaneous soul retrieval took place that evening. Her dreams had been telling her for years that a part of her was somewhere else and might be ready to return. She brought it home by going back inside her dream with full consciousness and the determination to resolve its issues. At the same time, she discovered a spiritual guide, in the form of a professor who had died eight years before.

━ CASE #3: MOTHER GOOSE

Paula had just learned she was about to become a grandmother; her daughter had told her she was two months pregnant. Paula had the following dream:

I am watching small animals inside a fish tank in a store. They could develop into birds, but there is something wrong in the tank. The water is too hot. It's going to kill all these little creatures. There is a goose beside me. She keeps laying eggs and burying them in sand. All these eggs are going to die, too. I want to do something to save the eggs, but this seems to be beyond my control. A man in the store is very laid-back and won't do anything to help.

When Paula shared this dream, I guessed that it might be preparing her for something beyond becoming a grandparent. The images of the dream—the hot tank, the dying creatures inside it, the wasted eggs outside the tank—all seemed to evoke menopause. But in her own associations, Paula veered far away from this possibility. As a mere man, I decided I would not put it to her directly. She was edgy about the dream and clearly needed to integrate its message. I asked her to formulate her main question about the dream. She decided her question was "Why am I doing nothing to save the eggs?" I asked her to try to go back inside the dream and put that question to whoever or whatever might best be able to answer it.

Paula's experience during dream reentry was brief but telling. "I saw that the things in the tank were destined to die. There was nothing I could do about it. The man was no help, and I couldn't find any other people to talk to. I thought the mother goose might be able to give me some answers, but when I tried to speak to her, she just laughed and honked at me."

The possible message, Paula concluded, was "Don't be a goose." She now remembered a second dream fragment from the same night, in which she saw herself and her husband as elderly people with white hair. In Paula's case, dream reentry helped her prepare for an inevitable life passage in a gentle way, by accepting the wisdom of her dreams.

Among its many uses, dream reentry is the most effective technique I know for dealing with nightmares. As we have seen, a nightmare is not just a "bad" dream; it is an *unfinished* dream, one from which the dreamer fled back to the imagined safety of the daylight world. It is a failed test. By retaking that test and passing it—as many shamanic traditions teach—we gain power and powerful allies. Through dream reentry, when we feel strong and prepared, we can return to the place of fear and slay our demons.

Bill, a once-heroic drinker who had broken plenty of hearts and made lots of enemies in his youth, ran away from recurring dream confrontations with a monstrous adversary. When he found the courage to confront his persecutor, the demon shrank to the proportions of a man he had once wronged, who still seemed to be consumed by hatred and bitterness. When Bill looked straight into his eyes and said, "I love you," all the wind seemed to go out of his adversary, and he crumpled to the ground like an empty cloak.

In cases like this, dream reentry may become an exercise in what Jung called "dreaming the dream onward." It is important to note that this is *not* the kind of "control dreaming" exercise in which we are instructed to reassure ourselves that this is "only a dream" and to manipulate the content of the dream in an artificial way. In a genuine dream reentry, we do not interfere with the authentic images of the original dream. We *are* open to fresh images that may now appear, and to conscious interaction with the whole cast of the dream. We have the advantage of coming prepared, fully conscious that we can make better choices than before and are able to call in help when the need arises.

➤ EXERCISE: LOCATION, LOCATION, LOCATION!

The realtors' familiar slogan applies to the technique of dream reentry as well as the property game. The easiest way for you to go back inside a dream is to hold your focus on the dream location. Your initial memories may be fuzzy, but a single landmark—even a single shape or color—may be sufficient to enable you to shift your consciousness into a vivid and complex scene.

Be open to possibility! The geography of the dream world is not that of the *Times* atlas or the Mobil guides. In dreams, you may find yourself in familiar locales, including places from your past—Grandpa's place, or your childhood home—that may or may not have changed. You may also visit unfamiliar but realistic locations, often clues that your dream contains precognitive or other "psychic" material. You may find yourself in scenes from a different historical epoch (past or future), in a different galaxy, in otherworldly locales, or in free-flowing situations where nothing conforms to the supposed laws of the physical world. One of the purposes of dream reentry is to establish *where in the worlds you are.* The typical dreamer, after waking, has no more idea where he spent the night than an amnesiac drunk.

The best time to try to reenter a dream is often immediately after you have come out of it. By snuggling down in bed and rehearsing the postures of sleep, you may be able to slide back into the dream in a gentle and natural way. But your work schedule may not allow you leisure to do this. And if your dream contains deeply disturbing material, you may need to wait until you are ready to deal with it. You may also feel you need the support of a partner or a drumming session.

But here is a simple technique for dream reentry you can use in the privacy of your bedroom or easy chair:

1. *Find your question.* What is your main question about the dream you wish to explore? Try to formulate that question as clearly and succinctly as possible. Write it down. This will help to establish your focus. During your exploration, you will use this question like a flashlight or a miner's lamp. It might be quite specific, or as general as, "What is this dream telling me?"

2. *Focus on your target.* Summon back as many details of your dream location as you can. This is the scene you are going to reenter. Maybe you have multisensory impressions of it. How does the air feel? What can you hear? Are there any distinctive smells?

3. *Ask yourself who or what inside the dream can best answer your question.* When you reenter the dream, you may be able to communicate directly with one of your dream figures.

4. *Relax.* Get into a comfortable position, sitting or lying down. Take some deep breaths. Breathe in through your nose, out through your mouth. As you exhale, try to release any pain or tension you are holding in your body and wish it outside your space. You may find it helps to count yourself down—from twenty to one—as you let your consciousness slide toward your remembered locale. Or you may wish to put on meditation music or a drumming tape.

5. Move into your dream locale. Look around carefully to identify exactly where you are. You may notice many details you forgot or overlooked before. Do you know this place? Do you feel you are inside a scene from another time, or another order of reality?

6. Let the action unfold. Don't interfere with the spontaneous flow of images. You have full power to choose how you will interact with your dream characters and respond to any challenges that are presented to you. Your dream reentry may take you beyond the point at which the original dream ended; if the first dream was unresolved or aborted, this is part of your design. Your new dream may also introduce characters and events that were not in the original dream. This is fine: your underlying purpose is not to reproduce the earlier version, but to move closer to the source from which dream images flow.

7. Dialogue with dream characters. You may find a dream character who can answer your questions. Your selection is not confined to humans. Dreams are full of "persons other than human" (to borrow an Ojibwa phrase).[4] There is no such thing as an inanimate object in dreams.

8. Expect the unexpected. Because the dream source is wiser than the ego, it may be telling you something more important than the question you decided to ask.

9. Map your journey. Pay attention to how you return from the dreamscape, as well as the paths you took through it.

5. DIALOGUE WITH DREAM CHARACTERS

One of the best ways to work out what your dream characters are telling you is to *ask* them. Though this is best accomplished through dream reentry, you can make fascinating discoveries by simply taking up a pen, addressing your question to a figure from the dream, and jotting down whatever comes to you on a piece of paper. Your question may be as simple as "What are you telling me?" You will need to decide who or what inside the dream may best be able to answer that question. You are not confined to dialoguing with human characters! Everything in dreams is *alive*. (Shamans know the same is true of waking life.) I once had an extraordinary dialogue with a Persian rug. Spirited facilitators of dream theater like Bill Pearlman and the late Jessica Allen, borrowing from Gestalt as well as from shamanism, invite participants to act out the role of every element from a dream, down to the doorknobs.[5]

I had a series of dreams in which I was constantly changing trains, getting off at the wrong stops and having to reverse direction, which was an accurate reflection of my dithering and indecision about some important matters at that time. In one of these dreams, after being squeezed into a third-class compartment where I could hardly breathe, I decided to find a better way of getting around. I left the station to hail a taxi. One pulled up immediately. It was a magnificent, Genevieve-style vintage roadster, its chrome lovingly polished. There was plenty of room inside for all the luggage I had been dragging around with me, piles of suitcases and steamer trunks. The driver was cheerful and friendly. At the end of my dream, I was completely confident I had finally found my way and woke in excellent spirits.

I was curious about the vintage cab, which had also appeared in previous dreams. I decided to ask the driver about this unusual mode of transportation. Here is part of the dialogue that ensued:

Dialogue with the Vintage-Cab Driver

R: Why are you in my dream? What are you telling me?

Driver: I'm telling you that you ought to pursue your plans to write more historical fiction. Your novels make a splendid vehicle, roomy enough for everything you want to put into them. I'll get you wherever you want to go. You don't belong on other people's tracks. The third-class compartment is an accurate image of how disgusted you feel when you submit to other people's agendas and expectations.

R: Okay. But my historical novels are set in the eighteenth century. So why didn't you come as a coachman, with horses?

Driver: Because I need to fit into the landscape of your dreams. You were riding on trains, around modern cities. A coach and horses would seem improbable, at best a tourist attraction. I wanted you to believe in me. Besides, I wanted to remind you that your historical fiction need not be confined to any period, or even to the past. You know from your dreams that the future, as well as the past, belongs to history—which is to say that both are with you, and accessible now.

Dialogue with dream characters is especially rewarding in dealing with scary dreams and nightmares. Dream pursuers and assailants are often bearers of messages we need to hear, and this is a way to tune in to these messages.

You may also want to try dialoguing with your dream self. If your dream self was more cowardly or passive than you perceive yourself to be, you might ask, "Why did you run away?" or "Why didn't you do something?" If your dream self was braver or wiser than you know yourself to be, you might ask, "How can I be more like you?"

6. TRACKING YOUR DREAM SELF

*W*ho are you in your dreams? Are you the protagonist or simply an observer? Are you younger or older? Male or female? Do you behave in your dreams the same way you behave in waking life? Do you flee from challenges or face up to them?

The character who appears in all of your dreams, even if only as a witness, is *you*. Yet strangely, this is the character most commonly neglected when we start trying to harvest the meaning of our dreams.

As Strephon Kaplan-Williams explains in his brilliant, quirky books *Dreamworking* and *The Elements of Dreamwork,* by tracking how your "dream ego" acts (or fails to act) you will learn to recognize your inner motivations, and you may lay the groundwork for improving your attitudes and making positive changes in waking life. You will certainly find yourself taking lessons in courage and choice. By monitoring your dream self as it evolves through many dreams, you will find you become more observant of the contents of your mind in waking life, and more conscious of how your attitudes shape the reality you think you inhabit.

A radio talk-show host I'll call Julia consulted me about a dream in which she was traveling with her mother, who had died several years before:

Broken Chains

We are visiting my mother's friends, a couple whose marriage is in trouble. I am hungry and sweaty. I need to eat and I'd really like to take a shower. But I do neither, because I'm not at my own place. I break a chain I am wearing. I want to throw the broken chain in the trash, but I can't even do that because the owners of the house are fussy about recycling. I stay more or less in the background. Finally my mother goes off to a fancy Italian restaurant with her friends. They don't invite me. I watch them as a spectator. At the end of the dream, I've become just a kind of disembodied presence.

As we talked, Julia made a number of associations. She had recently taken to wearing a silver chain that had once belonged to her mother. By an interesting synchronicity, this chain had snapped for no apparent reason a couple of weeks earlier; she had been meaning to have it repaired. She associated the Italian restaurant with her current partner and his ex-wife, a woman of Italian descent who was bitterly jealous of the relationship. Her immediate question for the dream was "How can I mend the chains that are broken?"

Now, "broken chains"—Julia's own title for the dream—are, for most people, a symbol of liberation. When I hear that phrase, I picture a slave stepping free from the fetters that have bound him.

But in her dream, Julia seemed to have consigned herself to a servile, secondary role. She's starving and needs to freshen up, but she does not honor her legitimate needs because she is not in her own place. Her dream self dwindles to the point where she is a lonely wraith watching other people enjoying themselves.

If this were my dream (I suggested), I would want to know why I am putting up with this situation. Do I behave the same way in waking life?

Why do I want to mend the "broken chains"? Aren't they something I need to get rid of?

These questions brought a shock of recognition. Julia now recognized that her dream might be warning her not to go on sacrificing her needs in her current relationships. She confessed that she had always felt her mother—a socialite who had seldom made time for her kids—had relegated her to "second-class status," and that she was now allowing someone else to do this. She resolved to express her feelings more openly to her partner. She also hit on a personal ritual for honoring her dream: instead of repairing her mother's chain, she put it in the trash.

Follow your dream self, and you are likely to find you have many selves. You may catch yourself changing sex or age or race. You could even find yourself body-hopping, as I seemed to do in the following sequence:

Body-Hopping

I am inside the body of a powerful, athletic black man, a basketball player younger than my present age. He/I has sex with a number of women, including a tall, voluptuous black woman with a teenage son. I show him how to shoot hoops. Much of this is taking place in a tough inner-city neighborhood. I stroll through it without fear; here, I am king.

Then somehow I jump into the body of a prosperous middle-aged white guy who spends a lot of time on the golf course. I find his life incredibly boring. He reminds me of Dan Quayle. I want to get out of this fast.

I slip into yet another identity. Now I seem to be inside the skin of an immensely learned scholar. I'm fascinated by his library, which is filled with works on alchemy and mythology. I smoke a pipe with him while he sorts through his letters, but I am oppressed by the physical pain he is experiencing. He's elderly and quite frail. His bones ache.

I ascend to a higher place and enjoy flying around, released from physical form.

Dreams in which we become "other people" often contain rich teaching lessons. For example, that our surface personality is only part of our larger identity, and that despite surface differences, we are connected to other people and are capable of understanding each other.

In dreaming, what we identify with is what we *become*. I suspect this is also true in waking life, though it may be manifested in subtler ways.

This is an excellent reason for taking a closer look at who you are in your dreams, and what you may become.

— CUE CARD: WHO ARE YOU, IN YOUR DREAMS?

1. Do you look different in your dreams? Maybe there's a "thin man" or a movie star inside you after all. Are you the same age and sex? Do you seem to be a completely different person, or even a member of another species?

2. Are you a participant or an observer?

3. Are you active or passive? Who is in the driver's seat?

4. Are you naked in public or improperly dressed? Do other people in the dream notice or care about it?

5. What are you doing, or not doing, in the dream? How do you feel about it? How would you describe your attitude?

6. Are the actions and attitudes of your dream self similar to those of your waking self, or different? Compare your answers to the previous questions with situations in waking life. When do you feel exposed? When do you take a backseat?

7. SYMBOL EXPLORATION

Symbols take us from the known to the unknown. In its root meaning, a *symbol* is a "bringing together." Dream symbols bring together ordinary awareness and deeper levels of knowing. Although the dream source tries to communicate with us as clearly as possible, it must often speak in symbols in order to carry us beyond the limitations of the everyday mind. Dream symbols also dramatize themes, lending us energy and rich entertainment—and a ticket to the world in which myths and great stories are born.

You don't want to take the juice out of a dream symbol by reducing it to an abstract concept, or the kind of translation you will find in the dream dictionaries they sell in drugstores. A symbol calls for exploration, not merely interpretation. You will find it just as rewarding to track the evolution of specific symbols in your dreams—the role of snakes or trains, your relationship with fire or water—as to monitor the progress of your dream self.

As your dream collection grows, you will notice recurring images. The meaning of these images may be quite different from the attributions you will find in dream dictionaries or encyclopedias of symbols. The same images might not mean the same things to a different dreamer. A dream of teeth falling out might evoke fears of death or job loss in one person, the memory of a boyhood fistfight in another, and the need for a routine dental checkup to a third. A snake might warn of a sneak attack, arouse sexual fears or energies, or signal potential for healing or transformation.

In my dreams, as you may already have noticed, I seem to spend far more time on trains and at train stations than I have ever done in waking life. Anyone fond of puns will pick up an underlying message: *train* as in *training*. My training, in these dreams, involves choosing the right line, dealing with luggage, finding the currency to purchase tickets, and the right way to deal with occasional customs officials. When I get on the wrong train, I end up spending more time than I would like at stations ("stationary"). Sometimes, I'm afraid I'm going to miss the train. In one dream, I was frustrated because there were endless doors blocking my passage from the station waiting room to the platform. After throwing open a dozen or more, only to find another thick glass plate in front of my face, I realized I could simply vault over the obstacle. On the platform, I was confused by a maze of train lines. It was impossible to know which line I should take—until I remembered I was dreaming and was not bound to a terrestrial perspective. I shot up into the air and made a leisurely aerial inspection of the railyard that enabled me to see where each track was likely to lead. This was a useful teaching dream, which caricatured my tendency (at that time) to go on banging at the same doors in my hurry to catch the express, without even clarifying that it was headed someplace I wanted to go.

The kitchen, in my dreams, is the place where the cooking gets done in more senses than one. Its condition often reflects the state of my creative work, especially my writing. During a more than usually disorganized period when I was working on four major projects at once, for example, I dreamed my kitchen was in total chaos, under murky light; nothing was in the right drawer, and the food on the stove was being cooked in the wrong containers, at the wrong temperatures. I took the hint from this dream, spent a day getting my projects sorted out, and was promptly rewarded by a follow-up dream in which I was pleased to see four prime sirloin steaks broiling superbly on a rotisserie grill.

Dream symbols are constantly evolving, spinning off new meanings and associations. How often have you dreamed of changing hats or clothes or shoes? There is a whole book to be written on the dream grammar of footwear. Shoes ground us and allow us to move about in relative comfort, but may hurt and confine; I know a Freudian psychiatrist who converted to dreamwork and Jungian analysis after she dreamed that her shoes were killing her. Shoes also have soles, and therein lies another fertile pun.

The symbolic language of our dreams can carry us deep into the *prima materia* of the collective unconscious. You are swallowed by a great fish and find yourself in the realm of Jonah, the Inuit shamans, or even Walt Disney's *Pinocchio*. Even incidental details in modern dreams can open a trail into the forests of ancient myth.

Going through a series of dream reports in which I clashed with opponents who ranged from inner-city muggers to concentration-camp guards, I noticed an odd motif. In many of the dreams in which I vanquished my adversaries—escaping from the prison camp, clearing a way through a dangerous neighborhood—my weapon was a ruler. Not a heroic broadsword or a hyperefficient Uzi, just a simple, old-fashioned ruler of the kind I used in elementary school. Sometimes the ruler is steel or wood, often it's merely plastic, highly unconvincing as a weapon in waking reality, but very efficient in the dreams.

What is a ruler? A tool for measurement, a way of drawing lines, of setting boundaries. Also something that rules. I gave only passing thought to these associations until I stumbled across an image of Tehuti—an aspect of the Egyptian god Thoth—in an old book. Tehuti is shown holding a measuring stick. The ruler is his emblem of office, because Tehuti is the embodiment of proportion, balance, and judgment. It is because he knows the true measure of things that he is called "the god of peace between the gods." This little discovery gave me a thrill and brought a four-thousand-year-old papyrus vividly alive. No wonder the dream ruler worked!

As you explore your dream symbols, be careful not to reduce your vital dream experience to a bloodless "text." Good popular discussions of how to work with dream imagery include books by Ann Faraday, Gayle Delaney, and Jeremy Taylor, all mentioned in the suggestions for further reading at the back of the book. You may wish to arm yourself with a good visual guide to archetypal symbols.[6] You may find it fun to compare your findings with those of the dream dictionaries, as long as you don't buy into their precooked associations; the best of all dream dictionaries (for my money) is still Artemidorus' *Interpretation of Dreams,* just eighteen centuries old.[7]

The following suggestions are an eclectic mix, drawn from several approaches to dreamwork and dream interpretation. They are not offered as an alternative to the core shamanic techniques described in this book, but as additional tools that may help you to harvest the full meaning of your dreams.

⟶ CUE CARD: EXPLORING DREAM SYMBOLS

1. Imagine you have to describe an object or character in your dream to a caveman or an extraterrestrial who has just been beamed down from Sirius. How would you describe Princess Di or a toaster oven to someone who has never heard of either?

2. Describe the key elements and personalities in your dream as if they are part of you. For example, in my "ruler" dreams: "The part of me that can get things in proportion overcomes the part of me that is aggressive or overcontrolling."

3. Monitor recurring images. Watch how they evolve and how they relate to situations in waking life. For example, how do you get around? Is someone else at the wheel? Are you in a group situation on a prearranged schedule (bus or train) or can you choose your own route (taxi) even if it might take longer (bicycle). Do you move from one form of transportation to another? Have you gotten rid of your excess luggage?

4. Hunt for counterparts for your dream images in mythology, nature, and the nearest zoo. If you keep dreaming about wolves, learn their habits. A woman's dream of dismemberment led her to study accounts of the initiation of Inuit and Siberian shamans, and eventually to her own shamanic initiation. Another woman's dream of a cup led her on a personal grail quest. Through an obscure word or visual detail, dreams often suggest specific lines of research.

8. "WHAT PART OF ME?"

*D*reams make us whole. They show us the many aspects of ourselves and help us to bring them under one roof. This is why it is often useful to ask "what part of me" different characters and elements in a dream might represent. Is the shadowy dream attacker an aspect of myself—maybe my anger or sexuality—that I have repressed or denied that is clamoring for my attention? Is my mother, in my dreams, the part of me that feels or judges as she does? Is the storm or fire or flood the force of my own emotions?

Fritz Perls, the Austrian-born psychiatrist who was one of the founders of gestalt therapy, maintained that *all* the elements in a dream are projections from the dreamer himself. He encouraged clients to play out the roles of all these dream elements, giving voice (in both words and body language) to natural forces, scenery, and "inanimate" objects as well as the cast of human players. In this way, the dreamer might be able to get in touch with many split-off aspects of his personality and bring them together.[8]

By asking, "Which parts of me are top dog and underdog in this dream?" we can sometimes clarify what point we have reached in the perennial contest for dominance between different aspects of ourselves. The gestalt approach makes for lively dream theater. It can help to build consciousness of the extent to which we create our own reality. And when gestalt role-players give voice to walls and mirrors and ocean waves, they move toward the shaman's understanding that everything is alive, in both the dreamworld and the physical world.

The game of "What part of me?" is an excellent game for beginners. I play it most often with workshop participants who have limited experience of working with dreams and may be starting out with limited dream recall. Christina, a middle-aged woman who was new to dreamwork, gave us this short dream report:

Dirty Snow

I am driving in the country with my friend Donna. It's a beautiful day. We are driving in spring sunlight, through fields that are bright with wildflowers. Suddenly there's a big change in the weather. Everything is covered up by dirty snow. I feel terrible. I am utterly alone.

The force of Christina's emotions indicated that this dream was more important than a simple summary might suggest. As she spoke, I noticed she was clutching at her solar plexus, just below the rib cage. I asked her to tell us how she felt. "When I woke up," she recalled, "the tension was clenching me in my gut. I guess it's tugging me now, when I try to describe that dirty snow."

We did a quick reality check. Christina had a friend called Donna and saw her often. She described Donna as a person who laughed a lot and loved gardening and the outdoors.

"Who's driving the car in your dream?"

"Donna."

"And where is Donna when the scene changes to dirty snow?"

"She's not there." Christina closed her eyes, trying to get back into the scene. "I think the snow came because she left."

"So who's at the wheel?"

"No one. There's no one at the wheel. All I can see is dirty snow." Chris was clutching at her stomach again.

I asked her to describe her friend Donna as a part of herself. She quickly responded, "Donna is the part of me that's vital and loves a good laugh." After further discussion, she added this thought: "When the part of me that's like Donna is at the wheel, everything is sunshine. When she goes away, I'm stuck and my world is gray and hazy."

This was enlightening, as far as it went, but we needed to deal with that dirty snow. Every time Christina mentioned it, she started clutching at her belly. I encouraged her to try some gestalt role-playing. It wasn't easy for her, because of the fear she was carrying. But she finally came up with this statement, speaking as the "dirty snow" in the dream: "I'm the crud you're left with at the end of a long, hard winter. I'm dirty because of all the muck you've been leaking out of your cars and your snowplows. You need to do a cleanup. And you ought to get your pipes fixed."

There was a health advisory here—which some of us had suspected because of Christina's body language and our own associations of "dirty snow" with spillage and pollution. Dreamwork, in this instance, was a gentle way for the dreamer to get the message for herself, within a supportive group.

I played the "What part of me?" game—after considerable groundlaying—with an Episcopalian priest who called me about a dream he found deeply troubling. The title for the dream emerged from our discussion:

In the Service

I'm peeking through a hole in a fence at a barracklike building that reminds me of my time in the service. There are people going up a ramp into this building, like cattle going to the slaughter. I edge through the fence to see what's going on. Inside the building, a huge, voluptuous blond woman is presiding over a horrifying scene. All these people are being butchered and slung up on meathooks. First their eyes are removed, then their brains. The blonde is very Aryan—she looks like a Nordic goddess—and completely nude. I do nothing to intervene.

The phrase *in the service* offered an initial key to this dream. I asked the priest if he could think of any way in which his *church* service might resemble the goings-on in that shed. Understandably, he was horrified by the suggestion! Then he shocked himself by making an analogy between the people moving up the ramp and the procession of his parishioners to the communion rail. He had noticed that the victims' eyes were removed first. Was there a sense in which the people in his services were losing their "I's"? He conceded that the form of his service did not allow room for self-expression; he had even minimized the time permitted for his congregants to pray in silence.

This left us to deal with the sexy blond dominatrix.

I took the risk that the priest might hang up by asking, "Can you describe her as a part of yourself?"

"That's out of the question!" he protested. To the priest, she represented paganism, raw sexuality, the Goddess—everything he rejected. He paused. "Are you telling me she's the part of me I've denied?"

"Only you can say that."

He had read some Jung and reluctantly conceded that the pagan blonde might be a spurned anima. I do not think he is at peace with her yet. But when we can recognize our connectedness with dream adversaries, we can start to make peace with them. This process was itself the theme of a dream in which I was once advised, "Happy is he who kills no person in himself or in others."

I am constantly impressed by the theatrical flair with which the dream source dramatizes the struggle between different aspects of the dreamer. In the period of my life when I felt torn between the pursuit of commercial success and the path of a teacher, my dreams were a battlefield:

Star Wars *Battle*

A tremendous battle is raging inside and around a huge complex of buildings, with towers and battlements. It looks like a fortress from the future, like something from Star Wars. *The bad guys are wearing blue-and-black uniforms. They have seized control of the fortress, but they are threatened by rebels inside the walls and an attack from without. They are holding important hostages, but the guards are nervous. The commander of the bad guys tells one of his men he will be kneecapped unless he carries out orders. Two files of startroopers are sent up into a tower to eliminate the rebel leader. The battle is unresolved when I wake up.*

In those shapeless, divided armies, I recognized the warring sides of myself. The conflict was recast in an everyday setting in another dream from this period in which I enter a handsome room where I am planning to present a talk on dreams and spiritual growth and am interrupted by an angry writer in the front row who yells at me, "You'll disappoint your fans!" One of my favorite dreams from this cycle—and a major step toward resolution of all this inner turmoil—invited me to stop taking the issues so seriously. In this dream, I found myself held up at Customs (a recurring motif). While I endeavored to explain myself to a severe Man in Authority, I noticed a "happy hooker" type breezing through the controls. Swathed in silks and furs, she reminded me of a Jackie Collins character. She waved and blew me kisses. She advised me, "We have to deal with people the way they are." She indicated that she, too, had had to pay her dues to get through Customs.

I woke up laughing. I recognized my "happy hooker" as someone closely related to me—maybe the part of me that was unembarrassed about giving the public what it wants, and collecting the worldly prizes for doing that. In pursuing my new path, I did not have to perceive this aspect of myself as an armed opponent; it was an old chum. We were going our separate ways, but we could still be friends and maybe even have good times together again.

In practice, I find I use the "What part of me?" approach on only a small proportion of my dreams, and only then in conjunction with other basic techniques, which *always* include a reality check. It would be foolish, for example, to interpret a hurricane in a dream as a "storm of emotion" until you have checked on whether a literal hurricane is in the offing. Frankly, the "What part of me?" game works best with short, relatively uncomplicated dreams, especially those that involve a symbolic house or landscape, the play of natural forces, battles and conflicts, or recurring generic figures like the hotel manager, the policeman, the taxi driver. The gestalt approach, even in this heavily modified form, is rarely satisfactory as a primary method because it tends to ignore both the transpersonal and the literal content of dreams and therefore misses urgent and empowering messages.

9. DREAM ENACTMENT

We should always do something with important dreams. Recording them, exploring them, and sharing them are good ways to begin. Here are some further suggestions for bringing the energy and insight of dreams into waking life:

1. Write a dream motto. See if you can come up with a one-line statement that summarizes what the dream is telling you. This simple technique, recommended by Aad van Ouwerkerk, is an excellent way to distill dream insights and may provide an immediate guideline for action in waking life.

I dreamed Fred Astaire was coming to one of my classes. Waking, I asked myself what I knew about Fred Astaire. The two most salient things were that he was dead and he was a great dancer. Since I was already working extensively with the theme of dream communication with the dead, I formulated the following dream motto: "I need to bring dance and movement into my classes."

A woman executive dreamed on a Friday night that she was being courted by three strange men. She became embarrassed when she realized she was wearing only a slip and no panties and ran into another room to put on more suitable clothes. The dream felt quite sexless to her; she associated the strangers with several companies with which her firm was negotiating for new business. She came up with the dream motto "I'm exposed and I need to cover myself"—and spent part of the weekend bringing herself up to speed on corporate developments. This put her ahead of the game when she was asked to make a presentation to prospective clients the following Monday.

2. Confirm your dream messages. Especially if your dream seems to contain a warning about a situation looming up in external reality, you may want to take steps to check the information. This may involve a more active reality check than just sitting around mulling things over. For example: A young woman noticed an earring she didn't recognize in her fiancé's bedroom. Her boyfriend fobbed off her inquiries with a story about sloppy houseguests. Then she dreamed the earring was *in* the bed, swollen to such colossal size it filled the whole space. This led her to confront her fiancé, who confessed he had been having an affair with another woman.

In many societies, confirming a dream message may involve consulting a shaman or a diviner. You may have a favorite system of your own, such as the tarot or the I Ching, that could give you a "second opinion." You may also want to experiment with the technique for "putting your question to the world" that is outlined in chapter 5.

3. Dream fulfillment or avoidance. If your dream seems to promise good things, you will want to figure out practical ways you can help to bring them to pass. If you don't like a future event you have glimpsed in a dream, you will want to consider how to get off the path that is leading you toward it. Many dreams call for *action* in ordinary life.

4. Personal rituals. Making a poem out of a dream report, drawing or painting the images you have seen, or constructing a personal shield or dream talisman are all excellent ways to honor the powers that speak to you through dreams. If the wolf is your dream ally, wear a piece of jewelry or a T-shirt with a wolf motif, study the habits of wolves in the wild, and read Clarissa Pinkola Estés and Barry Lopez on the subject. If a deceased relative appears in your dreams, light a candle for her and remember her on your birthday.

To give you more of a feel for this, I will share a poem that sprang almost fully formed from my journal report of a dream in which I saw myself carrying the corpse of my former self, looking for a safe place to bury it. Whatever its literary deficiencies, the poem underscores that dreamwork can be a profoundly transformative experience, and that any transformation has its price:

The Man with a Corpse on His Back

When you die to the old life
you must bury it well
or you'll stumble on
with the corpse of your old self
strapped to your back.

Bury it well and do your grieving.
Set right what can be set right
with those you hurt
and those who hurt you.
Give up the souls you've stolen.
Reclaim what was stolen from you.
Then walk on and don't look back.

Others will dig up your corpse.
Not only enemies and abandoned lovers
but your very best friends.
They'll exhume your bag of bones
and lash it to your shoulders
to prove you haven't changed.
You'll be dragged, down and back.
You'll need a second wake,
a second burial.

The grave-robbers will come for you
again and again
to chain you to your dead self
until you are changed so utterly
you can only be seen
by those who have changed their eyes.
You'll vanish into the sunlit spaces
where those who cling
to the ghost of what you were
can't find you anymore.

MINI-WORKSHOP

— NINE KEYS TO THE TURNING STAIR

When Diane's husband returned late at night from a business trip, she was waiting up for him in her favorite, sexiest nightgown, ready to give him a passionate homecoming. Instead, he asked her to sit down on the sofa in the living room and proceeded to tell her he was in love with another woman.

"I still love you," Diane's husband assured her. "And I want our marriage to continue. But I'm in love with Dana too. To give her up would be like cutting off one of my own limbs."

Shell-shocked, Diane had a hard time understanding what her husband was suggesting. *He wants us both,* she realized. *He thinks he can have it all.* She thought he was crazy.

She needed time alone with her husband, but circumstances made it easy for him to avoid her. Houseguests arrived. Then Diane's husband left for a conference, leaving her to sort through her rage and grief to find her way forward. Should she present her husband with an ultimatum, forcing a choice that might end in divorce?

In the midst of a crisis that threatened to destroy her home and her marriage, Diane had a powerful dream, richly layered and vividly experienced.

Here is her initial report:

The Turning Stair

I am one of a group of people riding in some kind of conveyance up to the top of a building. The conveyance reminds me of the kind of nontrack trains they have in zoos and amusement parks. No one in the group is especially familiar to me. They are all dressed in casual/business clothes. We are escorted by a male guide.

When we get to the top of the building, the guide tells us to sit still for a moment to regain our equilibrium; we are very high up. The group complies. Then people start leaving the train and getting ready to take the climb that leads down the outer side of the building.

I get out of the train and lean over the railing. I am immediately dizzy, struck by how high we are. My stomach gets that roller-coaster sink-then-rise feeling, and I grip the railing hard and sit down. I tell the tour leader I'm not ready for the downward hike. I need more time to regain my balance and make the adjustment. As I sit down, the ground beneath me seems to be moving. The people in the group move on ahead of me, and gradually disappear from view as they go down the stairs.

After a time, I feel steadier and decide I'm ready to go. But when I look over the railing again, I realize the stairs have no railing on the outer side; the only handholds are in the wall itself. So I need to leave the stuff I've brought with me: a handbag, a coat or sweater, a big paper bag like a shopping bag. I leave it all behind.

I begin my descent, very cautiously. The stair is narrow and pitches very steeply to the right, around the wall of the building. As I go down, it seems to me that the building is revolving counterclockwise, in the opposite direction from the direction I am taking. My heart is pounding and racing very fast. I feel lightheaded.

Finally I reach the bottom of the stair. The other people in the group are about to enter a building some distance away. I look back toward the staircase. I'm shocked and surprised to see that there is no steep staircase along the side of a very tall building. There is only a series of five or six shallow steps leading up to a very ordinary looking business-type hotel. There may be a red Ramada Inn sign out front.

I hurry to catch up with the group. I'm struck by the fact that there are far fewer people in the group than when I joined them—only two or three, instead of a whole trainful.

Diane was pulled out of this dream by her clock radio, her heart still pounding. Since her husband's revelation, she had been shuffling around in a daze, trying to sedate herself with alcohol, shopping, and family chores. What she had experienced in the dream, by contrast, was vividly *real*, and its energy spilled over into waking life. Though unsure what her dream was telling her, she felt stronger, more power-full, more alive.

As she started writing it down, she found elements of a second dream swimming up to her from deeper levels. She now remembered a scene in which she was walking with her child through narrow streets. Though they were not at the beach, this was a tidal area. In the midst of the town, she saw seaweed and sea creatures and sandy pools, as if the tide had just gone out. She noticed a hermit crab carrying a conch shell house on his back, and a large, oddly shaped turtle moving toward her in crablike fashion. The turtle seemed to be wearing a scallop shell. As he came closer, she saw that his right front leg was much longer than the other, and that this accounted for his scything motion. The turtle raised his head and peered closely at her.

When Diane shared these dream adventures, I had a hunch they might be scenes from a single dream, something we tested through dream reentry. I was struck by the confidence and energy Diane seemed to have derived from her dream. The crisis in her marriage was unresolved, her husband had left home to spend time with the other woman, and yet Diane seemed wonderfully centered, even in command. She felt that her dream had given her vital guidance; she was now eager to explore its many levels of meaning.

Because of its complexity and evident importance, Diane's dream invited the use of *all* the techniques described in the previous chapter.

First Key: I asked Diane to describe her *feelings* on waking from the dream. "I woke breathless and excited," she told me. "I felt *physically* as if I had been through this adventure. I also felt good that I had been able to overcome my fears in an unfamiliar situation." With that last sentence, welling out of her felt sense of the dream, we were already close to the heart of its meaning.

Second Key: Not surprisingly, Diane's *immediate associations* were with the critical life passage she had entered with her husband's announcement of his infidelity five days before.

"I think the dream is about *me*," Diane said after a moment's thought. "It reflects some of the grappling I've been going through trying to sort out how I want to proceed."

Third Key: Though Diane's dreamscape seemed heavily symbolic, we ran a *reality check* on all its main elements. The building—an ever-changing locale!—reminded her, at different stages, of several different sites in ordinary reality. At the outset, it resembled a modern skyscraper walled with "Texas glass"—"a Hyatt Regency–type structure that might have an outside elevator." When she got to the top, the railed-in observation deck reminded her of the Empire State Building. On the way down, the building appeared to be round and windowless, something ancient and rough-hewn, "like a castle." When she got her feet on the ground and looked back, she saw something more modest and familiar, like a Ramada Inn.

Picking over these impressions, we were soon able to identify a location (*not* the Ramada!) where her husband had been conducting his affair. Diana added that she went to a Ramada Inn for "local conventions."

Diane did not recognize individuals in the tour group; they were generic "convention people." She could not describe the guide. We agreed to look for him when we went back inside the dream.

Fourth Key: The *dream reentry* was assisted by drumming. One of many discoveries Diane made, when she went back inside the dream, was that she was escorted on her downward as well as her upward journey: "The guide was with me all along." She was able to have a fascinating extended conversation with him, summarized in the next section.

When she explored the locale at the foot of the turning stair, she discovered she was near the beach; the sea creatures and the turning stair belonged to the same dreamscape. When she looked back, the "Ramada Inn" was still the same. But for the first time, she noticed a palm tree that grew to enormous size. She sat down with her guide at the foot of this tree, and he drew pictures with his finger in the sand: a circle enclosed in a square, flanked by squares that proliferated upward as well as outward, forming a 3D model. He pointed to the center and told her, "This is you."

Looking into her dreamscape while drumming, I had a notably different vision of Diane's gyrating tower than the ones she had shared with me. As she spiraled down, I saw it as an immense phallus. I felt rather diffident about sharing an image any good Freudian might have offered at the outset, but followed my own rules by telling Diane what I had seen.

She blushed as she told me, "That's part of it." She revealed that the night before, she had made love to her husband for the first time since he had told her about the other woman, and had found this experience quite extraordinary: "I felt like I was outside my body observing this strange self doing and saying these amazing things. Our lovemaking was passionate and beautiful, better than since the first, rocky days of our relationship. I went with my body wisdom, but also my heart wisdom. Somewhere deep inside me, I knew this was really okay."

Fifth Key: Diane recounted more of her *dialogue with a dream character*: the mysterious tour guide.

During her reentry, he showed himself as a slightly chubby fellow with straight black hair, dressed in black, with wraparound sunglasses, and a gold-capped front tooth. Diane thought he looked Hispanic. He told her to call him Arthur. "He was carrying a wand or baton and a lantern. While he was guiding the group, he waved the baton like a conductor."

Diane's dream guide told her, "You need help in the easy bits. The hard bits you don't have any difficulty with. I need to be here to give you a nudge when you get faint-hearted, as you tend to do when the worst of the struggle is over. You have a tendency to wimp out when you should be in the home stretch."

Diane felt that Arthur was more than an aspect of herself. She saw him as a transpersonal figure. He had a trickster quality akin to that of Exu, the West African divine messenger who has quite a following in the Hispanic community. He told Diane, "I am always around."

At the end of their conversation, Arthur produced a huge ball of multicolored yarn and asked, "Now, what do you think is going to happen when this unravels?" He tossed the ball into the air, and a kitten rushed up and started to unravel it. He told Diane, "All of this is about what is happening to you. And you are still at the center. You have to remember this."

Sixth Key: I asked Diane to *track her dream self.* Had she acted differently in the dream from the way she behaves in waking life? She observed that she was often able to separate herself from "people of convention," as in the dream. In waking life, however, she had a deep aversion to outside stairways and elevators. She felt the way she was able to go up and down the *outside* of her dream building held a lesson for her.

In the dream, she left her baggage, including her pocketbook, behind. I asked if she would be prepared to do this in ordinary reality. She said, with deep resolution, "Faced with what I had to do, *yes.*" She got shivers as she said this.

Seventh Key: There was tremendous scope for *symbol exploration.* The changing structure, we agreed, was a metaphor for her marriage. She had gone up it in a vehicle shared with lots of "conventional" people. She had briefly been on top of the world, but knew her position was shaky, and needed to come down to earth.

Diane felt drawn to look at the pattern of the turning stair. In her dream, the narrow stairway was spiraling down, turning always to the right, while the tower building was spinning the other way. She thought of the double helix of DNA and the interlocking serpents of the caduceus, the staff of healing. "It is the pattern of life," she decided.

Eighth Key: We played the *"What Part of Me?"* game with the sea animals from the earlier dream episode.

What part of Diane was the hermit crab?

"The part of me that can change its shell when it has outgrown it."

What part of the dreamer was the odd-looking turtle?

"There's more of me in the turtle than the hermit crab. I like turtles, and I often notice that I hunker down inside my shell, turtlelike, when I'm challenged. *This* turtle could be the part of me that's ready to stop hiding and even change its shell."

Before we played the same game with the scallop shell, I asked Diane to describe a scallop shell to me as if I had just dropped in from another galaxy.

"It is the outside covering of a sea creature that does not have a skeleton. It's fan-shaped and has up-and-down edges. It opens on hinges. There's soft glob inside when you pry one open. But I've heard that if a sea scallop opens in the ocean, it can live. Maybe that's true for me too."

Ninth Key: As part of *dream enactment,* I asked Diane to formulate a series of dream mottos. What was the message of the turtle?

She formulated a three-part motto: "I've outgrown my old shell. If I'm ready to open myself to deeper ways of knowing, I can survive. This means leaving behind my old stuff."

The last statement resonated with the scything action of the turtle's arm, and also with leaving the baggage behind.

Diane decided that in order to bring the full energy and insight of her dream into waking life, she needed to "stay the course" and "be open to acting out of character"—as she did when she journeyed up and down outside her structure. She noted that when she had faced all her tests inside the dream, the building had been transformed. "There was still a structure in place, and there was nothing to fear. With hindsight, the dimensions of the challenge seemed almost trivial."

She resolved to weather the storms in her marriage while embarking on an adventurous program of personal study and spiritual exploration, ranging from yoga to tarot. Within the year, her husband decided to end his other relationship and renew his full commitment to Diane as his life partner. When she reported this to me, I remembered the scything motion of her dream turtle's crablike leg, and reflected that her husband was a Cancerian who had likened separating from his lover to "cutting off a limb." The couple emerged stronger and more loving than before, in a way that might have surprised the "convention people" from whom Diane parted company in the dream.

In exploring Diane's dream, as in all true dreamwork, the goal is never merely to *interpret* the dream—a process that can shrivel dreams into juiceless abstractions—but to tap into dream energy and bring it into waking life.

3

EXPLORING DREAMS
WITH PARTNERS

Dreaming itself is the workshop of evolution.
Sandor Ferenczi

Dreams never come to tell you just what you already know.
Jeremy Taylor

See yourself in others
Then whom can you hurt?
What harm can you do?
Dhammapada

IF IT WERE MY DREAM

If you think you know everything your dream is telling you right off the bat, you are probably missing something important. Dreams tell us more than we already know, in our everyday minds, and the dream source is constantly calling us to rise to a perspective beyond the narrow horizons of the ego. Sharing dreams with a partner is often rewarding because a second person can often spot something the dreamer is missing.

Sharing dreams with a group can be an even richer source of understanding, providing a variety of insights that may illuminate many levels of the dream. Dream-sharing within a group not only provides insight; it builds community and breaks down prejudice. If you start sharing dreams with other people, you will rapidly discover that you have a great deal in common with them. If you are a newcomer to a dream group, you may find that you make that discovery at the beginning of the very first session, when others start sharing the themes or titles of their dreams, and you recognize something of yourself in a phrase like "Naked in Public" or "My Three Selves" or "Phone Call from My Dead Mother." If you can feel your way into another person's dream and allow them right of passage into yours, you will quickly find that you can imagine yourself in that person's situation. If all of us were able to dream ourselves members of another sex, race, or religious community, there would be far less room for the prejudice that divides us. Dream-sharing is a tool for building habitats for humanity on the level of soul.

Whether you are going to work with a single partner or a whole circle of fellow explorers, dream-sharing requires mutual trust and respect. If you are going to bare your soul to others, you must have the assurance that you are in a place where you are protected and supported. A vital element in your protection is that everyone involved should be ready to share in the same way, including the group leader (if there is one); if you permit others to enter your dreams, then they must allow you the same right of access. Whether there are just two of you or twenty, it is also important that you take care to set the tone for each dream-sharing session. At the start of each of my workshops, we light a candle, perform exercises to center ourselves and call in Light energy, and join in a formal affirmation of purpose. These simple rituals serve to define as sacred ground the space in which we will share dreams and seek renewed guidance from the dream source, where we will seek to act in the spirit of love and healing.

In commenting on each other's dreams, we need to respect an agreed code of etiquette. Working independently, Jeremy Taylor and Montague Ullman,[1] two liberating forces in the modern dreamwork movement, have suggested basic guidelines that might be stated as follows:

➤ THE ETIQUETTE OF DREAM-SHARING

1. You are the final authority on the meaning of your dream.

2. You cannot tell anyone else what his or her dream is about. You can only tell them what it would mean to you if it were *your* dream. You should preface any comments you make about someone else's dream with the phrase "If it were my dream . . ."

3. Sharing dreams does not mean giving up your right to privacy. How much or how little you share of your private life is your decision. You should not ask other dreamers for personal details they have not volunteered, and you should not tolerate snooping by others.

4. Dreams shared within the circle should not be told to outsiders without the dreamer's permission.

RITUALS OF DREAM-SHARING

*O*nce you start working with a dream group, you will come to expect the unexpected. There is no way of telling where the energy of the circle, or the exploration of an individual dream, will carry you (unless, perhaps, you dreamed it). The constant element of surprise, spiced by synchronicity, is part of the adventure of sharing dreams. But if you are going to share dreams with a group on a regular basis, you will want to develop a rhythm that allows you a reasonable chance of getting the essential work done. This requires time limits and traffic control. As my own workshops have evolved, I notice they tend to move through seven distinct phases.

⟶ 1. OPENING THE CIRCLE

The group forms a circle. By having participants gather in a circle, you ensure that no one is placed above, or apart from, the others. By lighting a candle, you signal that you are entering a sacred space and evoke the firepit at which our ancestors shared dreams. The candle should be placed at the center of the group.

Spend a few moments letting your consciousness flow with your breathing. As you breathe out, release any pain or stress or anxiety you may be carrying and wish it out of the space.

The group leader may now suggest a visualization to raise the energy of the circle. Here are two that I frequently use together:

Calling Earth Energy

Stand or sit with your feet on the ground. Try to see and feel yourself reaching down through your feet, into the deep earth below. As you breathe in, let the energy of the earth rise into your body. Let it rise up through your legs, through your pelvis, through your solar plexus. Let the energy of earth rise all the way through your body to the top of your head.

Now let it fall around you as a gentle mist, returning to its source. (Pause)

And let it rise again . . . and flow back again . . . renewing and returning, in an endless cycle. (Pause)

And with each breath, feel your energy grow, and that of the whole circle. . . .

Calling Light Energy

As you breathe in, see the light moving into you. As you breathe out, let the light spread through every part of your body. (Pause)

Now you may begin to see a radiant light above your head, moving down toward you. You may see it as a cone of light, pointing toward the crown of your head.

You are beginning to open yourself to the light energy of All-That-Is. Let it flow into your body through the crown of your head. Let it move down through all your energy centers, shining. Let it roll down in waves of light through your forehead, your throat, your heart, your solar plexus. Let it move through your pelvis and flow down through your legs . . .

And exit through the soles of your feet . . .

And move beneath you and behind you, flowing up the back of your legs . . . up your spine . . . up the back of your neck and your head . . . and reenter you through the crown of your head . . .

And roll through you again, pooling at your natural centers . . . and move around you again . . .

So that at this time and in this place, where there is only now, you are within the Light and you are surrounded by the Light. You are in a place where you are loved and protected.

Members of the group should now join hands and visualize the energy flowing between all the members of the circle.

The facilitator may offer an affirmation on behalf of everyone present. Part of an invocation I often use (which you are welcome to borrow or adapt) runs as follows:

We come together in a sacred and loving way
to honor the wisdom of our dreams
to seek counsel and healing for ourselves and others
to align ourselves with our Higher Self
to remember who we are and what we may become.

— 2. CALLING THE DREAMS

The next step is for members of the group to introduce (or reintroduce) themselves. You may wish to invite participants to describe how they feel and to report any unusual experiences they may have had since the last meeting. At this stage, each person may share the title of a dream (if they have one) and indicate whether they would like to work on that dream during the session.

In an Active Dreaming workshop, we will drum to call up the dreams that will be worked on during the session.

⟶ 3. SHARING

The dreamers who choose (or are chosen by the group) to share dreams now take turns to present their reports.

If you are recounting a dream, you should tell it in the present tense, as if the events are unfolding *now*. You should speak fairly slowly so the rest of the group can keep up with you. If at all possible, avoid *reading* your dream report; try to draw your listeners into your original experience rather than present them with a finished text.

At the end of the first telling, others in the group may ask you questions to clarify their understanding of the dream, but should *not* offer interpretations.

Afterward, you may be asked to retell your dream, or the group may decide to ask others to tell your dream as if it were their dream.

The dreamer should now express her principal question about the dream.

⟶ 4. RESONATING

Other participants in the group may now offer their sense of the dream and its principal images—always remembering to say, "If it were my dream . . ."

In a typical dream group, this process results in a game of shared associations. As long as this remains a head game, it has limited value and can lead away from the authentic dream experience into thickets of irrelevancy. Empathy and intuition are surer guides; they come fully alive within a group as participants drop their barriers and learn to offer associations without passing judgment.

Example: Spilled Orange Juice

Celia dreamed an unidentified woman put something in her orange juice that spoiled it. She threw her juice on the table and walked out the door. Later, when she hailed a taxi to go back to the hotel where she was staying, she had trouble remembering its name. She woke full of anger and became angry again as she shared her dream with the group.

Celia added an interesting piece of information; she did not drink orange juice.

We worked initially with the question "What is orange juice?"

The answers included: "Breakfast time." "Health and vitamin C." "Sunshine." "Energy."

These associations led Celia to formulate the following question about her dream: "Who is taking the sunshine out of my day?"

She now came up with a further association of her own, dating all the way back to early childhood. She remembered admiring a picture of a glass of orange juice on a wall poster on her "first day at school," in kindergarten. She realized she made a personal connection between orange juice and the pleasure and challenge of learning in new environments.

Was there a sense in which she had gone back to school?

Celia had an immediate answer: she had recently started attending the dream group and had also taken up art classes. She felt she had raised her energy level, in midlife, by striking out in these new directions.

So who was poisoning her juice?

The "breakfast time" association held the clue. At 8 A.M. the morning after her dream, Celia now remembered, she had received a phone call from her sister, whom she described as a very negative person "who is always trashing my efforts to learn something new."

We had more work to do to identify the forgotten place where the dreamer was staying. But by this point Celia was already alive to a dream message that might call for action. After encounters with her sister, she told us, she often felt drained, low on "juice." Celia now resolved to limit contact with this naysayer until they achieved a better understanding.

When real empathy is flowing within the group, the game of associations will soon tap into deeper sources. *Echoing*—an exercise to which I was first introduced by Naomi Matthis, a therapist in Santa Fe—is an effective device for speeding this process. It works like this:

After the dreamer shares her dream (and perhaps defines her question) members of the group call out the names of the key elements in the dream. From Celia's dream, for instance, you might select "orange juice," "poison," "unidentified woman," "taxi," and "hotel." While the group echoes the key words, you will choose the dream element that seems most likely to unlock the underlying message. Maybe you would choose "hotel" rather than "orange juice"; where does the dreamer think she is going, anyway? When you have made your selection, you will write a few lines from the perspective of the dream element you have chosen. You might begin simply, "I am here to tell you that . . ."

Even if what you produce, by any process of association, is a million miles removed from the dreamer's sense of her dream, it may be helpful in eliminating false trails. When Lisa shared the dream in which her bathtub overflowed and she vomited "red stuff" (recounted in chapter 2), several women in the group made associations with "control issues" and "power struggles." Even before Lisa was certain her dream was about pregnancy, she knew it was not about any of *that*.

— 5. EXPLORING

Dream exploration may lead in any direction. In group work, the dreamer should *always* be encouraged to run a reality check on the dream content—although she should never be pressured to share all her findings (which may surface painful or embarrassing personal material) with the circle if that is against her inclination.

The closer we can approach the full experience of the dream, the closer we are likely to come to its meaning. This is why dream reentry is one of the most rewarding means of exploration. Dream reentry can be a shared experience. Indeed, many dreamers find it much easier to go back inside the dreamspace with the support of a partner or a group, either because they have difficulty shifting consciousness to a dreamlike state when alone, or because they balk at confronting dream adversaries by themselves.

In Active Dreaming workshops, we use two principal techniques for going back inside the dreamscape. The first is *guided reentry*, the theme for the remainder of this section. The second is *reentry with the aid of shamanic drumming*. This is actually a shamanic journey through the gateway of a remembered dream, in which the dreamer may be accompanied by a partner who will serve as an ally and seek to develop further information that may be helpful for the dreamer. Shamanic journeying, a powerful technique for exploring the dreamworlds in a waking state, is explained in chapter 5.

In all forms of dream reentry, you will not go far wrong if you remember that realtors' slogan: *location, location, location.*

Guided Reentry A: A Hug on a Deserted Street

Cathy offered a dream group this brief report:

> *I am walking on a deserted street. Everything is cold and gray. I start climbing the steps of a row house. Then David comes out the door and gives me a big hug. He doesn't invite me inside the house. Instead, he leads me to a business office. When we come out, he hugs me again and I wake up.*

In response to questions, Cathy explained that her friend David was "a huggy, touchy guy who always made me feel good." She also told us that David had been dead for four years—which alerted all of us to the possibility of an important message here.

I asked Cathy to relax, with her eyes closed, and focus on her breathing.

After a few minutes, I asked her to put herself back on the "deserted street" in her dream and tell us where she was.

"I don't have the faintest idea," Cathy reported after looking around.

"Are there any people you recognize?"

"No people at all, until David comes out of the house."

"Tell us what you hear. Can you hear traffic? Or dogs? Or the subway?"

Mention of the subway triggered something. "I can't hear it, exactly. It's more like vibrations from under the street. Oh, Lord!" Cathy suddenly burst out. "It's Brooklyn."

This called back childhood memories. She had lived in Brooklyn as a kid. She could not think of anyone close to her who lived in Brooklyn now. "Only very dead people, like my grandmother."

More than a verbal exchange was taking place. All of us were sitting with our eyes closed, opening ourselves to the images from Cathy's dream. I glimpsed children's toys—a tricycle, maybe a rocking horse—behind the half-open door of David's house.

When I mentioned this sighting, Cathy got shivers. She told us she could feel her young daughter's presence in the dream, though she had not recalled this before and did not see her daughter now.

Still focused on the dream location, I asked Cathy to walk from the row house to the business office.

"I can't," she announced. "There's something missing."

We soon established a huge gap was in her dream report. To get to the business office, she had to picture herself flying. She realized the office was not in Brooklyn but in another city that felt Southern. She now felt her dead friend had somehow flown her down here without need of an airplane.

I asked her to walk round the office and describe what she saw.

"Computers and picture frames."

Another member of the group, putting these together, asked Cathy whether she was in the office of a graphic design company.

Cathy made an important connection. She told us her ex-husband had just taken a job at a graphic design company in North Carolina.

"Stay with the office for a moment," I encouraged her. "Can you see your ex?"

"Yes. He's talking to David, while I talk to Sue."

We now had two living people who were not in the dream report.

"Tell us about Sue."

"She works in insurance."

Before Cathy could go any farther, a newcomer to the group volunteered an association. "If this were my dream, I would think this is about my need to protect myself. We've got dead people, my ex-husband, and a woman who works in insurance. This could be telling me I need to make sure I'm properly covered in case of death or disability."

Cathy again got goose bumps.

After further discussion, we agreed on a practical step she would take, based on this possible insight: she would check to ensure that her ex-husband had kept current with the premiums due on several insurance policies. This turned out to be prudent. She subsequently discovered that her ex had stopped paying the premiums on her homeowner's policy. The policy was about to lapse, although nobody had informed Cathy—except via her dream.

Cathy regarded the dead friend in her dream as an angel in the literal sense of the word, which means "messenger." However, his message remained buried in a fragmentary report until a guided reentry—illuminated by the intuition of another member of the group—brought us closer to the dream experience itself.

Dream Reentry B: Getting into Men's Pants

Terri volunteered the following dream:

> *I'm in a gymnasium. I have to change because I'm wearing street clothes. A woman tells me there are clothes I can use outside the door. I find a box full of men's clothes. There's also a trunk with personal effects. There's a red logo on some books or brochures, a pattern with a square and a triangle and words that read either* Mad Dog *or* Wild Dog.
>
> *I put on a man's pants and top. When I go back in the gym, I feel bulky and out of place.*
>
> *I want to go on an Exercycle and I walk directly over to the bikes. An attractive young woman is pedaling away. She's boasting about time she has spent with my lover. I am stunned and deeply hurt that I am the last person who seems to know about this.*

On waking, Terri felt wounded, shocked, and deeply alone. Before sharing the dream, she also mentioned she was suffering from acute sciatica pains. She said she did not recognize the gym in her dream, but she knew that her lover had been working out with a female trainer.

She reported that an interesting synchronicity had taken place the night after the dream. At a downtown concert, she ran into a woman friend from her aerobics class who took her to a singles bar where they were doing a promotion for Red Dog beer. Terri had kept a glass with the Red Dog logo as a souvenir; she felt sure this was the logo she had seen in the trunk in her dream.

It seemed quite significant that the overlap between Terri's dream and an incident in waking life had taken place at a singles bar. This suggested one line of dream exploration, as well as the possible need to take some elements in the dream fairly literally. But the first need was to bring back more of the dream itself.

I asked Terri to relax and go back inside the gym. She could not get a fix on the woman who told her where to get clothes for her workout. But the scene came alive when she imagined herself going out through the side door. She now found herself in a "woodsy scene" that made her think of her lover's "country retreat"—a place she had never seen in waking life; Terri revealed in private that they were both married and had tried to keep their affair under wraps.

I asked her to look inside the box.

"I see lots and lots of folded pants, men's pants. They're stacked like files, so I just see the creases until I take a pair out. They are starched and stiff. The cotton chafes my skin." She rubbed her thighs as she spoke.

"What about the trunk?"

"It's somehow attached to the box."

"What's inside?"

She produced a detailed inventory—an entire "gent's wardrobe," with folded blazer and chinos, hiking boots, heavy socks, as well as books and letters, tied together in stacks. She clutched at her upper arms, evidently uncomfortable. The way things were packed in the trunk reminded her of her husband, who was obsessively neat and kept his personal possessions to a minimum. "It's what he would take if he left," she now felt. "Like his going-away bag."

"Can you describe the outside of the trunk?"

"It's rough plywood, like the box, with a utilitarian hasp. It looks like a cheap coffin."

She was uneasy, but determined to go on with the reentry. She wanted to confront the young woman on the bicycle.

I asked Terri to mime her actions as she dressed in the clothes from the box and describe her sensations. A stylish woman, Terri squirmed with distaste and discomfort. "They're *awful!* They make me look like my bottom is sagging. Nothing fits! I don't fit!"

Now that she was getting mad, her spirits began to lift. She was ready to take on the competition.

She moved her attention back inside the gym. She crossed the space, describing several people she had not previously mentioned. She took a long cool look at the younger woman, whom she now described as "late twenties, Mediterranean, with flowing dark hair."

"Do you want to ask her name?"

"I know her name. It's Adrianna."

"Do you know her?"

"I've never seen her before."

"Do you want to talk to her?"

"I think I'll stay out of sight, like before." As in the original dream, Terri moved behind a second bike that blocked the younger woman's line of sight. She mimicked "Adrianna's" speech and body movements as she talked about her relationship with Terri's lover. We noted no direct suggestion of a sexual liaison. What came through for Terri now was the depth of her own feelings of jealousy and sexual frustration.

"Do you want to do what you came to do?"

Terri nodded. She took a step beyond her original dream by imagining herself getting on one of the exercise bikes and pedaling away vigorously. She mimed the cycling actions with her legs.

Terri came back glowing. "Adrianna couldn't keep up with me," she reported. She stretched her limbs and noticed with delight that her sciatica pains had vanished during her dream workout.

We discussed several layers of meaning that had been opened up in the course of the reentry. There might be a *literal* caution that another woman was interested in her lover; Terri filed away the name Adrianna for future reference. As bodytalk, the dream called attention to Terri's need for sexual fulfillment, which was not being adequately served by the combination of a sterile marriage and a furtive, intermittent affair. At the same time, the dream provided a humorous commentary on Terri's inclination to wander with the image of all the men's pants "filed" in the box; she acknowledged, with a naughty grin, that "getting into men's pants" might be the title for the dream.

There was a more somber warning about the state of her marriage, in the image of the coffinlike trunk that might be her husband's "going-away bag." But her strongest associations of all were with the stiff, unsatisfactory man's clothing she had agreed to wear.

I observed that in my dreams, the way I dress often seems to reflect my social identity, the way I appear, or seek to appear, to others. Terri saw her ill-fitting clothes as a possible metaphor for her unsatisfactory marriage, but also for another theme in her life, which gave her the dream motto she finally adopted: "I am trying to claim my masculine power and I stick to this doggedly even though it's uncomfortable."

Our dreamwork remained open-ended, as is so often the case. It also seemed to amount to spontaneous therapy. For all the evident complications of Terri's life, she emerged from this sharing full of bounce, her sense of humor richly alive, and her physical aches and pains utterly forgotten.

⬤ 6. DREAM GAMES

It is not enough to decide what your dream means; you need to do something to bring the energy and insight of the dream into your waking life and to honor the source from which it comes. Dream-sharing is already a step in this direction, especially when it results (as in Terri's case) in spontaneous playacting.

The best dream groups are also playgrounds where people are constantly improvising new games to play with their dreams. *Dream guessing* is an ancient game; you might have the dreamer mime the actions of the dream while the others try to figure out what's going on. *Guessing the outcome* is a variant, still played by traditional Iroquois Indians on the Onondaga reservation; you have the dreamer tell part of the dream, and the others guess how it comes out.

Dream dance moves with the energy of the dream. It works best if you have a real dancer in the group to help establish the choreography and suggest a range of movements. But once a flow is established, even die-hard "nondancers" will abandon their conceptions of what they can do. The simplest variant, appropriate for group celebration, is to *dance your dream animals*. Drumming helps to get people out of their left-brain inhibitions and beating wings or stamping hooves.

Dream theater is perhaps the best game of all. I usually ask the dreamer to play casting director, selecting members of the group to portray the various elements in her dream, including the dreamer herself. Here is a fairly straightforward example of a dream performance that helped to release the full power of a dream experience that hinted at a personal calling. Carol shared the following dream with the group:

Terminal Patient

I am in a hospital room, standing on the right side of a man who is lying under a sheet, covered by a glass lung. There are two other people in the room: an ethereal-looking woman, dressed in a flowing gown, and a man standing at the foot of the bed.

I feel that all of us are dying.

The ethereal woman removes the lid from the bed and carries it over to a second bed. There is nobody in the other bed. I feel that this woman is being selfish. The man under the sheet cannot breathe.

I pick up the lid and put it back on the glass lung.

For the first time, the patient speaks. "Turn—the switch." He makes a hoarse, rasping sound, deep down in his throat. He says again, "Turn—the switch."

The man at the foot of the bed does what he asks. There is a distinct click *as he throws the switch.*

Now I realize the ceiling is gone. I see a brilliant ball of light moving toward me. The light streams into my right hand and I am thrilled by its power. I lay this hand over the patient's left hand. I see his features move almost imperceptibly into an expression of satisfaction. I know he is passing over.

We clarified one element in the story line: the action of the switch. Carol had been confused about whether the patient wanted the switch turned off or on. After discussion, she felt that he wanted his respirator turned off. She remained puzzled about her negative feelings toward the "ethereal woman," who may have tried to bring about the same effect by removing the "lid" of the "glass lung."

Carol chose the cast: first the woman who would play her, then the patient, the ethereal woman, and the second man. She also chose actors to portray the ball of light, the bed, the glass lid, the second bed, and the ceiling that fell away.

The cast went into a huddle with the codirectors—the dreamer and the workshop leader—to work out the choreography. It was agreed, for example, that the glass lid would be portrayed by two participants crouched on either side of the patient, with hands linked. Someone found a flashlight for the "ball of light" to shine on the actor playing Carol in the climactic scene.

The performance corresponded closely to Carol's dream report. It released tremendous emotions, in both the dreamer and the cast. Someone said that the group centered on the dying man looked like a Nativity scene when the light came down.

After the reenactment, actors spoke from the viewpoint of the dream figures they had portrayed. The actor who had played the ethereal woman defended her actions, firmly rejecting the dream ego's belief that they were selfishly motivated. "I removed the lid because it was the right thing to do," she insisted. "The patient was ready to move on."

These dialogues led the dreamer to recognize the ethereal woman and the man at the foot of the bed as "aspects of myself, or personal guides." The performance led Carol to focus on the situation of a male friend who was seriously ill in the hospital at the time. It deepened her sense that she might have been called to play a healing role in relation to others. She told us that she felt "awed" that she might have been chosen to assist the dying in making their transition to the next life. Nobody in that group was surprised when Carol reported several weeks later that the night before her friend in the hospital died, she had a strong impression of his spirit passing over her head.

Our theater with Carol's dream did not require rescripting. But quite frequently, the dreamer may want to make changes in the story line after the first performance, to incorporate new insights, returning memories, or attempt at a better ending.

━ 7. CLOSING THE CIRCLE

Just as group work should begin by defining a sacred space, it should end by returning the participants to their roads in life, hopefully with heightened energy. I usually suggest some assignments for homeplay (*never* homework!). These may include dream telepathy games, experiments with interactive dreaming, or dreamwork with the symbols of everyday life.

The last step is to join hands and give thanks for the shared adventure and the wisdom of dreams.

FORMING A DREAM PARTNERSHIP

*T*here are those who believe that the ideal size for a dream group is just two people, and this is often true. But chances are that you and your regular partner know each other fairly well and tend to look at things the same way, which may prevent you from bringing the benefit of fresh perspectives to the dreams you share. I work one-on-one with many of my own dreams. One of my favorite partners is a psychically gifted woman who frequently dreams about future events and shares my interest in dream precognition. Because we are both so highly attuned to the *literal* content of dreams, we sometimes fail to help each other to recognize other possible layers of meaning. For example, I once spent half an hour with this friend discussing a dream in which Rupert Murdoch sent me a fax letter telling me that I ought to cut down on my teaching commitments so I would have more time to write books. I had once interviewed Rupert Murdoch (as a student editor in Australia), and I knew that he owned a publishing house. My friend and I were both inclined to take my dream fairly literally, as a message that somebody powerful in publishing (not necessarily Murdoch) might one day tender similar advice. A second friend then offered an insight that had escaped me and my original partner. She pointed out that Rupert Murdoch and I share the same initials and were both born in Australia, and also that I had acquired a fax machine (for the first time) shortly before this dream. "If it were my dream," she suggested, "I would ask myself what part of me thinks like Rupert Murdoch."

To have even a single partner with whom you can share dreams with complete trust and intimacy is already a gift. Work with her! However, if you are going to work one-on-one with your dreams, try to familiarize yourself with several different approaches, and experiment with all of them. As your network widens (as it *will*, because when you become an active dreamer, complete strangers seem drawn to share dreams with you even before you announce your interest), you may still prefer to work with a single partner. You should now consider the merits of serial monogamy. By moving from one partner to another, you bring a multiplicity of viewpoints to bear on the multiple worlds of dreaming.

If you are interested in forming a dream group, there are several organizations (listed in the resources section) that can help you with guidelines and contacts. You will need to answer four basic questions: *how many, how often, how long,* and *who's in charge?*

If you want each member of your group to have time to work on a dream in depth within the whole circle at every session, you will have to keep your numbers small; six to eight would probably be the maximum. But you may find that in practice, not everyone needs (or wishes) to work on a dream in depth every time. By agreeing to focus on the most pressing dreams that are volunteered at each session, you could expand your group to twelve to fourteen and benefit from the greater energy and multiplicity of viewpoints of the larger circle. If you work with partner exercises, you could conceivably accommodate much larger numbers, at least for basic training purposes.

Whatever the size of the group, the members should be asked to make a commitment to attend regular sessions over a set time. You might allow for a "trial marriage," while participants are getting to know each other. Members should then be asked to commit themselves to attend weekly meetings for no less than six weeks. A typical group session is likely to run for two to three hours, on an evening or over the weekend.

There are no "experts" in dreamwork, but inevitably there are leaders. Dreamwork is inherently antiauthoritarian, yet it is foolish to ignore the reality, and positive applications, of the personal authority that flows from character, learning, and direct experience of the dreamworld and its inhabitants. Jeremy Taylor, an inspiring teacher who carries great personal magnetism, addresses this issue frankly in his book *Where People Fly and Water Runs Uphill*. In my experience, the best dream groups—like Rita Dwyer's dream network in the Washington area or Jeremy's on the West Coast—center on a seasoned guide who plays the role of teacher without presuming to lecture or lay down the law. No doubt egos will always get in the way. But the purpose of dream-sharing, as of the dream source, is to lead us beyond the ego to a more spirited and generous way of seeing and being.

4

CONSCIOUS DREAMING

Our normal waking consciousness is but one special type of consciousness, while all about it parted by the filmiest of screens there lie potential forms of consciousness entirely different. . . . Apply the requisite stimulus and at a touch they are there in all their completeness. . . . They forbid our premature closing of accounts with possibility.

William James, The Varieties of Religious Experience

Our truest life is when we are in dreams awake.
Henry David Thoreau

He who binds to himself a joy
Does the wingèd life destroy;
But he who kisses the joy as it flies
Lives in eternity's sunrise.
William Blake

AWAKE AND DREAMING

*T*o dream consciously is to be aware you are dreaming while you are dreaming. It is a triune, rather than a dual, state of awareness: you are aware that your body is lying on a bed, you are aware of the contents of your dream, and you are aware of watching yourself dreaming. In a state of conscious dreaming, you are likely to shift back and forth between these foci of awareness; you may get so caught up in dream events that you forget you are dreaming, or feel the need to check on the state of that body in the bed. Once you learn to dream consciously, you may find you are able to move into levels of dreaming that were previously beyond your comprehension. You may perceive this progression as a sequence of dreams within dreams, nested like Russian *matreshka* dolls. Your return to ordinary reality may now be a series of false awakenings. To use a different analogy, if you have ascended from a Level One dream to (say) a Level Five dream, coming back to the waking world may be rather like descending from a mountaintop through a series of base camps, each of which you may temporarily identify as "home."

I prefer the phrase *conscious dreaming* to the widely used term *lucid dreaming,* for two reasons. First of all, some of the recent enthusiasts for "lucid dreaming" have given the impression that their aim is to practice *dream control:* to manipulate dreams to serve the agendas of the waking ego. Though Stephen LaBerge has labored to correct this impression in his excellent second book, *Exploring the World of Lucid Dreaming,* the desirability of "controlling your dreams" is still promoted by other advocates of lucid dreaming. The point is that dreams are wiser than our everyday minds and come from an infinitely deeper source. To try to "control" this source, to interfere with the authentic flow of dreams and to justify this on the grounds that they are "only dreams," is the ultimate delusion of the control freak who lives in the ego. Fortunately, it is an attempt that can never succeed. One way or another, the dream source *will* remind us that we are not the masters of the universe. If it were truly possible to put the ego in charge of dreams, the effect would be to divorce us from soul and spirit.[1]

My second dissatisfaction with the term *lucid dreaming* is that it is now widely understood as a technique for programming yourself to wake up inside the dreamstate. We are advised to do this by telling ourselves, over and over, that we are going to do it; by memorizing "dreamsigns" (e.g., "If I see my hands, I will ask myself if I am dreaming"—the Castaneda method); or even by strapping on an expensive pair of goggles with a flashing red light that is supposed to alert us to the fact that we are dreaming. All these techniques may work at some times, for some people, but they are not the simplest or most rewarding way to become a conscious dreamer.[2]

Spontaneous lucidity, inside a dream, may be triggered by various things. You may find yourself doing something it would be difficult or impossible to do in your physical body, like flying or walking on water, and this may jolt you into becoming aware you are dreaming. You may catch a glimpse of yourself and notice you are younger or thinner or a different sex or color from your everyday self. A woman dreamer realized she was dreaming when she looked at herself in a bathroom mirror, inside her dream, and was startled to observe that her face was covered with shaving cream and she was holding a razor.

Many dreamers are startled into lucidity by an auditory signal inside the dream: a doorbell, a ringing telephone, a siren, or a voice. The voice may be that of a dream guide who is actively inviting you to become conscious you are dreaming. In one powerful dream, a companion I had not previously noticed asked me, "Where is your body?"—making me aware that I was dreaming and that I was outside my body. One of my favorite accounts of spontaneous dream lucidity comes from a woman dreamer who found herself making out with a pop music star. Here is her dream report:

The Wrong Beatle

I'm in a movie theater, cuddling with one of the Beatles. It gets hot and heavy. Then I realize I'm with the wrong Beatle. I'm with Ringo Starr, the only member of the group I never found cute. This wakes me up

to the fact I'm dreaming. I tell myself, "I'm dreaming so I can switch Bea-
tles." But at the end of the dream, I'm still stuck with Ringo.

There are other ways you may become conscious, inside the dreamstate, you are dreaming. A false awakening may be the trigger. However
it comes about, your consciousness that you are dreaming will give you
endless possibilities for creative play, for developing skills and rehearsing
for future challenges in waking life, and for investigating the nature of
reality itself. You may find you are able to return to a special place of
training and exploration relevant to your interests. I know a computer
programmer who likes to visit a software laboratory that he describes as
Dream Windows. I visit a Dream Library where I can read books that
have not yet been published, and a locale I think of as the Gallery of
Time, where symbols from different cultures and periods provide doorways through which I can travel backward or forward in time. I know an
artist who likes to go to a Dream Gallery where she gets ideas for paintings she has not yet done—she often sees them as finished works—and
can experiment with new media without having to wash off her brushes.

Such return visits to a dream locale are often accomplished in the twilight zone of consciousness, between sleep and waking, and the mode of
travel may be rather similar to the shaman's journeys into nonordinary
reality. Despite the claims made for blinking goggles and other artificial
prods, the easiest way to become a conscious dreamer is to start experimenting with the images that will come to you, entirely naturally, on the
cusp between sleep and waking, if you can open yourself to receiving
them. If you want a ten-dollar word to describe these experiences, you
may call them hypnagogia. If you are comfortable with such language,
you will want to distinguish hypnagogic images—received in the state
"leading toward sleep"—from hypnopompic sightings, which come in
the state "leading away from sleep," i.e., after you wake up. Creative
people are often quite familiar with these twilight states of consciousness. Robert Louis Stevenson received the ideas for many of his best-
known tales, including the whole plot of *Dr. Jekyll and Mr. Hyde,* from
"brownies" who visited him while he lay on his bed in a state of reverie.
Einstein said that his greatest breakthroughs came to him in this state.
The Russian philosopher P. D. Ouspensky wrote an interesting essay on
his observations in the twilight zone.[3]

EXERCISE: FUN IN THE TWILIGHT ZONE

*O*n a night when you are not so tired you are likely to fall asleep straightaway, and your belly is not drum-tight with food and drink, lie in bed and relax.

Focus on the flow of images and impressions that come to you as you relax with your eyes closed.

You may find yourself looking at a succession of faces that change as soon as they take form. You may see a series of childlike drawings or photographs, falling as fast as autumn leaves in a high wind. You may simply see hazy shapes and colors. You might see a whole theater of characters waiting to introduce themselves.

You have begun to look into a gallery of possibilities.

When you see something that catches your fancy—a face, a scene, a picture barely formed—try to hold it in focus. If you can hold your attention on the image you have chosen, you can follow it into a full-fledged dream, while retaining awareness that you are dreaming.

Move gently into this sequence. Tarthang Tulku, a teacher of Tibetan dream yoga, puts it well: "While delicately observing the mind, lead it gently into the dreamstate, as though you were leading a child by the hand."[4]

Do not try to manipulate the flow of images in a crude or artificial way. Because you are conscious, you are able to choose your direction and your mode of operations. If you run into a situation you don't like, of course you are free to leave the dream. But a dream is never "only a dream," and there are good reasons for staying with the dream and trying to resolve any problems that come up on its own ground. You can always ask for help.

At this point, you should find it easy to get airborne. You may choose to use your initial dream as a launching pad from which you can fly off to visit a person or place at a distance from you, or to explore deeper levels of dreaming. You may find yourself drawn to move toward a point of light at the edge of your field of perception. As you go toward it, you may find you are entering a tunnel, traveling faster and faster. Go with the flow. Be open to whatever may be waiting for you on the other side. In an entirely natural, spontaneous way, you may find yourself crossing through one of the doorways into the dreamworlds of the shamans.

You are likely to reach a point where you will become so absorbed in the dream events that you will forget you are dreaming. Alternatively, if you let your attention falter or your inner critic comes to the fore, you may fall out of the dream.

The challenge is to stay with it and open up new territory.

As you develop confidence and skill, you will find you can not only return to stable locales in the dreamscape; you can arrange to meet other people there, both dream companions and partners from waking life with whom you can share fun and adventure.

As you become a more conscious dreamer, you will bring the gifts of greater consciousness into your everyday life, which is also a dream. Through conscious dreaming, you will learn to observe the contents of your mind and to stand outside your ordinary personality. When you can stand outside your ordinary personality, you can change it.

DREAM JOURNEYS OUT OF THE BODY

*I*f you wake up to the fact that you are dreaming, you may also notice that you are not in your regular body.

If this experience is new to you, your first instinct will probably be to jump back into your body, which will also pull you out of the dream. With practice, you can learn to master your initial fears that you won't be able to get back to your body, or won't be able to cope with whatever is waiting out there on the astral planes. You will now be ready to make some important discoveries.

You may observe that when you journey outside the physical body, you are using a second body (or dreambody) that retains the semblance of physical form. When you use this vehicle to visit people and places on the physical plane—say, to drop in on your boyfriend in Chicago—you will probably be invisible to them unless they are dreaming or unusually receptive. In other dimensions of reality, you will be right at home. On the astral plane, your dreambody is your natural body. This is where many of your encounters are likely to take place with other people who are moving around in their dreambodies. These include other dreamers, dead people, and entities that never had physical form. Because the dreambody is extremely malleable—once you recognize that it will assume the shape of your thoughts and desires—travelers on the astral plane can present themselves in a fantastic variety of forms.

You may be drawn to paradoxical locales. You may find yourself in a setting that seems thoroughly "real," where you can share fully in the lives of the people around you, but the strange thing is that while you think you are out of your body, they think this is physical reality. A doctor friend reported an experience of this kind:

> *I woke up to the fact that I was dreaming and out of my body and started running around yelling to everyone, "I'm having a lucid dream! I'm having a lucid dream!" The only people who paid any attention looked at me as if I might be mildly deranged. I felt a consuming desire to have sex and went looking for a woman. I found a couple of attractive women, both sexually experienced. I said to myself,* This is my dream and I can do anything I like, *and tried to embrace them. They pushed me away as if I were some kind of sex maniac. I told them,* This is my dream and I can make love to you if I want. *They didn't believe me. I became embarrassed and apologetic, as I would have done in waking life, and left the dream.*

I do not think the doctor was simply running away from a sex fantasy (we'll get to sex and the dreambody in a moment). I think that, through a conscious dream, he became aware that he was spending time in a dimension that was literal reality for its inhabitants, but not for him. Perhaps they exist in a parallel reality that conforms to physical laws. Perhaps they are people who have passed on and are currently living in a transitional community they believe to be "real." Perhaps they exist in *this* physical reality—in which case the doctor must have succeeded either in transferring his consciousness to the body of another person, or in projecting a dreambody that seemed fully corporeal to the people around him.

Chances are you have already had any number of spontaneous out-of-body experiences during your night dreams. Do you dream of flying, or falling? Have you ever dreamed of being stuck in your car on top of a mountain, like the Jeep in the TV commercials? Do your dreams switch from black and white to color? Have you woken with a jolt, feeling that something has dropped inside your body? Do you have dreams within dreams and wake up only to find you are still dreaming? Such experiences often contain trace memories of journeys outside the body.

You can learn to induce, in a waking state, what you are probably already doing in your sleep. Robert Monroe, whose book *Journeys out of the Body* has helped greatly to demystify the whole subject, suggests that this is something almost anyone can do, and I believe he is right.

To induce a *voluntary* journey out of the body—which the old books call astral projection—you need four basic elements. The first is *relaxation* in a protected space where you will not be disturbed. The second is *conditions for liftoff.* These may include special breathing, visualization, sexual arousal, and other stimuli intended to change the flow within your energy field and loosen the connection between the physical body and the dreambody. The third element is the *ability to overcome the barrier of fear.* The final element required to sustain the journey is *clarity of purpose:* the ability to resist a swarm of diversions and possible sources of confusion along the way.

At one stage in my own experiments, I noticed a tendency to get too caught up in the mechanics of the process. This is probably typical of beginners, but was a curious segue for me, since journeys out of the body had never seemed either exotic or difficult to me; I suppose my childhood illnesses had helped to shake my dreambody loose from the physical. For much of my life, I seemed to be able to shift consciousness and simply project myself in the direction of a chosen target in an entirely smooth and natural way, without the bumps and grinds and flashing lights described by Monroe. When I decided to try out some of Monroe's techniques, I had rather different experiences, as the following excerpt from my journals will illustrate:

Wednesday, June 15, 1988

    I lie on my back on the bed in the guest room and fall into a relaxed state, fully conscious. The image of a beautiful woman who visited me in a dream the night before returns to me. I become sexually aroused. I focus my intention on using this sexual charge to achieve liftoff from my physical body.

The vibrations come quickly, beginning at the toes. My legs are soon vibrating quite violently. The vibrations move all through my body, up to my head. I attempt separation too soon, too jerkily—and am diverted by noises outside (a barking dog, a train passing).

I look at the clock. 45 minutes have elapsed. My mouth is quite dry. I realize that for all this time, I have been breathing through my mouth, making a rasping noise.

I lie down on my side, to make a second attempt at separation. This time, the vibrations are most powerful in my head. Behind closed eyelids, I see flashes of light high up above my head, at the very edge of my field of vision. I have the sense of receiving a painless electric shock.

I have the impression of an owl's face, pressed close to my own—beautiful, soft, glossy feathers. Is the bird connected with the woman I used as a focus?

My concentration is again broken by noises outside the house.

In my third try, I feel a definite sensation of stretching, as of rubber or elastic, especially around my head. I have a strong sense of extending myself beyond the limits of my physical body.

I again focus on the woman. Each time I call her mentally, there is another electric flash. I now see her vividly, dressed as a priestess in a light, diaphanous robe. I feel an even stronger sexual charge, pulsing through my second body. I am certain now that this will give me liftoff. I feel I am becoming something else. My arms are turning into wings.

This time I am interrupted by a male presence. When he enters my consciousness, I recognize him as an ally. His intention is loving but firm. He wants me to go back and return when I am better prepared. I'm slightly embarrassed that he has caught me in the middle of a sexual adventure, though I explain that it's all in the aid of research.

This less than highly evolved, and notably unsuccessful, experiment consumed several hours. I have included it here as a cautionary example of the penalty for getting stuck in the mechanics of a process that will unfold quite naturally when the circumstances are right. The vibrations, the light effects, and the stretching sensations I experienced paralleled

Monroe's account of his own early liftoff procedure. So did the power of the sexual drive as a means of propulsion.

One of the charms of Monroe's work is that he is refreshingly candid and down-to-earth about the importance of the sex drive in inducing out-of-body experiences, and in directing (or distorting) subsequent adventures. Monroe notes, "There seemed to be a direct relationship between what I interpreted as the sexual drive and the 'force' that permitted me to dissociate from the physical body."[5] His frankness is a welcome antidote to the winks and nudges and hints of dark secrets you find in old occultist stuff about astral projection. In fact, Monroe is expressing an open secret, well-known to genuine psychic explorers of every tradition. One of the most ancient and most celebrated images of the shaman is a scene that was painted in the Lascaux temple cave twenty thousand years ago. It depicts a male figure, arms spread like wings, with an erect penis. Behind him is his bird-staff; tossing its horns before him, an enormous bull. The shaman is journeying in ecstatic trance. Sleep-laboratory technicians started noticing back in the 1950s that penile erection in men is often associated with the REM state; they are just getting round to observing the corresponding, but subtler, symptoms in women. What the men in white coats have not told us is what was known to the artist of Lascaux, twenty thousand years before EEGs: that penile erection (in men) is the most consistent physical reaction associated with a journey out of the body. This is more than a casual side effect. The same energy that may be released in the physical act of sex is harnessed and used like a jet propellant. In the language of the East, this is the raising of kundalini, the "serpent power," and it is at the heart of all real magic.[6]

One of the easiest ways to initiate a journey outside your physical body is to allow yourself to become sexually aroused without expending that energy in immediate physical gratification. You can do this alone, through fantasy, or with the help of an adventurous partner (who does not need to be with you in the same physical space). If you are experimenting alone, you should try to withhold orgasm completely and switch the energy to the second plane, beyond the physical. If you are in bed with a partner, you should delay physical release for as long as possible and again focus on switching the energy to move into a different dimension. If both of you are bold spirits, you might try to arrange an astral assignation, which you will both attend in your dreambodies. In addition to play, you may then be able to undertake all sorts of joint experiments and explorations and compare the results.

There is a dual challenge in this. The first is to honor your natural sex energy without fear or guilt, *without confusing the underlying force with the purely physical expression of sexuality.* The second is to avoid losing your fundamental purpose in the party scenes you may encounter on the lower levels of the astral planes.

There is a reason why Eastern mystics sometimes call the dreambody the "desire body." Once it is released from the physical body, its desires and appetites can become ravening. I suspect that this is how people land in the different situations in which they find themselves after physical death. I had a conscious dream about this that was quite instructional for me. In the dream, I found myself in a hospital emergency room. Several people who had just died were roaming around outside their physical bodies, lost and bewildered. Someone asked me to help, so I started escorting them toward the Light, hoping that their guides or relatives would come to meet us. We journeyed through several locales—one contained bars and honky-tonks, another a Club Med–style singles scene—where most of my gang took off to have sex or pursue old habits. By the time I reached a locale familiar to me on a higher level (a place of education that resembles a pleasant Midwestern college), only one of the people who had died was still with me. Emanuel Swedenborg, the Swedish scientist-turned-mystic, came to believe as a result of his journeys outside the body that we create heavens and hells from our desires.[7] This is why yogis, mystics, and shamans all practice the art of conscious dreaming as a preparation for the conditions the soul will encounter after physical death. It is why conscious dreaming is fundamentally a spiritual practice.

If the last statement seems like a vertiginous leap from my earlier comments about the importance of the sexual drive in these areas, it is only because our society has confused the nature of both spirituality and sexuality and set them falsely at odds with each other.

In my continuing experiments with conscious dreaming, I find that the transfer of consciousness to and from the dreambody is fluid and natural, without the jarring vibrations of my "early Monroe" phase. It may be accompanied by the sound of rushing air, or by the impression of a flashing light above and slightly behind my head. In a successful experiment two months after the botched attempt I reported earlier, I had the impression of being drawn up through a cone of light:

Through the Cone of Light

Wednesday, August 31, 1988

As soon as I lay down and closed my eyes, I saw a dancing figure of blue light, inside a blue circle, reminiscent of a hologram.

I had the brief sensation of something sliding away from my body— like a soft serpent—and heard the rush of air. Then I was outside the house, wandering around the west side of the property. I decided to go and check on some relatives. I entered the house through the top story. The new baby was in a cot at the foot of the bed. When it started to cry, the father got up to fix a bottle. Nobody noticed me except one of the older daughters. When I spoke to her, she simply seemed to rise up out of her sleeping body and gave me a hug.

I got up to make notes, feeling I needed to check some of these details to make sure I was not simply imagining this stuff.

When I got back in bed, I again had an impression of the "blue lady." White lights began to flash at the top of my head. I had the sensation of being pulled up into a cone of light and visualized this as the inside of a pyramid, with an opening at the top.

I found myself in a long, narrow chamber—very light, with many tall windows—hung with masks and sculpted heads. It had the quality of a gallery or museum, suspended somewhere in space. A rounded doorway was at the end of the gallery. As I moved toward it, I was startled by an enormous face: the face of an attractive woman, but of giant proportions. I backed away, despite the woman's beauty and welcoming expression.

Then came another shock. I glimpsed the feeler, or part of the leg, of an insect that was also blown up to giant size. I wasn't happy about dealing with a bug this big, so I concentrated on expanding myself to comparable proportions.

I found the reverse process taking effect. I was now shrinking incredibly fast. The insect's leg now looked as big as a tree. The shrinking continued to accelerate. I realized that, in becoming infinitely small, I was also harnessing immense energy and happily acquiesced in this process. I saw "planets" spin by and realized I must be traveling in the space between atoms and molecules. This space was as vast as the galaxy.

I saw an intense pinpoint of white light. In some way, I became it. I was traveling unbelievably fast.

Through swirling cloudbanks, I saw another world. Its sun was a great white disk, much closer to the surface of the planet than our sun is to Earth. The planet was screened from its burning rays, to some extent, by dense gaseous clouds. I was looking at a dramatic, jagged range of mountains.

I knew I was in the presence of a life force. I could not visualize it clearly. I picked up a fleeting image of a humanoid creature with an enormous head. I realized the life-forms of this place are not focused on material reality in the way that we are. They put on images as we put on clothes.

I had an extended "conversation" with the presence. Its thoughts seemed deep and heavy as a mountain. I did not hear it speak; it did not communicate in language as we know it. Its thoughts were not expressed in linear form, yet I seemed to receive them without need of a mediator. However, some of the translations were far from easy, and I think I missed a great deal. I was told, "You were born an interpreter."

When we parted, I had strong sensations of a deep exchange of affection, less personal than love, yet strong and empowering.

I have omitted much of this report, including the substance of my dialogue on the world beyond the "white hole." In this conscious dream, I was able to explore several kinds of territory. At the outset, I seemed to be wandering about—outside my body—in the ordinary world, and nobody saw me except the girl who was dreaming. (I was later able to confirm some of the details I had picked up.) When I went up through the cone of light and entered the "gallery in space," I was in a different dimension of reality that evidently conformed to different laws. Later I felt I had entered a different galaxy. I could not tell whether it existed only in inner space, in the dreamtime, or whether in some way inner space and outer space might be one and the same.

Just one more observation about this particular experience. I had the strong feeling that I had been "called." This came from the early appearance of the "blue lady," and her return when I had finished rambling about in the middle world. Of all the ways of initiating conscious dream journeys, the most powerful—more powerful even than sex!—is that of being *called*.

From many adventures of this kind, I found I was developing personal maps of paths and landscapes inside the dreamworlds, places to which I could return. As you become a conscious dreamer, you will develop your own geography and form your own understanding of the conditions that apply in different orders of reality.

STABLE LOCALES IN THE DREAMSCAPE

*M*aybe you already find yourself returning again and again to dream locations that do not have a counterpart in ordinary reality or seem to belong to an order of reality where the rules are completely different. Despite what you may have been told about the fluid, fleeting nature of dreams, some of these locations appear quite stable. They have structure and form and offer the possibility of multisensory experience. You can explore their paths on visit after visit. You can rendezvous with other dreamers.

In this way, you can learn about worlds beyond physical reality. You can begin to recover knowledge you may have had before you were born. You can explore the possible conditions of life after physical death. You can go back to special places for specific guidance or healing.

You may wonder how many of these dream locales are "imaginary," the work of your own imagination or that of other dreamers. You will notice that some have a manufactured quality, like movie sets. Some of these dream environments are certainly created by other people. But they are not "imaginary" in the diminished sense of that much misused word. In the language of the Persian philosophers, they are *imaginal*, which means something rather different.

In their visionary works, Avicenna and Sohrawadi described a nonordinary reality they called the *alam al-mithal*, or imaginal realm.[8] It exists on the astral plane, beyond physical reality. But it has form and dimension, and as in the physical realm, structures are built there by human effort and vision: gardens and deserts, cities and caverns, even heavens and hells. You can visit them and return to them as often as you like, once you know the paths and are prepared for the gatekeepers, who may challenge your right to be there.

Shamans know a good deal about these things. Among indigenous peoples, apprentice shamans are required to make ecstatic journeys through a metageography created and mapped by previous voyagers. They are given limited directions, but are expected to report back in elaborate detail. Their courage and competence will be judged by how closely their reports correspond to their mentors' knowledge of these territories in nonordinary reality. Among the Warao Indians, for example, the shaman-to-be is required to make a trance journey in which he must face and overcome various terrifying ordeals. If he survives, he is expected to reach a series of magical waterholes. He must select one as his own. This becomes his special spot: a place of power to which he will return in dreaming to cleanse himself and renew his energy. He is also required to visit and report on the houses of spirit beings, like the House of Smoke in the east and the dark house of hungry ghosts in the west. Above all, he must learn the paths into and out of the Dreamtime where his most important training will take place.[9]

Homer's *Odyssey* describes a created locale in the dreamscape that was used for similar purposes by the Mystery schools. When the adventurer Odysseus, the "man of many ways," is returning to ordinary reality after his long voyage among gods and spirits, he is washed up naked on the Phaeacian shore. The Phaeacians are a people of dreams. Their wild, rocky coast is a liminal zone, on the borders between sleep and waking.[10] In the Western Mystery traditions, the Phaeacian coast was long used, and is still used, as a way station and meeting point for adventurers in consciousness. It is a stable locale in the dreamscape, created and maintained by the shared intention of many generations of dreamers. You can explore it for yourself, when you are ready or when you are called. I have been there in dreams. I can still taste the wild figs.

USES OF CONSCIOUS DREAMING

*J*ulie became aware she was dreaming when she noticed two anomalies in her dream situation. First, a male classmate from high school was in the bathroom with her—an invasion of privacy she would not have tolerated in waking life. Second, when she picked up a book from the stand next to the toilet, she noticed something unusual about it. The book resembled a proof copy; it had a light green cover with a picture of a candle. As she looked more closely at the candle, she realized it was not a cover illustration, but a "real" candle flame, inside the book itself.

Now aware she was dreaming, Julie reported, "I start doing some of the stuff I usually try when I become lucid inside a dream. I try flying out the window, getting caught up in the putty around the frame. I decide to visit my mother and deal with some of the rage I've been carrying because of her. This doesn't prosper."

When we discussed her experience, Julie recognized she might have done better to have stayed with her original dream, using her awareness she was dreaming to explore the "light inside the book." When we did this through dream reentry, she realized her dream might be prodding her to start working with old journals and letters—"the book of my life." Over the years, she had given up a great deal of her energy trying to deny the rage and pain caused by recurring patterns of abuse and neglect. Julie had some writing ambitions, but it had not occurred to her until now that the story she might have to tell was her own. By setting out to rewrite "the book of my life" into a literal book (the "proof copy" of the dream), she might now be able to bring the gift of self-awareness into waking life and break with those recurring patterns.

When I am asked, "What is the point of conscious dreaming?" I am tempted to give the reply Ben Franklin made when a woman asked what was the point of electricity: "What, madam, is the point of a newborn child?" An expansion of consciousness is very much like a new birth. It brings new worlds of possibility. To be truly *conscious* is to be aware of how your thoughts and emotions shape the worlds you inhabit—and that you have the power to change them. As you become more conscious in dreams, you become more conscious in life.

Where your explorations in conscious dreaming will take you will be determined by your purpose, your courage, and your familiarity with the many levels of dreaming. After attending some of my programs, a Wall Street attorney reports a series of fascinating experiments in "folding time" through conscious dreaming. He recently hooked up with a physician in Victorian London, circa 1870, and says they have been investigating the nature of time travel together. A young man whose mother was undergoing major surgery decided he would try to help her by making a conscious dream journey to the operating theater and trying to enter her dreams. When he found her, he was surprised and delighted to realize that several other dream visitors were present, including his deceased grandfather and some close friends, who were focused on sending healing energy to the patient at that time.[11]

Conscious dreaming facilitates *shared dreaming:* your ability to join a partner in your dreams.[12] You might set up a "dream date" with a rendezvous at a locale familiar to both of you either in ordinary or nonordinary reality. Or you might simply focus on your intention to get together and let things unfold. In one experiment, one of my students and I had an interactive dream in which the woman took me to visit an apricot orchard on the farm where she had grown up. In my dream, I encouraged her to pick a fruit and replace it on the stem to verify that we were dreaming the same dream. Instead, she chose to transform the apricot tree into a beautiful silver birch.

Wherever spirituality is alive, conscious dreaming is recognized as the most important source of instruction on the soul's survival of death and its conditions in the afterlife. The detailed account of the *bardo* states through which the soul will travel after death that is presented in the Tibetan Book of the Dead is based on the conscious dreaming of generations of dream yogis.[13] Even St. Augustine—who had problems with dreams when he abandoned his lover for the church and decided that sex was disgusting—recommended paying the closest attention to dreams in which the dreamer is conscious he is outside his body. In a letter he wrote while he was working on *The City of God,* Augustine quoted the experience of one Gennadius, "a physician of Carthage." In a dream, Gennadius encountered a radiant young man who escorted him to an otherworldly city were he heard singing "so exquisitely sweet as to surpass anything he had ever heard." Waking, the doctor dismissed his experience as "only a dream." His radiant visitor returned the following night and asked Gennadius whether he had been asleep or awake when they had met before. At this point, the doctor became aware that he was dreaming. When his guide asked him, "Where is your body now?" he became aware that he was also having an out-of-body experience. This was the preliminary to a teaching session in which he learned that the soul's condition after death is similar to its condition in dreams, and he lost his doubts about life after life.[14]

The story of Gennadius finds echoes in the experiences of conscious dreamers today.[15] In a dream that was the gateway to many further explorations, I found myself in a large room where a circle of people were waiting for me. An electric blue fire burned in an alcove. A radiant guide indicated that I was to lead them through it. As we danced into the fire, my guide asked, "Where is your body?" Now aware both that I was dreaming and out of the body, I was briefly tempted to rush back to check on the inert form on the bed. But I managed to stay with the dream and was shown a number of places of teaching for people who seemed to have passed on. At one of these teaching facilities, students of all ages joined their voices in songs of extraordinary beauty. The chorus of one of these songs stirs in me now:

> What cannot be seen in the dream
> Cannot be seen in its glory.

EXERCISE: THE TREE GATE

Shamans have a special doorway into the dreamworlds. In the next chapter, we will walk through it.

But first, I would like to pause and invite you to perform a simple visualization that I frequently offer at the start of my Active Dreaming workshops:

Sit or stand with your back straight and your feet on the ground. Breathe in deeply and let your diaphragm expand. Hold your breath for a moment, then exhale slowly, releasing all the air from deep down inside you. As you breathe out, get rid of any negative thoughts or feelings you may be holding and wish them out of your space.

Now you can begin to reach down below the soles of your feet and feel your connection with the deep earth below you. As you breathe in, let the energy of Mother Earth rise up through the soles of your feet. Let the earth energy rise through your legs . . . through your pelvis . . . through your solar plexus . . . Let the earth energy move all the way up through your body to the crown of your head . . .

And see it returning to the earth in a fine mist . . .

And rising again through the soles of your feet . . . and moving all the way up through your body . . .

And returning to the earth like a gentle rain . . .

Rising and returning, in an endless cycle.

Now you can begin to reach even further down into the earth. Feel your toes reaching down like the roots of a tree. Feel the sap rising within you.

Now you are calling back the picture of a tree that you love.

It might be a tree you loved in childhood. It might be a tree you have seen at a special place in nature, or a tree in your yard. It might be a tree you know only in dreaming.

Your tree could be a mighty oak that stands strong in all seasons. It might be a swaying willow. Or a hazel, giver of wisdom. Maybe it is a beautiful silver birch or an evergreen, or a fruit tree, full of juice. Maybe it is a holly, the tree of willing sacrifice.

Find your tree.

Feel how your roots go deep into the soil and draw up the energy of earth. Feel the earth energy rising through your body again . . . and returning in a gentle mist . . .

Feel yourself becoming one with your tree.

Feel the air as it moves through your leaves and your branches. Is it warm or cool? Moist or dry?

What can you smell?

What do you taste?

Can you hear birdcalls or running water or the rush of the wind in your leaves? What can you hear?

Look all around you, up and down. What can you see?

Feel how your arms spread far and wide, reaching for the sky. Let the light flow down through your canopy and fill you. Feel how you feed on sunfire and breathe for the world.

Feel how your body fills the whole expanse between earth and sky. Your roots go deep, all the way down to the Lower World. You rise through the Middle World to touch the sky.

Relax into the deep dream of your heartwood . . .

Maybe there are memories returning to you now . . . things about your deepest self that you forgot . . . clues to who you are . . .

When you are ready, gently return the way you came.

If the tree you have found is one you know in the natural world, make time to sit with it. If the tree springs from your dreaming, look for its counterpart in nature. Sit with it and be still. Ask for its wisdom.

If you have found your special tree—*truly* found it, with all your inner senses—then you can return to it anytime you choose, in *dreaming*. You can find a passage through its roots to the Lower World, to seek your animal guardians. You can rise from its upper limbs to seek spiritual guidance and healing in the many dimensions of the Upper World. You can make this your starting point for Middle World journeys to scout out the future and visit people and places at a distance from you.

As I write, I think of many special trees that have been doorways into dreaming during different passages in my life: of the singing she-oaks and an ancient grass tree that brought me voices and visions of the dreamtime in my native Australia; of the oak that called me to my farm in the Hudson Valley; of the holly that offered me the cup of communion and sacrifice in a Celtic gathering; of the wild figs of the Phaeacian shore; of the maple linked to an Iroquois shaman of long ago; of magical times in the New Forest in England; of the hemlock on a rich man's estate that brought me an appeal for help from a lost soul; of the gifts of hazel and ash, willow and yew.

If you have any Celtic blood, you will not need persuading that there is magic in trees and a special connection between trees and dreamers. But all dreamers know this. Mapuche shamans, in southern Chile, climb a tree ladder in ecstatic trance. The prophet Elijah is visited by an angel while he is sleeping under a juniper; Old Testament angels (and the people who could see them) also favored oaks and myrtles. Odin hangs suspended for nine days—like the Hanged Man of the tarot—on the world-ash, Ygddrasil, to gain wisdom. The druid is literally the "oak-seer," i.e., one who sees with the aid of the oak. For the cabalists, the secrets of the cosmos are contained in the multidimensional Tree of Life, whose roots are in the Above. Malidoma Somé, a West African shaman, says simply that trees are wiser than people, and I think he is close to the truth.[16]

Walk through the Tree Gate, and you are already at home in the three-tiered cosmos of the shamans.

5

SHAMANIC DREAMING

I had to have dreams before being able to act.

Isaac Tens, Gitskan shaman

Our greatest blessings come to us by way of madness, providing the madness is given as a divine gift.

Socrates

Last night the moon came dropping its clothes in the street
I took it as a sign to start singing
falling *up* into the bowl of the sky.

Rumi

DREAM CALLINGS

*T*he shaman's calling is often announced in dreams, and much of his or her training is the work of guides inside the dreamworld.

Stanley Krippner and Bruce Carpenter have published a riveting report of their encounters with a traditional healer, or *dukun,* on the Indonesian island of Sulawesi, who was called to her vocation by dreams.[1] When she was about thirty, Rohanna Ler's son fell ill with an eye infection that local physicians were unable to treat. Then an aged man appeared to Rohanna in a dream. He told her it was her destiny to become a healer and that her son would be her first client. He warned her that if she refused her calling, her son would go blind and never recover his sight. He put a stone in her hand and instructed her to place it on her son's eyes to extract the hidden source of the disease.

Waking, Rohanna found a stone in her bed. She placed it on her son's eyes, as she had been told to do in the dream. He soon made a full recovery.

However, her husband, a devout Muslim as well as a prosperous businessman, refused to allow Rohanna to practice as a shaman. He found conventional explanations for their son's recovery. Three years passed, and Rohanna received a more insistent summons. In a "dreamlike vision" a young couple demanded to know why she had not followed her calling. When she explained her husband's opposition, they took her out of the house and showed her a tremendous fire that threatened to consume her husband's business. They told her the fire would come if she continued to refuse her call. They gave her a large ring and told her she could use this in the same way she had used the stone. Waking, she found an unfamiliar ring in her hand.

Rohanna's husband eventually gave in and allowed her to practice as a healer, on condition that she did not hang out a shingle and gave the money she earned to charity. When Krippner and Carpenter visited her, they found Rohanna operating a busy practice. She specialized in casting out evil spirits and in the direct transfer of psychic energy.

Death and rebirth, abduction and dismemberment by hostile spirits, are common themes in the initiatory dreams of shamans-to-be. Some of these dream reports are reminiscent of the stories of contemporary Westerners who claim to have been abducted and subjected to medical experimentation and implants by space aliens.

Even in dreaming cultures, not everyone welcomes the call to become a shaman. The shaman's path involves many ordeals. In many societies, at the instigation of rival priests or medical practitioners, traditional healers have been reviled, persecuted, or butchered, as they were during the European witch-craze. Among indigenous cultures that are in transition, as in mainstream Western society, people often resist a shamanic dream calling because they fear it conflicts with another religious affiliation or could jeopardize their social position. But if the calling is genuine, the penalty for rejecting it can be high. The ethnographic literature is full of accounts of reluctant shamans who were hounded by death and misfortune until they agreed to enact their dreams.

The great Arctic explorer Knud Rasmussen once asked an Inuit guide if he was a shaman. The Inuit replied that he could not be a shaman because he had never been ill and did not remember his dreams.[2] This theme of a dual calling and initiation, through dreams and a psychophysical crisis, echoes through many accounts of how shamans are made. The initiatory illness, explained and ultimately healed through *dreaming,* is one of the shaman's central qualifications to practice. Shamans are wounded healers; they deal with problems they have encountered and overcome in the depths of their own beings.

A Zulu woman called Dorcas was confined to a sickbed for three years. Local doctors could neither explain her condition nor heal it. Several members of her family, including her grandfather, had been shamans, or *sangomas*. But Dorcas, a Christian, had accepted the view of her minister that the *sangomas* were witch doctors and would have nothing to do with them. It seemed her ancestors had other plans for her.

"No one becomes a *sangoma* without first getting sick," she said later. "Everyone who is called by the spirits gets the sickness, a bad sickness."

Her time of illness was dominated by dreams. "At night I would leave my body, and my spirit would go far, far away to other places that my body never sees." Since conventional medicines had failed to help, Dorcas was advised to consult traditional healers. But she was inhibited by her orthodox Christian beliefs.

Then she had a dream visit from her deceased grandfather. He told her she was sick because she was resisting a calling to help her people. If she agreed to follow his path, he would join her and help her become a *sangoma*. He told her, "You will do my work."

Dorcas was scared and hostile. "I wanted none of that *sangoma* business."

Her sickness worsened, and she received more dream visitors. "At night the *sangomas* would come in my dreams and shout at me that I must become *sangoma*." She had her bed moved to another room, but this did not solve her problem. In dreams and dreamlike states, the spirits came after her. "They became so strong it was like at the cinema. The pictures came before my eyes just like they were real."

The dream visitors conducted teaching sessions. They showed Dorcas the tools of a Zulu shaman's trade: herbs for healing, bones for divination. One night, she saw a whole crowd of spirits rocking the bench at the end of her bed with their singing and clapping. An enormously fat female shaman was among them. She yelled at Dorcas, "Get up! Get up and sing! You are *sangoma*, you are not sick! Wake up—you must wake up and teach!"

Dorcas was told to weave herself a shaman's headdress from beads and hair. This time, she complied. But she still held back, refusing to put on the headdress until her grandfather returned in a terrifying dream and threatened to end her life unless she accepted her calling.

When she put on the headdress, everything changed. Her illness was lifted. She went to an aunt's house and danced wildly for hours, though she had not walked for three years. She had become a shaman.[3]

Isaac Tens, a Gitskan Indian from the Pacific Northwest, was another reluctant shaman. Aged thirty, he started falling into deeply disturbing trance states. An enormous owl grabbed his face and threw him to the ground; he woke with blood streaming from his mouth. He was pursued by crowds of people, by spirit animals, by tall trees that crawled and slithered like snakes. He was caught up in a whirlpool; he saw his flesh boil. These visions were accompanied by strange events and coincidences in waking life. As in the case of Rohanna, the Indonesian healer, a spiritual emergency seems to have been accompanied by a breakdown of the normal barriers between different orders of reality.

Isaac reported these terrifying disturbances to the shamans of his own people, the *halaaits*. Instead of telling him he was crazy, they instructed him to accept his terrifying experiences as proof that the spirits were calling him to practice as a shaman. Isaac was not enthused; the shaman's life is not easy. He tried to go back to his previous way of life, but the spirits pursued him, this time with the gift of song. His dream guides taught him healing chants. When he finally agreed to follow his calling, these songs of power became the heart of his healing practice.

When Isaac agreed to become a *halaait,* he was isolated from the community for a full year. His task during these months of isolation was to dream. "I had to have dreams before being able to act," he recalled. In his dreams, he received guidance from the spirits on healing operations, especially shamanic extraction techniques for removing the hidden sources of illness. When he was ready to treat patients, he practiced dream incubation to diagnose their complaints and decide on the appropriate course of treatment.[4]

Among Australian Aborigines, "spirit men" and "clever men" are also called by dreams and serve their apprenticeship inside the dreamworld. Among the Kurnai of Gippsland, shamans were traditionally selected and "made" by ancestral spirits who appeared to them in their dreams. Through dreams, the ancestors taught the novice sacred songs, how to work with quartz crystals and talismans, and the geography of the spirit worlds. These preparatory dreams were sometimes followed by a ritual in a cave where both the living and the dead were present. A. P. Elkin describes one such ceremony:

> One individual, after dreaming of his father three times, was carried by a cord tied around his neck and waist to Wilson's Promontory. There he was blindfolded and led into a great cave, where it was bright as day. All the old men were round about. The initiate's father showed him a lot of shining things on the wall, and told him to take some. He was taught outside the cave how to make them go in and out of his legs. The ghosts then carried him back and left him up in a tree, where he found himself on waking.

He was able to throw the shining things received in the cave, "like light in the evening."⁵

Among the Aborigines at Walcott Inlet, it was believed that the high god, Unggud, summoned potential shamans through dreams. Those who had the courage to answer their calling faced a terrifying trance-initiation in which they saw themselves killed and dismembered. The potential "man of knowledge" is reborn from this ordeal with a new brain, filled with inner light, and a new body, filled with shining quartz crystals. He now has the ability to send his dream double, or *ya-yari*, outside his body to gather information. His shamanic powers are described by an interesting term, *miriru*. Elkin explains its meaning as follows: "Fundamentally it is the capacity bestowed on a medicine man to go into a dream state or trance with its possibilities."⁶

Some elements in the stories I have just recounted may seem alien or exotic to those of us who live in modern urban environments. Yet modern Westerners, hooked up to the Internet or the morning commute, are also called and initiated in dreams in ways that are remarkably similar to the experiences of tribal shamans.

Take the case of Carl Gustav Jung, the founder of analytical psychology and one of the greatest liberators of the Western imagination in the twentieth century. Jung's path to his most important work and teaching led through a psychospiritual crisis at midlife in which he was pursued by the spirits in dreams and visions and saw part of his soul carried off into the realm of the ancestors. As in shamanic initiation crises, Jung's inner experiences were accompanied by strange phenomena and the play of sychronicity in his physical environment; in the thick of his dream visitations from the dead, he became convinced that his house was haunted. Lacking a shamanic model to explain the storms that threatened to overwhelm him, he feared he was going insane. He found the teacher he desperately needed in the dreamworld, which is where shamans always find their true teachers and their truest initiation. The guide Jung called Philemon helped him to realize his calling and integrate his experiences—a process that took seven years and the invention of a new conceptual vocabulary. Jung perceived *his* Philemon as an old man with blue wings and the horns of a bull. Toward the end of his life, Jung said this about his guide:

Philemon and other figures of my fantasies brought home to me the crucial insight that there are things in the psyche which I do not produce, but which produce themselves and have their own life. . . . It was he who taught me psychic objectivity, the reality of the psyche. . . . At times he seemed to me quite real, as if he were a living personality. I went walking up and down the garden with him.[7]

Even in this late confessional work, Jung is cautious about how he describes certain experiences; he was raised in a respectable Swiss German household, in a city of bankers and cuckoo clocks, and his professional peers prided themselves on being people of science. Yet the fundamental experience—of being called by the spirits through dreams—is profoundly shamanic. Jung recognized the depth of his affinity with the ancient ways of the shamans on a visit to Africa, where he recognized a landscape he had seen in dreams as it might have been thousands of years before and (forgetting his bourgeois inhibitions) joined in the dances and medicine rituals of a tribe he was meeting for the first time.[8] Part of Jung's greatness was that instead of "going native," as he confessed he was tempted to do, or isolating himself in some alternative community, he proceeded to harness the power of his visions to the needs and modes of understanding of the society in which he lived. It was this ability that made Jung most truly a shaman of the West. Shamans have walked alone where the earth is narrow (as the Iroquois say), but they become true shamans only when they use their gifts for the benefit of a community, and to do that they must know its ways and bring their dreaming to where the people live.

Though Jung's intellectual and creative gifts—and therefore his ability to put his dream experiences to work—were extraordinary, his dream calling and initiation was no more unique than those of the tribal shamans we discussed before. People in all walks of life, with condos and car payments, are called by dream visitors in the same way. The spiritual guides who reveal themselves in dreams may take many forms. But two sources of dream calling are almost universal. More than likely, you have encountered them already, especially if you are being called to a shamanic path. If you choose to follow that path, you will certainly be required to deal with both kinds of dream visitors. The first are spirits of the departed, especially departed members of your family, including distant ancestors. The second are spirits associated with the place where you live, who may include spirits of the first inhabitants of your country, spirits of departed shamans or spiritual practitioners who once lived in the area, animal guardians, and nature spirits.

A New York woman who had survived a life-threatening illness with the help of healing dreams started dreaming of her deceased grandmother, who had practiced as an herbalist. In a series of powerful dreams, her grandmother passed on some of her tradecraft and urged the granddaughter to take on a healing practice of her own. Here is one dream from the cycle:

Lessons from My Dead Grandmother

I am ambling down the mountain in a place I love, behind my grandmother's old house. I start wondering, in the dream, what my grandmother would say if I asked her for a definition of the soul.

She appears the moment I have that thought. She is holding a fallen walnut in her hand, still sheathed in the multiple layers of shells. She begins peeling the difficult layers of shell away until she reaches the fruit. She makes this process seem quite effortless. She allows the shells to fall to the ground. She takes the walnut, closes her hand around it, and squeezes. The walnut pieces fly into the air, and they are no longer exactly solid. They sparkle a little. They seem to be the essence of the walnut. I realize my grandmother has just demonstrated the nature of the soul—its many shells, its sparkling essence.

Now she leads me to a place at the foot of the hillside where she used to conduct healings. A man is stretched out on the ground, arms folded over his chest almost as if he were dead. My grandmother shows me a tall plant I have never seen before. The leaves are large, long, and thin, and they seem almost joined in pairs along the stem. The flower is bright yellow, quite flamboyant. It is level with my face. As I admire it, my grandmother smiles and says the flower is like the sun. She takes the leaves and soaks them until they are almost black and a little slimy. Then she places them in layers over the upper body of the supine man. She says the leaves will restore him.

The dreamer could not identify the flowering plant in her dream. Then two weeks later, while picking raspberries in a country field, she felt she walked into her dream. The neighboring meadow was filled with tall plants she had never seen before—except in the dream. The flamboyant yellow flowers nodded at eye level. She discovered that the plant was *Silphium perfoliatum,* or Indian cup, and had many recognized uses in native medicine (including treatment of chest and lung complaints) and spiritual cleansing. But her subsequent experiments were guided by her dream teacher: her departed grandmother.

On the theme of dream visitations from spirits associated with specific places, I will share a brief account of an experience I had on a visit to a Seneca Indian site near Rochester, New York.

I woke with a start in my motel room soon after 4 A.M., with fleeting dream images of deerhoof rattles and little native medicine pouches. After taking a shower, I returned to bed and let myself slide into this conscious dream:

Seneca Burial Place

I am flying over dense woodland. The trees assume collective identity, taking on the form of huge bears and wolves that seem to advance toward the cleared land. I fly over formal gardens, toward a greenhouse cluttered with plants and tools. I am drawn to a trapdoor near this greenhouse. It opens, and I realize I am at a burial site. There are two maskettes— miniature Iroquois False Faces—inside the grave.

A Native American man hovers over the site. He gives me his personal name, and I know he is a Seneca Indian medicine man. He says clearly and distinctly, "I will teach you about HON-WA-DEE-OH."

He shows me scenes from his life, of buffalo hunting, maybe somewhere out West, of hard drinking in his earlier years, and of something like death and rebirth. I glimpse a silver object, shaped like a thunderbird, an equal-armed cross, and a full-size mask with shells for eyepieces. The Indian says, "Burn tobacco for me."

After we part company, I see a number of white people, including an animated red-haired woman, and another native figure. He is wearing a magnificent circlet of bright orange feathers radiating outward from his head. His outfit puzzles me, because it seems to belong to an entirely different culture. He looks like an Amazonian Indian.

This conscious dream gave me a number of interesting leads. I was able to follow them up almost at once. I had an appointment that morning with Peter Jemison, a Seneca Indian artist who was also the manager of Ganondagan, the site of a Seneca village burned by the French in the 1600s. When Pete welcomed me into his kitchen, I stared at the unfinished painting on the table. He was painting an Amazonian Indian with a sunburst of feathers around his head—the last figure I had glimpsed in my conscious dream.

I asked Pete a series of questions about my dream. He recognized the formal gardens as the Sonnenberg Gardens, in nearby Canandaigua, and told me it was "almost certain" there were Seneca Indian burials there. He became very intent when I repeated the Seneca phrases I had taken down phonetically. "Ho-non-di-ho," he corrected my rendering of the key phrase.

"What does it mean?"

"They are above the faithkeepers. They are in charge of the most important Longhouse ceremonies." Pete became guarded at this point. I learned only later that the Honondiho are the keepers of the famous Little Water Medicine, the most powerful of the traditional medicines of the Seneca people, whose secret is closely guarded and passed from the keeper to his chosen successor.

I had no doubt after this exchange—and the further synchronicity of meeting the redhead from my dream when Pete walked me over to the office—that I had received a "visit," apparently from a deceased shaman who had lived in the area I was visiting. This led me into further explorations that deepened my understanding of shamanic practice, particularly in the traditions of the First Peoples of the region where I was now living.

Spiritual guides may appear in many guises in your dreams. We will examine the many masks they assume, and the challenges involved in working with them, in part two. First we need to explore the methods shamans use to maintain contact with dream guides, gain entry to the many worlds they inhabit, and apply their counsel to the problems of daily life.

THE SHAMAN'S GATEWAY

*I*f "everyone who dreams is a little bit shaman," as the Kagwahiv say, then *every* approach to dreamwork that honors dreams as coming from a source beyond the ego might be considered "shamanic." For example, we have seen how the gestalt approach that treats everything inside a dream as a living entity with a voice of its own parallels the shamanic perception that *everything* is alive and ensouled. However, we now come to techniques that take us deeper into the dreaming of the shamans. These go beyond the exercises described in previous chapters, and beyond the practice of most Western therapists.

The word *shaman* is borrowed from the language of a shamanic people, the Tungus of Siberia, and is usually translated to mean "one who is exalted, or lifted up"—i.e., a person who has the ability to go outside himself in ecstatic trance.[9] This clearly implies the ability to journey outside the body in an altered state. In the midst of the shamanic revival in our society, there is a good deal of confusion about who "shamans" are and what they do. Many people seem to believe that shamans are people who hold sweat lodges and burn lots of sage. If you are a North American Indian, or wanna-be, this may be the case, but external rituals have little to do with the heart of shamanic practice, which is *dreaming*. So what is *shamanic dreaming?* After considering and rejecting many definitions, I suggest the following cross-cultural description: *A shamanic dreamer is a conscious dreamer who has developed the ability to enter the dreamworld at will to communicate with dream guides, to journey across time and space and into other orders of reality, and brings back gifts of healing and insight for the benefit of others.*

How do shamanic dreamers "enter the dreamworld at will"?

A master shaman may do this simply by *shifting attention* in a relaxed state.

But few of us are master shamans, and even master shamans, on an average day, can use stimulation or prompts.

In tribal cultures, shamans may employ many techniques for shifting consciousness. They use breath control, fasting, sweats, sleep deprivation, solitary vision quests at special locations (such as "power places" in nature or burial mounds), dancing, chanting, and (in some cultures) the ingestion of psychotropic drugs. They also use visualization devices, focusing on a symbol or image that may provide a doorway for a dream journey to one of the many dimensions of nonordinary reality. But cross-culturally, the shaman's characteristic device for shifting consciousness is monotonous percussion, especially drumming.

There is magic in noise, as Mircea Eliade, the pioneer scholar of shamanism, observed. Shamanic drumming, perhaps the oldest technology for transcendence, seems to work amazingly well with rational, Western-educated people in the post-postindustrial era. Michael Harner, who has introduced thousands of people to the "core techniques" of shamanic journeywork, notes that the vast majority of participants at his workshops report vivid and useful experiences during their first drumming session. I regularly notice the same phenomenon in my own Active Dreaming workshops. If the exercise is properly framed, and the purpose is clearly stated, nine out of ten participants embark on powerful, fully conscious dream journeys on their first exposure to a drumming session that may last no longer than twelve to fifteen minutes. This seems to happen almost regardless of the religious background, education, or belief systems of the people who take part. At a conference in Holland, a pair of Freudian analysts chased after me after attending one of my Active Dreaming workshops to tell me they had just seen the most vivid images they could recall and had gained strong experiential proof of telepathy. The people who have most difficulty with the drumming are individuals who need to be in control all the time. "Control freaks" are also the people who find it hardest to recall and work with sleep dreams. They cling to their ego defenses, terrified that if they open themselves to the source energy that speaks through dreams, they will be swamped and overwhelmed. When they finally let themselves relax into the rhythms of the drum, they are usually able to go home and start working with their dreams.

Shamanic drumming is not concert music. At its simplest, it is one or more drummers beating at a steady rate, usually four to seven beats per second. This drumming may produce striking vibratory effects. In my workshops, people often ask about singing voices, other musical instruments—sometimes whole orchestras—they seem to hear in the pulse of a single drum. In a dream, I was once astonished and delighted to find that many primal instruments, including a sistrum and a didgeridoo, had been cunningly built into my drum and were playing along with it—a neat commentary on this vibratory effect. But in ordinary terms, shamanic drumming is not "making music." It is a means of opening a doorway through sound.

The steady, peremptory beat serves as a focus for concentration. It helps to get rid of clutter. It quiets the chatterer and numbs the skeptic who live in our heads. It reduces the tendency of the "monkey mind" to wander off in any direction. It overrides old mental patterns. A female business executive told me after her first session, "When the drum got hard, I finally got out of my left brain."

Some physiologists believe that shamanic drumming may harmonize neural activity inside the brain with the frequency of the beat, an effect that is also described as "sonic driving." The pace of the drumbeat corresponds to brain-wave frequencies in the theta band (four to eight hertz) associated with the hypnagogic state and its dreamlike imagery. The theory is that during exposure to shamanic drumming, our brain waves get in step with the beat, carrying us into the patterns of the theta state and the corresponding flow of images.[10]

According to your preferred model, you can choose to believe that shamanic drumming works because "sonic driving" herds brain waves into the theta band, or because it helps the dreambody to get loose from the physical body, or because you have spirit guides who are eager to communicate and will give you a lift as soon as you open yourself up to them. What matters, demonstrably, is that shamanic drumming *works*—faster, more reliably, and more safely than certain alternative techniques for inducing altered states of consciousness. It is certainly a welcome alternative to "improving the mind through chemicals." It may also be better adapted than Eastern methods of meditation in assisting Westerners, with our endemic hurry-sickness, to get beyond our left brains.

The classic shamanic cosmos is three-tiered, as it is clearly pictured on a Lapland shaman's drum in a Berlin museum. There is an Upper World and a Lower World—not to be confused with heaven and hell—beyond the Middle World in which humans spend much of their waking lives. The Lapp shaman is shown as a primal Santa Claus, flying between the worlds on a magic sleigh, drawn by his power animal, the reindeer.*

In typical beginners' exercises, as developed by Michael Harner and his colleagues at the Foundation for Shamanic Studies, shamanic journeyers are taught to find a visual focus for entry into one of these three realms. To enter the Lower World, to make contact with an animal guardian, they might be asked to picture a passage leading down into the earth, like a cave or tunnel or an animal's burrow. To rise to the Upper World in search of a spiritual teacher, they might be asked to picture a means of ascent: to imagine themselves on top of a mountain or a tree, or being shot out of a volcano or scooped up and carried away by a twister, the way Dorothy got out of Kansas. Since we live on the cusp of the twenty-first century, there is no harm in using images of our times. I find some people can launch themselves quite effectively on an Upper World journey by picturing themselves riding up in an open or glass-sided elevator (the "Hyatt Regency Method").

The Tree Gate exercise offered at the end of chapter 4 provides a visual focus for a dream journey into any of the three standard zones of the shamanic cosmos and recalls the World Tree, or *axis mundi*, that is a frequent motif on Siberian and *saami* drums.

The visual images that are selected—as in pathworking, a method taught by Western esoteric orders that may involve the use of tarot symbols, the images of sacred sites, or the building of Inner Temples in the imagination[11]—constitute the gateway into a conscious dream. The drumming opens the gate and fuels the journey.

In Active Dreaming workshops, we call up the images of a remembered dream to construct our gateways for conscious journeys into the many worlds of dreaming. While the visualizations suggested by a group leader may be artificial (or simply the wrong doors for us to use at this time) our dream images come from our personal source. They open the paths it is right for us to follow now. They lead to the guides who have already been seeking to communicate to us. By working with our per-

---

* The original Santa Claus was almost certainly a shaman, a fact that might surprise the greeting-card industry. His red coat evokes the flayed skin of a reindeer.

sonal dream images in this way, we ensure that we will not be carried away into the realm of other people's suggestions and projections.

We choose our own dream gates and use drumming to go through them into territory we have already scouted in dreams and beyond it, into larger forests of possibility. In my workshops, dreamers who journey in this way often choose partners who will escort them, track them through the dreamscape, and afterward share "my dream of your dream." This usually yields valuable insights and is often a powerful introduction to *shared dreaming,* another shamanic technique.

EXERCISE: JOURNEYING AND TRACKING INSIDE THE DREAMSCAPE

*F*or this exercise, you should wear loose-fitting clothes and choose a space where you and your partner(s) can lie full length on the floor. Make sure you will not be disturbed; switch off the phone if there is one in the room. You might want to arm yourselves with cushions and blankets to get comfortable and keep warm. (You may find your perception of temperature changes during the exercise.) Other essential supplies include a notebook to record your experiences and newsprint or art paper on which to draw your dream images and map your journeys.

Drumming is not strictly necessary for this exercise, especially if you and your partner(s) are already conscious dreamers and have developed personal techniques for shifting awareness. However, the use of shamanic drumming tends to deepen and accelerate the experience for *everyone* who participates.

Ideally, at least one of you will be able to lay hands on an appropriate drum—a single-headed frame drum with a long-handled beater is best for these purposes. However, if nobody in your group has a drum, or if you lack confidence in your drumming abilities, you may wish to experiment with a drumming tape (see the resources section).

This exercise will work best with at least three people, so that one can drum while the others journey. Most of my examples come from my work with considerably larger groups. However, the heart of the exercise is an adventure for two.

— STEP ONE: CLEARING A SPACE

As in all work with partners, you should begin by gathering in a circle and clearing space for your explorations through breathing and energy-raising exercises. By lighting a candle, you signal that you are opening a sacred space and are ready to receive guidance from transpersonal sources. You may wish to affirm your shared purpose: to invoke the wisdom of the dream source and the powers that speak through dreams.

Here is an affirmation I frequently use in shamanic dream circles that you may wish to adapt for your purposes:

> In the presence of earth and air, fire and water
> In the presence of the unseen
> We come together in a sacred and loving way
> To seek the counsel of our true spiritual guides
> To honor the wisdom of our dreams
> To walk the path of soul and spirit in this lifetime.

You may wish to invoke the protection of spiritual allies, for yourself and the circle, by names that are meaningful to *you*.

If you are working with a single partner, you should sit facing each other and join hands during the affirmation.

— STEP TWO: CALLING BACK THE DREAM

We call back the dreams we need to work on *now* with the help of shamanic drumming. Apart from the person who will drum for the group, you should lie on your backs with your eyes covered during the drumming. (If you have back problems, make yourself comfortable as best you can.)

The initial drumming session should be kept short; ten to twelve minutes should be sufficient. The object at this stage is not to embark on a full-fledged journey but to get everyone acclimatized to the effects of the drum and to allow each of you to identify the dream that is calling you at this moment. This dream may have come from the night before or may rise out of your earliest memories of childhood. Or it may be a stream of images that seem completely fresh, from a new dream borning in this room.

Trust the images that come to you.

At the end of the drumming, draw a picture from your dream. Don't worry about your artistic abilities; this is not an art competition. The best pictures, for our present purposes, will evoke the setting or a central figure in the dream: a house, an island, a train, a bear.

⟶ STEP THREE: SHARING WITH PARTNERS

Now you are ready to share your dream image, and the story behind it. If you are working in a group, find a partner. Decide who's going to go first. If you are on first, show your picture and tell your dream story as simply and clearly as possible, in the present tense. Your partner's main job at this point is to help you decide your main question about the dream. Do *not* get involved in dream interpretation and head games. All you really need to communicate, in this initial sharing, is an image that will help both of you to go back inside the dreamscape, and a question that will guide your explorations.

⟶ STEP FOUR: REENTRY AND TRACKING

During the next drumming session, both of you will seek to reenter the same person's dream. You should focus on two things: the dream *location* and any dream *characters* who might be able to answer the question you need to resolve.

The same basic instructions apply to both the original dreamer and the tracker: When you get back inside the dream, look around you carefully and try to establish exactly where you are. Look for who or what inside the dreamscape might be best equipped to answer the question. Hold that question in your awareness, as you would hold a flashlight in the dark. (But don't be confined by it, especially if you are the tracker; you may feel the question your partner has about her dream is less important than the question the dream may be putting to her.)

During the drumming, you may find it helpful to lie next to each other, touching lightly at shoulder, hip, and ankle, to reinforce your connection.

This time, you are embarking on a full dream journey. You will want to allow time to explore the territory in depth and bring back your prizes. This will require a longer drumming session, perhaps twenty to twenty-five minutes. The drummer should remember to sound a strong recall signal (a pattern of four peremptory beats, repeated several times) to bring everyone back to the circle.

➳ STEP FIVE: COMPARING TRAVEL REPORTS

After the drumming, you and your partner will take turns to share your travel reports. I usually ask the tracker to go first. If you are playing this role, you need to remember two things. First, all you can offer is "my dream of your dream": you have been permitted privileged access to your partner's dream, but you still cannot tell her what it means. Second, trust your images; what you have brought back might seem confusing or irrelevant to you, but may go to the heart of her situation (see "The Peach Pit Principle" below).

The overlap between these travel reports often provides rich experiential evidence of what Jung called the "objective psyche."

➳ STEP SIX: ROLE REVERSAL

You and your partner now swap roles and do the exercise the other way round.

➳ STEP SEVEN: HONORING THE DREAMS

If you are working with a group, you are now ready to share experience with the whole circle, which may lead to spontaneous rituals to honor the dreams—for example, through dance, dream theater, healing ceremonies, or the creation of dream talismans.

➳ DOUBTING THOMAS

When I was first experimenting with this exercise, I learned something about its power from a businessman who attended one of my workshops at a community college. Thomas was a large, confident man, a self-made millionaire with rugged good looks. But before the start of play that morning, he confided that he was nervous. "I don't know if I can do this dream stuff," he told me. When I asked why he had come, he confessed that his wife had signed him up. "She says I need to get in touch with my inner self." I tried to reassure him that all he needed to do was to allow himself to go with the flow.

Thomas partnered Phyllis, who shared the following dream:

I Can't Get Down to Earth

I'm stuck in a place where I feel confined. I manage to get out through a window and I'm flying around, free as a bird. I feel wonderful! Then I realize I have to get back to earth. I can't get down because power lines are blocking me. There are people who are holding these power lines in place, but I can't see who they are.

Her question about the dream was "Who is blocking me?" Thomas was more inclined to ask "What is stopping me from coming down to earth?"

Thomas was skeptical about his ability to go inside another person's dream. But at the end of the drumming, he let out an almighty war whoop.

"What happened to me?" he boomed.

We invited him to tell us about it.

"I just became an eagle inside Phyllis's dream," he told us with rising excitement. "It was totally real. I saw everything." He proceeded to describe the dream location in great detail, adding many elements the dreamer had not shared but was now able to confirm. He gave precise personal descriptions that enabled her to identify a work supervisor and a family member who might be the source of serious problems, including possible job loss.

— THE PEACH PIT PRINCIPLE

To apply your natural intuition to someone else's situation or problems, in dream reentry or everyday life, you must learn to trust your impressions, even when they are faint and do not make sense to you. Obviously you are going to check any information you pick up. But don't dismiss it out of hand because it seems weird or trivial before you have gone through the checking process. Things that are meaningless to you may be quite central to another person. Because you are not that other person, you may be unable to make sense of these things until you have shared them. You do have access to information of this kind, nonetheless, because on a deep level we are all connected, because intuition is your birthright and because at times it comes fully alive.

I summarize what I am trying to explain here as the Peach Pit Principle, from one of my experiences of dream reentry with a partner. A woman artist reported a complex dream of a house that was and was not her own. The house had different sections; one resembled a busy coffee shop with an industrial-sized kitchen. The kitchen she recognized as her own was in complete chaos. She wandered through it looking for a place to dump some trash she was carrying in her hand, but soon got confused because food and garbage seemed to be jumbled up together. Before we did the reentry, we agreed that a possible dream motto might be "I need to sort out the garbage in my life." The dreamer also confessed that her literal kitchen, like the one in the dream, was a total mess, in need of expensive repairs she had delayed making because she felt her marriage was on the rocks and was not sure how long she would be staying in that house. A literal element in the dream seemed to be pointing the dreamer toward a metaphor in waking life: the state of the place where she was nourished and fed.

When I entered the artist's dreamscape, I noticed that the trash she was trying to dump looked like a stack of old letters. I also picked up the strong image of a peach pit, with shreds of the fruit still attached. It was much larger than a normal peach stone.

When we discussed our experiences, I had no hesitation about mentioning the letters. This triggered some useful associations; the dreamer had been wavering over whether to get rid of letters her husband had sent her during their courtship—another metaphor from waking life.

However, I almost failed to mention the peach pit, which had no significance for me except in connection with the messy state of the kitchen. I was glad I followed the rule about going with faint impressions. When I reported the image, the woman told me she had a large painting of a peach pit in her living room. The painting was by an art professor who had once offered her advice on a job possibility she had ignored at the time. The nudge she received from our dream reentry led her to contact the professor. Within twenty-four hours, she had found a new job opening, and a new artistic medium (fabric painting) in which the artist-professor was highly gifted.

⟶ GETTING THE RIGHT ADDRESS

How often have you woken from a dream without the faintest idea where you were? We emerge from many dreams like partial amnesiacs or drunks after a bender.

Even if you have a fairly exact memory of your dream location and are fairly sure it was a "real" place (i.e., a place in ordinary reality), you may not be able to get the address.

A partner who knows that place better or knows how to dial directory inquiries may be able to give you that address. This can be another good reason for taking a partner into your dreams. A mother reported the following dream:

> *I am with my daughter at a shopping mall at closing time. Our car is parked a long way from the doors. Two men follow us, yelling dirty things at my daughter. We run into some kind of disco to get away from them. But they follow us in and shoot at us. I think my daughter is hit.*

During the shared reentry, the dreamer's partner was able to identify the shopping mall, one the dreamer had visited only once or twice. There was a disco at this mall that stayed open late. The mother subsequently discovered that, unknown to her, her daughter had been hanging out at this mall with drug users and alleged dope pushers. This led the mother to have some stern words with her daughter about personal safety. Several months later, however, it appeared that her daughter had already been "shot." The mother discovered her daughter was pregnant by the man she was dating at the mall disco.

Your ability to bring back information of this kind for others will grow as you develop a closer relationship with one of the shaman's closest dream allies: your power animal.

SHAPE-SHIFTING

"*Y*our guide might send a bird or an animal to get you out of your body so you can begin to *see*," advises Island Woman, the Iroquois shaman I introduced under the mask of fiction in my novel *The Fire-keeper*.

In many tribal societies, to be born into a clan is to be born with a special relationship with its totem animal. If you are a traditional Mohawk, for example, you are born into the Wolf Clan, the Bear Clan, or the Turtle Clan, and your relationship with the presiding animal is part of your group identity.

In dreaming cultures, you are encouraged to explore your personal relationships with other guardian animals and birds. They may come to you in dreams as messengers or helpers. They may reveal themselves during a vision quest, or through an unusual encounter in nature. These connections are important. They are part of your *power*. Adversaries, in waking life as well as in dreaming, certainly seem smaller when you are walking with a lion or a wolf!

For shamans, a power animal means more than this. Shamans are reputed to be able to shape-shift into the form of an animal or bird familiar, or to project a dream double in this form to pursue their work at a distance. This double is called a *nagual* in Mexico and an *oyaron* by traditional Iroquoians. At one level of understanding, the conditions for producing it are not so difficult to explain. Your dreambody, as noted in the previous chapter, is rather plastic. As you become a conscious dreamer, you will notice you have the ability to give it different forms. Shamanic dreamers may be able to replicate the dreambody and send out doubles (or triples) in several different forms—one of the reasons why tribal shamans are often reputed to have *several* souls.

Is this truly so alien to the experience of contemporary Westerners? In modern society, few of us see wild animals larger than squirrels outside a zoo, apart from the occasional white-tailed deer browsing on suburban lawns. Yet animals and birds frequently appear as important dream messengers.

The role of the animal messenger in the dreams of modern city-dwellers is often to recall us to our wild side, and the natural path of our energy. A familiar motif is discovering a wild creature in the place where you live. A woman dreams of driving home and being shocked to find a sleeping lioness curled up with her cubs on the front porch. Another dreams she comes across a ravenous tiger in her backyard and has to feed it one of her pets to escape being devoured herself. Dreams of this kind are self-revealing—i.e., they reveal more of the dreamer's character and potential than she has brought to bear in waking life.

They may bring further gifts, including the gift of shape-shifting.

Savannah was seventeen and still in high school when she started running with the wolves in her dreams:

Wolf Girl

The first time the wolves came, I was scared. There seemed to be a huge she-wolf in my bedroom, right next to me. Then I realized she didn't mean me any harm. She led me to the rest of her pack. I started to run with the pack.

Next time the she-wolf came for me she brought fresh kill and invited me to share. It tasted real good. The wolves told me they would take me across the mountains—they looked like the Rockies—and show me places most people don't get to see.

Rather than trying to interpret this sequence, I encouraged the high school senior simply to honor her dreams in any way that seemed natural. She decided to spend part of her school vacation as a volunteer at a nature observatory. She has since become a crusader for wildlife preservation.

The first dream encounters with an animal guide can be shocking to our ordinary sensibilities. Savannah was invited to eat fresh kill. Some dreamers find themselves literally torn apart by their animal visitor, as in this dream of a female therapist:

Claws of the Panther

I loved panthers as a child. But when Panther came to me, in a state between sleep and waking, I was terrified. I felt movement in the room and rolled onto my left side. I found myself staring into his jaws. In an instant, I was shredded and lay in pieces all over the room. Yet I felt no pain. I was conscious of my heart beating, but it no longer seemed attached to my body. I saw other animals moving toward me—Bear, Hawk, and Wolf. Behind them came an ancient woman, a person I knew from previous dreams. I think of her as the Ancient Mother.

I thought, "They must be going to put me back together."

But when Hawk flew down, he started tearing at my flesh and eating it. I thought, "This is disgusting." The other animals started eating me, too.

I was scared. I wondered how I was going to get myself back together. For a fleeting moment, it occurred to me I could wake myself up and get out of this. But I realized I needed to stay with this even though I had no idea how it was going to come out.

Then a light shone over the place where my body had been ravaged and eaten. The animals and birds that had torn into me went to the center of the light. They became translucent, blending into the heart of the Ancient Mother. She, in turn, became translucent, then one with the Light.

Now there was only Light. From its center came a beautiful stream of light pouring radiance on the place where I had lain. When this was over, I was intact. I awakened, gasping for air before I relaxed into deep, easy breathing. I felt whole and renewed. I felt every cell in my body had been made over.

This dream was a profound healing experience. It was also an initiation of a kind familiar to shamans. The experience of dismemberment—of being torn limb from limb, or filleted like a fish, to be given a new body, filled with light or glowing quartz crystals—is a common theme in shamanic traditions. In a terrifying, indelible dream visitation during my childhood, I saw myself torn apart by the horns of a bull I knew to be more than an ordinary animal. In the case of the therapist, the dream encounter with the panther cleared the way for rich new experiences on the inner planes, in which she established contact with a higher spiritual guide and with a deceased relative—a great-aunt whose identity had previously been unknown to her, who became a source of helpful and practical advice on family and health matters.

I am now alert, in dreams and dreamlike states, to visits from special birds or animals that seem to be connected to someone other than myself. Since I have worked with shamans and frequently journey in the shamans' worlds, such meetings are in no way strange to me, though they are often surprising. A Mayan shaman who lives in Belize introduced himself to me in this fashion.

Jaguar Messenger

In my bedroom on the cusp of sleep, I noticed a wild, feral tang and a thickening in the air. When I opened my eyes, I saw the room was empty. But behind closed eyelids, I saw feline eyes, pressed close to my own. From the animal's spotted coat and stocky build, I realized he was a jaguar. Though I feel close to all big cats, I knew this was not one of my own. He indicated he had come to guide me to the person who had sent him.

I journeyed with him to a ruined temple in a tropical jungle, where I had the first of a series of encounters with a Mayan shaman who gave me his name and demonstrated methods of healing and divination that were previously unfamiliar to me. He showed me how he used a stone mirror, a concave surface of blue-green jadeite, as "a place to see." He recited long passages from a chilam balam, *a Mayan book of prophecy, that I was able to note on a pad, scribbling furiously with my eyes closed. He showed me scenes of the rape of Mayan country and the burning of the sacred books by the Spanish colonizers. He spoke of a secretive order of shaman-priests dedicated to preserving ancient wisdom for the sake of the earth and all the species that share life on it. He warned, "Without our work, the Fifth Sun will end, as Four Suns ended before it. We are the sun-makers."*

I did not know the Mayan shaman at the time, in ordinary reality. But through a series of interesting synchronicities, I was able to confirm much of the information he gave me in these dream visitations, facilitated by his jaguar helper.

Your first personal experience of shape-shifting may be the gift of a spontaneous night dream, as in the case of Louise, a divorced mother and college administrator. She became aware of her transformation when she woke up to the fact that she was dreaming and not in her regular body:

Eye of the Hawk

I am looking down on a rocky pinnacle, rising from a cliff. This is the focal point of my vision; I am revolving around it. I ask myself, "What could perceive this place in this way?" The answer can only be: a circling bird. I accept what seems to be obvious, that I am a bird, and land on the tall rock. I look down at my feet and they are scaly red claws. I thought, "Well, that does it. I know I'm a bird, and I'm pretty sure the bird is a hawk."

Far below me is a canopy of trees. The midday sun is very hot. The heat is reflected off the shiny green leaves. I can feel how the trees protect the stream that flows beneath their branches from drying up, and how the stream thanks them by keeping their roots cool and moist. I feel drawn to a dead gray branch down there and ride an air draft down to it.

Louise felt certain, on waking, that she had visited a physical location, somewhere out West. Flying as the hawk was the preliminary to a powerful dream within the dream. She was drawn to a scene being played out in an open-sided shelter, in which native women were tending a dying person she felt was herself. Her consciousness slipped in and out of the dreams of the dying woman. She saw scenes from the woman's childhood, scenes of laughter and games in a native village. Then she was again watching the scene from the outside:

They are covering me with blankets, sprinkling me with sandy earth. They lay small leafy branches on top of the blankets.

A medicine man comes, wearing buffalo horns. He dances and taps the earth with a rattle as long as a staff. I hear a keening song. I think it is my death song. My spirit "pops" out of my chest like a piece of invisible material, the size of a handkerchief. It looks like a line drawing as it floats up into a beautiful starry sky.

This powerful experience led Louise on a personal quest that has made her a full-fledged shamanic dreamer, capable of guiding others on the paths of dreaming.

My personal relationships with the animal powers have evolved since I have been living in North America. I do not remember the Bear as an important presence in my youth, except as a cozy stuffed toy, but since my first encounters with the Woodland Indians, in the mid-1980s, he has become a frequent visitor and guide in my dreams. In one conscious dream, an enormous standing grizzly caught me up in his embrace, danced with me, and showed me that we were joined at the heart. We swapped skins. He showed me how to locate entry points for disease within the human energy field, and how to work on repairing them. Since then, if I am facilitating a healing circle, I call Okwari—the Bear—into the room.

SOUL REMEMBERING

The shamanic dream journey may lead in many directions, toward many possible sources of guidance and healing. As you explore these paths, you may find that its most important gift is the rediscovery of knowledge and power that belonged to you before you entered this life experience. "When the soul begins to mount," as Plotinus instructed, "it does not come to something alien but to its very Self."

You will come to recognize that some of the geography you are discovering is the geography of your deeper self. Once again, you may find that the door is already open to you, through a dream that came unbidden.

When I started experimenting with shamanic techniques from other cultures, I had a powerful dream in which I began to explore a house I did not know. This dream was different in quality and style from the dreams of a literal house that drew me to my home in Troy.

I am in a European city with many bridges and canals. I am meeting a shamanic teacher. He ushers me into a grand town house. It appears to

*have been built in the seventeenth century, if not earlier. I am fascinated
by the books and artworks in the library. I examine a couple of entries in
a Scottish dictionary of biography, and a morocco-bound volume,* La Vie
en Rome. *The teacher leaves me, speaking of an appointment elsewhere.*

*I am very curious about the identity of the owner of this house. I go
into the next room and see a marvelous, whimsical machine protected by
a glass case. The parts are like those of an antique clock. I know this is a
magical device, and that it is still in working order, though a bit out-
dated. I read the maker's signature: Israel Regardie.*

*In the master bedroom, I am struck by a magnificent Persian rug, only
partly unrolled. At this point, the teacher returns. He asks in high excitement, "When did this arrive?" I tell him the rug was just delivered. Its
colors are blue and silver.*

This dream really stirred me up, far beyond what a bald account of its
contents can convey. I knew that Israel Regardie had been a practitioner
of high magic and a leading figure in the Hermetic Order of the Golden
Dawn. The dream led me, among other things, to experiment with the
Golden Dawn tarot, which Regardie had made public prior to his death.

But many other elements in the dream did not yield their meaning all
at once. I suspected that the mysterious owner of the house must be myself. But I also wondered if the house had a literal counterpart in a city
of canals like Venice or Amsterdam. I was fascinated by my dream
teacher's excitement over the rug. I wanted to know about the rest of the
house.

Beyond all this, I felt the dream was tugging me to follow a certain
path, at a time when I still had many hesitations.

When I reentered the dream, with the aid of shamanic drumming,
my initial question reflected these hesitations: "Am I supposed to live in
this house?" The answer came back immediately: "The house already
belongs to you! It's a matter of when you are going to wake up to what
it contains."

I sped back to the bedroom to get a better look at that Persian rug.
Fully unrolled, it revealed a magnificent mythological firebird that came
to life and swooped me away on many explorations. He showed me a vision of the Magi journeying from the East to Bethlehem to honor the
holy child whose coming had been announced by prophetic dreams and
the flight of a star. The beauty and freshness of this vision filled me with

tears of joy. I felt both humbled and cleansed. I knew I was in the presence of a power that was utterly beyond my ordinary self.

With this experience came a renewed sense of vocation, in particular, of a calling to interpret between peoples of different traditions, and to offer the magic carpet of dreams to whoever was ready for flight.

RITUALS OF ENACTMENT AND AVOIDANCE

*I*n dreaming traditions, dreamwork is always oriented toward action. The principal task of the shaman, as a dream specialist, is to confirm the meaning of the dream and clarify the steps the dreamer should now take to honor the dream. *Dream confirmation* may require getting a second opinion. The shaman may journey to his own spirit guides, use a system of divination, or "put the question to the world" by observing the subsequent play of coincidence. By these means, the course of action the dreamer should follow to avert any evil consequences foreseen in the dream—and to honor or propitiate the powers that speak through the dream—will be clarified.

The shaman may now undertake a journey on behalf of the client to deal with a problem reflected in the dream. If the dream indicates soul-loss, the shaman will journey to locate the soul parts that have been lost or stolen and bring them home. If the dream suggests the intrusion of earthbound spirits, the shaman may journey to contact the lost souls and guide them on the paths to the afterworld.

A healing ceremony, cleansing, or initiation may be indicated. In many cultures, there are recognized rituals for releasing and transforming any negative energies that may remain with the dreamer after a "bad" dream. The Hopi Indians simply "spit it out." The ancient Assyrians practiced cleansing rituals with fire or water to remove the negative influence of evil dreams. For example, the Assyrians might tell their bad dream to a stick or reed, which was then burned; the dreamer was instructed to keep blowing into the flames until the material was consumed.[12] Significantly, in the language of the Assyrians the same verb (*pasaru*) means to "tell" a dream, to discover its meaning, and to dispel or release its effects.[13]

Among dreaming peoples, rituals of dream enactment or avoidance might involve the support of the whole community. Among American Indians, certain dreams—and the illnesses that may flow from them unless they are honored—are recognized as callings to initiation and membership in medicine societies.

According to tradition, the Eagle Medicine Society of the Seneca Indians originated from a dream that came to the mother of a sick boy whom no one could cure. She dreamed that her son should make an offering of soup and native tobacco to the mystical Dew Eagle, who taught the woman healing songs in the same dream.[14] Among Seneca traditionalists today, a dream of a great white bird with its head spattered with blood is an initiatory call to the Eagle Society. Similarly, a dream of a False Face mask is regarded as a summons to practice the rituals and obligations of the False Face Society.[15]

— THE IROQUOIS WAY: PLAYACTING TO CONTAIN A DREAM EVENT

Iroquois traditionalists believe strongly in dream precognition and respect the ability of a gifted dreamer to provide information about future events that may be vital to the survival and well-being of the people as a whole. On the early northern frontier, it was not unusual for whole Iroquoian communities to base life-or-death decisions on the prophetic dreams of individuals who had a proven ability to "dream true." Father Bruyas, an early Jesuit missionary among the Oneida, complained about the influence of a woman who was revered for her ability to dream future events. On one occasion, she advised the elders that she had dreamed that a southern tribe had taken the warpath against her nation, but could be ambushed at a certain place. In her dream, she had seen the enemy warchief, whom she named, captured by her people and ceremonially put to death. The Oneida sent out a war party in accordance with her dream and were so confident of the predicted victory that they fired up the kettles in advance for a celebration.[16]

Similarly, the Iroquois turned to their *dreamers* for guidance on the hunt and the weather.

Another blackrobe commented that "they believe, from a sure and infallible experience that, when they have dreamed something and have failed to perform it, there always befalls them a misfortune which was mysteriously expressed in the dream."[17]

Given these beliefs, the obvious question arises: What do you do if the dream portends trouble or disaster?

The Iroquois believed that it was sometimes possible to change the outcome of a precognitive dream by playacting the event that the dreamer, or the whole community, wished to avert. Sometimes this was taken to almost incredible extremes. A Mohawk warrior who dreamed that he was taken captive and fire-tortured to death by his enemies insisted that his fellow villagers should bind him and burn him with red-hot knives and axes.[18] This was evidently an attempt to contain a future event perceived in a dream.

PUTTING YOUR QUESTION TO THE WORLD

*T*here are shamans who believe that *nothing* happens in waking life before it is dreamed. Though this may sound heretical to scientifically educated minds, you can test the belief for yourself, through the techniques suggested in the next chapter.

Shamanic dreamers recognize that waking life is also a dream, and that the world will speak to us in the manner of a dream if we know how to attend to it.

Maybe we need to take dreams more literally and the events of waking life more symbolically. Just as shamanic dreamers recognize dreams as real experiences, they pay close attention to the symbolic meanings of the incidents and patterns of external reality. "As within, so without." Everything has meaning, everything is related.

As the Chinese put it, "There are things that like to happen together." Coincidences are never "only" coincidences. "Whatever is born or done in this moment of time has the quality of this moment of time," as Jung came to formulate the principle he called synchronicity after his experiments with the I Ching.[19] As you become more alert to the play of synchronicity around you, you will learn to use coincidences, as well as dreams, as navigational tools in daily life.

We can learn a lesson about this from the ancient Greeks. In the ancient Greek city of Pharai, in Achaia, there was a busy market, enclosed by a high stone wall. At the very center of the market, among the press of grain merchants and fish sellers, was a rough-hewn statue of the god Hermes, the divine messenger. The Greeks called Hermes "the friendliest of gods to men." He is the herald and interpreter for more remote Olympians, speeding back and forth between the surface world and the spirit worlds in his winged sandals. He presides over chance encounters and happy coincidences. He is lord of journeys, the special patron of travelers, including merchants, gamblers, and thieves. You will often encounter him in border areas, places of transition: at crossroads, gateways, and on the road itself. He also presides over the border zone between sleep and waking—he frequently communicates with humans through dreams and dreamlike states—and over the liminal zone between the living and the dead.[20]

The oracle of Hermes worked like this:

The Market Oracle

Around dusk, when business is winding down and the last vendors are closing up shop, you bring your question to the statue of Hermes. Your question might range from "Will I be healed?" to "Is my husband cheating on me?" or "What will be the price of olive oil next season?"—perfectly appropriate, since Hermes is also the patron of commerce. All that matters is that your question reflect what is truly important to you at this time.

You will want to bring some oil for the lamps, to show respect for the god. You might burn a little incense. But there are no dues to pay, and no priests to collect them. What is going on here is between you and the god, one to one, and between the two of you and the world.

You have made your modest offerings. You are ready to approach the statue. You will speak your question quietly into the right ear of the god. This should be shared with no one else.

Your next step is to stuff your hands over your ears, blocking out external sounds. You will walk like this all the way to the gate through which you entered the walled market.

As soon as you have stepped outside the market, you will unblock your ears. The first words of human speech you overhear will give you the answer to your question. The words might be a simple yes or no, or an enigmatic phrase that will set you scrabbling for associations, as you might do with a fragment from a dream. Whatever you pick up will relate to your question. You have made sure of that by evoking the Hermes energy, the power of synchronicity.[21]

The Greeks of Pharai knew, as shamanic dreamers know, that the tools of divination are all about us: in the flight of birds, in a chance encounter, in a snatch of a stranger's conversation overheard on the street. The world speaks to us in many voices, in the manner of dreams. These voices often seem a cacophony, because we persist in dismissing messages that defy linear sequence and logic. You have a better chance of collecting your messages from the world—as from your dreams—if you can create a *frame for synchronicity* that will bring events into focus. The easiest way to do this (as the people of Pharai knew, when they whispered into the ear of the god) is to find the question you need answered now. In all likelihood, this is also the question that is being put to you by your dreams.

⟶ EXERCISE: PUTTING YOUR QUESTION TO THE WORLD

1. Find your question. Decide what you need to explore *now*. Having the right question is more important than any number of answers. As Picasso observed, computers will never take over the world so long as they only give us answers. Many of our problems stem from the fact that we do not know what we truly want, even less what we need. A shamanic practitioner I know was once consulted by a man who asked whether the shaman could work some magic to get him a 20 percent pay raise. The shaman told the man to get out of his house. "If that man had asked for wealth and abundance," the shaman reported, "I might have had something to say to him. We don't bother the spirits for a twenty percent pay raise."

So take a moment to relax. Flow with your breathing, release any stress and negative thoughts or feelings. Clear your mind. Let the right question form itself. It might seem impossibly big ("What is my life purpose?" "What happens when I die?") or absurdly small ("Should I let the dentist pull my wisdom tooth?") What matters is that you find the question you really need to work on now.

When the question comes to you, put it into the simplest, most specific words you can find. Write it down.

2. Carry your question into the world. You are now going to carry your question with you in everyday life for a fixed time. Put the written question in your pocket or pocketbook and glance at it from time to time; this will help you to keep your focus. You need to decide how long you will give yourself to get an answer from the world. You may adopt a sudden-death, hit-or-miss approach, like the people of Pharai, by simply telling yourself, "The first unusual thing that comes to my attention will give me the answer to my question." If you are quite intuitive, or practiced at this sort of thing or just plain lucky, this will work fine. If you are new to such games or nailed to a schedule that preempts unusual events (which may be the commentary you are looking for), you may wish to allow yourself a full day, even a week if your question is a big one.

You have now created a frame for synchronicity. Whatever happens to you or around you during the time you have allotted may have some direct bearing on your question. A tarot reader does something quite similar when she takes a question and spreads the cards. But your deck is not limited to seventy-eight picture cards. For as long as you choose to focus on your question, you can work with anything that enters your field of consciousness.

3. Read the sign language of the world. Now you should be alert for anything unusual that happens in your environment. Anything striking or unexpected, an accident, chance meeting, or unexpected delay may be the sign you are seeking. Pay special attention to any chance encounters; they may not only shed light on your question but may actually hold the solution to your problems. Once you decide to work with coincidence, you invite new energy patterns into your life. You not only observe events in a new way; you actually draw events and people toward you in a way that is different from before.

If you fail to spot anything unusual or significant, if your life trundles on in its old grooves, maybe this will help you to see the root of your problem. Keep putting out a welcome mat, as you did when you resolved to catch and work with your dreams. Now you have invited in the power of synchronicity, it *will* speak to you, at the proper time.

Remember that within the frame of your question, anything the world gives you may be an answering voice.

— WHEN THE DEAD BIRD FLEW

This exercise should give you specific guidance. It should also help you to recognize the extent to which you create your reality through your thoughts, beliefs, and expectations. You will learn that when you change your attitudes, you literally draw different people and events toward you. You will see that you are only stuck if you insist on being stuck. This, too, is practical magic. Once you recognize that *everything* has meaning, you mobilize energies that can help you change whatever you need to change.

A talented graphic designer I know tried this method at a time she felt blocked in her marriage and career. The question weighing on Joanne was a big one: "How can I live fully and creatively?"

For most of the day, nothing remarkable happened. She went to the office; the hours passed in a familiar cycle of phone calls and coffee breaks. At the end of her workday, she sat on a bench in a neighborhood park in New York City feeling sorry for herself. She noticed a bird on the ground near her foot. The pigeon lay on its side, apparently dead. Her gloom deepened because she thought she had found the sign from the world she had been encouraged to seek.

Joanne told herself, "I am like that dead bird. I forgot how to fly, and then the life went out of me."

She started sketching the dead bird. After half an hour or so, a man she knew slightly walked by on his way home from the office. He saw the drawing and asked the woman about her work. She explained that her best ideas, for her graphic design business as well as her paintings, often came to her in dreams. The man was keenly interested, and she realized she was making a new friend. Her zest returned as she shared more and more of her dreams, and their function as a creative source.

As she talked to her new friend, they were both astonished to see the dead pigeon shake its feathers, stand up, and start waddling away. The bird took a few clumsy steps. Then it flapped its wings and took off.

Joanne's commentary was pithy: "That was truly a message for me. Once I opened myself to taking a risk with a virtual stranger and expressing my truest passions, my bird came to life and found its wings."

— SPEEDING ADVISORY

Putting your question to the world works equally well with smaller, quite specific issues.

On a visit to the Boston area, I was troubled by some tensions that had arisen within a group. I wondered if I had been too hasty in speaking my mind on some delicate matters, and whether this might have unpleasant consequences.

I decided that the first unusual thing that happened during my ride home would give me guidance on this issue.

It was a fine sunny day, and the traffic was scudding smoothly along the Mass Pike. Fairly soon my speedometer, not closely watched by me, had wound up to 90 mph.

I glanced out my window and saw an unmarked car cruising parallel to mine. The driver was wearing a state trooper's hat and staring at me with lively interest through his aviator shades.

I eased off the gas pedal. For a couple of miles, as I dropped speed, the trooper matched my pace, staring at me all the while. When I was down to the Massachusetts speed limit, sixty-five, he tipped a finger to his hat, slammed down his accelerator, and took off.

Through my relief at this reprieve, I realized I had just received a message from the world. I recorded it in my journal like this: "You have been given a warning not to go too fast. You won't be punished this time, but you'd need to be more careful."

⟶ NAVIGATING BY SYNCHRONICITY

The more you work with dreams, the more attentive you will become to the symbols and synchronicities of everyday life—and vice versa.

I sometimes suggest the game of "putting your question to the world" to people who are blocking their dreams because they are scared of what their dream source may be telling them.

A woman who came to one of my workshops told us she had once been an active dreamer, but had had no dream recall for several months. We soon established the source of her fear: she worked for a department of state government that was threatened with closure because of new budget cuts and was terrified of finding herself out of a job. Instead of exploring alternative options, she clung to the hope that lobbying efforts might save her department.

Since she was not listening to her dreams, I suggested she might try listening to the world, by framing her question—"Will I keep my job?"—and keeping it in mind for the rest of the evening. Anything striking or unexpected—maybe the first phrase she heard on the car radio—might be her answer from the world.

"I got my answer right away," she reported the following week. Though she knew the geography of the neighborhood quite well, she had found herself driving the wrong way on a one-way street. She had driven three blocks against traffic before the driver of a huge semitrailer alerted her to her mistake by turning on his high beams and leaning on his horn. She got an unmistakable answer: "I need to get off this street and go with the traffic." The scare also opened her up to her dream source. She caught a dream that night in which she saw herself at a conference in Washington, D.C. The dream puzzled her because the conference was on transportation, an area in which she felt she had little or no expertise. As we worked with the dream, we discovered that, while she might not know much about transportation, she did seem to have extensive experience in organizing conferences. Another lightbulb came on. The dreamer checked out some job possibilities in Washington. Before the end of the month, she had landed a higher-paid job that basically entailed organizing conferences.

Working with coincidence brought her back to working with dream radar, as real dreamers have done since the origin of our species.

Part Two

DREAMS OF POWER

The soul has the ability to conform to her character the destiny that is allotted to her.

Plotinus

6

USING DREAM RADAR

Dreams must be heeded and accepted, for a great many of them come true.

Paracelsus

It is a poor kind of memory that only works backwards.
The White Queen, in Through the Looking-Glass

The future can be seen, and because it can be seen, it can be changed.
J. B. Priestley, Man and Time

DREAMING TRUE

$\mathcal{P}$aula, a young publishing executive, had a dream in which she became conscious she was dreaming:

> *I seemed to be flying over Manhattan. I decided to drop in on a friend I hadn't seen in a few weeks. I entered her apartment through a window. She was in bed, asleep, and I couldn't get her to wake up. It was totally boring and I decided to take off. As I was leaving, I noticed something weird. There were these Alice in Wonderland characters in her bedroom. I wondered what they were doing in my dream.*

In the morning, Paula called her friend, who told her that the previous day her mother had presented her with a small family treasure: a set of porcelain characters from Alice in Wonderland. Unknown to Paula, her friend had installed these on a new shelf in her bedroom before going to sleep the previous evening.

A nurse in Hawaii dreamed she got inside a terminal patient's body to share the experience of dying. She felt an energy jolt at the top of her head. She felt warm sensations flooding through her body. She sat up and saw that the patient had separated from her body and was being guided upward by a radiant being. She asked this guide if her patient had died, and he nodded. When she woke, she got a phone call, telling her the patient had passed away.[1]

I dreamed I was on an expedition to Antarctica, wearing a special explorer's outfit. The ice glinted like mica. This was an exciting dream adventure, but I could not relate it to anything in my waking life. When I picked up my local newspaper, however, I saw that the front page of the lifestyle section was devoted to a reporter's trip to Antarctica. Then one week later I got a call from a friend from whom I had not heard in more than four years. He was a keen sailor and naturalist. He told me that he had an opportunity to make an expedition to Antarctica and wondered if I would like to come along.

These dreams are examples of the three principal ways in which hypersensory perception (HSP) is often at work in dreams. Paula's dream appears to be a clear case of dream *clairvoyance,* which is also called remote viewing; it is probably also a case of an out-of-body experience during a dream. The nurse's dream is an example of *telepathy,* which literally means fellow feeling at a distance. When we pick up other people's thoughts and feelings, in dreams or in waking life, we often confuse them with our own. For example, my wife once reported feeling as if someone were hacking off her torso with a saw; she discovered the next day that a friend had undergone open-heart surgery at the time she experienced these sensations.

In the nurse's dream, however, the dreamer was able to share another person's sensations without muddling them up with her own. My dream is an example of dream *precognition,* the main theme of this chapter. As with many of the other cases that will be discussed, it could be argued that my Antarctica dream could just as easily be classified as an example of remote viewing (i.e., picking up the cover spread in the newspaper that was being delivered to my box) or telepathy (picking up my friend's intentions before he made the phone call). These distinctions are of secondary interest. The common factor in such dreams—and their usefulness in our lives—is that they provide us with accurate information about people and events in external reality to which we did not previously have access.

Dreams of these types are often cited as possible cases of ESP. In fact, they probably reflect *hyper*sensory, rather than *extra*sensory, perception.[2] Shamans would say that such dreams are often the result of a journey in the dreambody, or the gift of a dream visitor who may be a spirit. (Before we shy away from the word *spirit,* let's remember that living people are spirits that have bodies, whether or not they remember.)

There is another common characteristic of the dreams cited above. They are *clear dreams:* their content is fairly literal, describing a situation in outer reality that is distant from the dreamer in space or time and is reported reasonably accurately. Such HSP material is common in dreams because the dream source is constantly preparing us for challenges that lie around the corner. In dreams we not only witness distant events; we explore possible futures and can choose whether to fulfill or avoid a dream event in waking life. By learning to check dream messages and taking appropriate action in ordinary reality, we can develop a powerful guidance system for living a more successful and more soul-full life.

THE CASE OF THE BISHOP'S PIG

*T*he scientific investigation of dream precognition begins, in modern times, with the case of the bishop's pig. Frank Podmore, an indefatigable researcher of paranormal phenomena in Victorian England, investigated a dream report sent in by Mrs. Atlay, the wife of an Anglican bishop. The bishop's wife dreamed that a jolly fat pig was stuck between the table and the wall in her dining room. Over Sunday breakfast, she regaled her family with this comical episode, which she took to be nothing more than a nonsense dream. The family then set off for church. On their return, they were astonished to discover a large-as-life pink pig jammed between the dining table and the wall. While they were out, a neighboring farmer's pig had escaped and managed to run inside the bishop's house.[3]

I like this story because it is a humorous antidote to the false impression, widespread among people with mediocre dream recall, that dreams of the future mostly involve death and disasters beyond the dreamer's control. This impression has been reinforced by the fact that the prophetic dreams that are mentioned in history books usually involve the impending death of famous men. When the classics were still a common inheritance, every schoolchild knew that Calpurnia, the wife of Julius Caesar, had two dreams in a single night—one symbolic, one entirely literal—that both warned of her husband's assassination. That the message was repeated the same night would have been taken by any Roman dream interpreter worth his olive oil as a signal that it was to be taken with the utmost seriousness, Caesar failed to heed the warning, with notorious results. Most American schoolchildren know that Abraham Lincoln dreamed he saw his own body, laid out in a coffin in the East Room of the White House, two weeks before he was shot and killed in Ford's Theatre. Lincoln believed in dreams and discussed this one with his wife and friends, but was unable to avoid its fulfillment—partly because he chose not to hide himself away from the public, partly also (perhaps) because his dream message was not sufficiently specific.[4]

It is also widely known that many people have dream precognition of mass disasters: the sinking of the *Titanic,* a coal mine tragedy in Wales, an earthquake in California, a civil war in Africa or the Balkans.

When we dream about world events that do not directly involve us, sometimes we are given a dream preview in the form of a TV news report or an advance copy of a newspaper. J. W. Dunne, the British scientist and Army officer who logged his own precognitive dreams with military rigor, noticed this phenomenon back in 1902, when he was on campaign in South Africa during the Boer War. He dreamed he was standing on a volcano on an island threatened with imminent disaster. He tried desperately, inside the dream, to persuade French colonial officials on a nearby island to gather ships to evacuate the people who were at risk. He heard an ominous message repeated over and over: "Four thousand people will be killed." A few days later, when Dunne received a batch of newspapers on the mail boat from London, he read the *Daily Telegraph* headline, "Volcano Disaster in Martinique," with the subheading, "Probable Loss of 40,000 Lives." Dunne's dream report was off by one zero, but otherwise accurate. He did not actually have dream precognition of the volcano disaster, which had already occurred at the time of his dream. But in his dream, he did manage to read the news before it arrived.[5] You may have noticed some similar occurrence in your own dreams.

Though the most celebrated cases of dream precognition involve death and disaster, we receive HSP material in our dreams about things large and small, happy and sad, almost every night of the week—whether or not we remember this information, recognize it, and work with it. It is easy to understand why people who generally forget their dreams tend to remember the scary ones, whether these are nightmares with symbolic motifs or clearer dreams about impending disaster. The dream source is trying to get an urgent message across that may relate to the dreamer's health and safety, or those of people close to him. By contrast, active dreamers may find they are getting more messages than they can use.

Clear dreams are entirely natural. They may carry messages of life-or-death importance or be incidental souvenirs from a night ramble through space and time. Precognitive dreams are most helpful when they are recognized as rehearsals for a possible future the dreamer may be able to improve or avoid.

One of the best general statements of what is at work in this type of dream comes from Montague Ullman and Stanley Krippner, pioneer researchers of dream telepathy. They observe that some aspects of dreaming may be described as a "vigilance operation" that involves "paranormal search operations" to prepare the dreamer for situations that lie ahead. "The orientation of the sleeping subject is not primarily to his own past, but to the kind of immediate future situation to which he may awaken." Hence the dreamer's future, more than his or her past, is the organizing principle of many dreams, and even the glimpses of the past that return to us in dreams may be giving us tactical advice on how to cope with a new development that is just emerging.[6]

Shamans, of course, would go further. They would say that precognitive dreams are *memories of the future* that we can explore in dreams because when we are outside our bodies, we are not bound by space-time.

TRACKING CLEAR DREAMS

*J*ohn Hotchin, M.D., a leading medical researcher, has made himself a case study in the workings of dream radar, rather in the manner of J. W. Dunne. I describe John's moving dreams of his dead wife in the next chapter. He has perfected a simple technique for checking the accuracy of your dream radar that I recommend highly for active dream explorers. When he dreams of an unfamiliar location, he tries to map it as faithfully as possible, in a simple line drawing in his journal. When he later comes upon his dream locale in waking life, as quite frequently happens, he compares the sketch with the physical scene, which he photographs when he has a camera handy. He worked this way with the following dream:

The Narrow Street

I dreamed I was in a village of ancient stone houses, with an unfamiliar woman. We parted company, and I found myself lost in a maze of narrow streets. The walls of the street I was on narrowed sharply, so that a cart obstructed passage. I was wondering which way to turn when a small boy, who has played guide for me in other dream situations, bobbed up and led me off along a side alley I hadn't noticed.

On waking, John sketched the street scene, but had no idea where he had been. A couple of months later, through an unexpected invitation, he traveled to Scotland, where he was introduced to a woman who resembled his dream companion. She took him to the village of Crail, near Edinburgh, of whose existence he had previously been unaware. They parted company, he became lost—and found himself in the narrow street from the dream. Because of his dream, he was able to find his way through the alley back to the village center. The photo he took of the street scene was almost identical to his sketch.

With practice, you will soon develop an intuitive feel for precognitive and other HSP material in your dreams. You will be less likely to miss important messages of this kind if you habitually run a reality check on all your remembered dreams. Always ask the basic questions: Could this happen? Could it be happening to someone else?

Since (contrary to Freud's opinions) the dream source tries to communicate with the ordinary mind as clearly as possible, your dreams are probably already giving you many cues about when to check for a message about external reality. These cues are rather like the flashing "message waiting" light on a telephone answering machine. Once you begin to recognize these signals, you will find it progressively easier to hit the right button and play back your messages. Here are the cues to HSP material I look for in dreams:

— CHECKING YOUR DREAM MESSAGES

1. Unfamiliar but realistic locales. Where is the dream taking place? If the dream locale is unfamiliar but realistic (no melting clocks and fire-belching dragons), chances are you have glimpsed a scene from the future, or a situation at a distance from you in external reality.

2. Communications themes. Did you receive a phone call, a fax, or a letter in your dream? This may be signaling you that a message is coming through. It may also be a literal glimpse of what you will be receiving in the mailbox or over the wires. If you see a newspaper item or TV report in your dream, this may contain "news" you can put to use. It can also help you to date future events you perceive in the dream.

3. Dream characters from your past. Does your dream feature someone from your past with whom you have long since lost contact? If this is a living person (you may need to check), the fact that she or he has turned up in your dream could mean your paths are about to cross again. Even more likely, your dream may be telling you that somebody new will come into your life who resembles the person you knew before (see "Dead Ringers"). A dream about an old flame might be preparing you for a new romantic encounter. Somebody you are about to meet may look like a person you once knew or may play a similar role in your life.

4. Dream events from another person's life. We are often more objective about other people's issues than our own, in our dream memories as in waking life. When your dream centers on events in the life of another living person, your dream source may of course be helping you make a comparison between your situation and the other person's. It may also be giving you information on what is going on behind the scenes, so you can better assess the other person's motives and actions. If you are especially receptive, you may also be given dream messages that are intended for that other person.

5. The dream message is repeated the same night. If the dream message is important, it may come to you more than once in the same night. This could be dubbed the Calpurnia syndrome, but the message does not have to be negative! I worked with one lucky dreamer who dreamed the results of a horse race and was cautioned by a dream character, in a later scene the same night, not to forget the name of the winner.

6. *You incubated a dream on a specific issue.* When you ask for direct guidance from your dream source, you announce that you are willing to work with your dreams and thereby increase your chances of receiving information that will help you resolve your problems. Your question is also a viewfinder through which it may be easier for you to read your dream messages.

7. *The message comes in the twilight zone.* Hypersensory perception is often highly active when you are in the receptive state between sleep and waking. This is when some of the clearest dream messages come through.

LOGGING DREAM RADAR

The only way to become proficient at this is to do it! On-the-job training is the only training required, and the only instruction that works. I keep a running log of dreams that seem to contain HSP messages, large and small, and the correspondences with later events and situations that I detect. If a major change or testing time in my life is looming, I have noticed that I may have dozens of preparatory dreams, couched in different vocabularies. In addition to clear dreams of external events, these might include various kinds of dream rehearsals, replays of past situations from which I might be able to learn something now, glimpses of possible other life experiences that could be relevant, archetypal dramas, and teaching sessions with dream guides. To maintain our focus for now on the way HSP material shows up in dreams, I confine the excerpts from my journals that follow to clear dreams whose content was essentially literal and proved to contain information about future events and events taking place at a distance that was not available to me prior to the dream. I have drawn these excerpts from my dream logs from April 1992 to August 1994. I have excluded dreams that involved powerful emotions and highly personal issues. I have also omitted dreams that seem to me to have been clearly precognitive but were couched in symbolic language. Finally, I have excluded dreams whose fulfillment essentially depended on my own actions.

The result is a simple, stripped-down chronicle that includes notes on my reality checks on the dream messages and/or how they were subsequently confirmed by waking events. The lag between the dream and the subsequent event, in this series, ranges from a few hours to a few weeks. Later in this chapter, however, I describe a dream whose enactment took six years.

There is nothing of earth-shattering consequence going on in this dream series, just small moving objects showing up on the dream radar. I include the list simply to underscore that dream precognition and telepathy are not only entirely natural, but quite *routine* phenomena. The only wonder is that in our culture, so many of us have allowed our dream radar to gather cobwebs.

━ PERSONAL REPORT: AN OPERATOR'S LOG

Dream #1: I am both observer and participant in a violent domestic drama centering on a husband's infidelity with the au pair. The man's name is Bowman or Bowhill, something beginning with *Bow*. I struggle to get this name right, because everything seems to depend on it. (4/5/92)

Reality check: The next evening, I gave a talk at the Chicago Public Library and was invited to coffee afterward by three women I had not previously met. One of them told me she had been reading a mystery novel in which the characters are struggling to guess a surname beginning with *Bow*. (4/6/92)

Dream #2: I see a Native American wearing a magnificent headdress of bright orange feathers that radiate out from his head like the rays of the sun. (4/30/92)

Reality check: The next day, I met Pete Jemison, a Seneca artist, for the first time. When I walked into his kitchen, he was finishing up a painting whose central figure was an Indian wearing a headdress of bright orange feathers. Pete told me the Indian belonged to the Kayapo, an Amazonian tribe. (5/1/92)

Dream #3: I become angry because a woman who has been decorating a row house has left a window on the stair landing open. The window descends almost to floor level. I am very worried a toddler in the house could fall through it. (7/18/92)

Reality check: The dream house reminded me of a type of row house in London. I knew a London family who had just moved into such a house and also had a toddler. I called a mutual friend and asked her to check on the windows. She found a window on the landing open, as in the dream, and suggested security measures. (7/19/92)

Dream #4: A woman in a red car is driving erratically among the trees at the front of my property. I'm worried she will smash into my Jeep, which is overcharging. (8/11/92)

Follow-up: I failed to get this dream message. Two days later, my Jeep was totaled by a woman in a red car who ran a red light near the Albany Public Library, where I had been doing some research ("my property"?). (8/13/92)

Dream #5: My wife is shocked because one of my English daughters is photographed topless, sunning herself by a pool. (8/19/92)

Reading the news: The next day, the media were full of the scandal caused by the publication of topless photos of Fergie—the duchess of York—in the London tabloids. Although not strictly a "clear dream," I have included this as a specimen of reading the news before it comes out. (8/20/92)

Dream #6: I have a lengthy theoretical discussion about something described as the Stutter Effect with a scientist with an unusual name, something like Zans or Zanssers. (3/7/93)

Reality check: Three weeks later, I was invited to lunch with a theoretical physicist named Michael Zenzen, whose name was previously unknown to me. He developed an impromptu theory of precognition based on the Spread Effect. (3/29 and 5/5/93)

Dream #7: I am trying to present a lecture but people cannot hear me because of an incredibly noisy fan. (4/18/93)

Reality check: I had this dream in Europe. As soon as I returned to the United States, I rushed over to the college where I was scheduled to speak and asked them to turn on the air-conditioning in the auditorium. The noise was insufferable. They agreed to move my lecture to another space. (4/23/93)

Dream #8: I dream that forty-six people have signed up for a workshop I decided to limit to thirty-five. (8/15/93)

Follow-up: The series began two months later. Class limits had already been announced, and I forgot about the dream until the host organization sent me a list of students. They had registered thirty-five, plus eleven on a waiting list, giving the forty-six total of the dream (10/10/93)

Dream #9: A svelte blond Englishwoman I haven't seen in fifteen years waves to me in front of a grand country house, set among manicured lawns and gardens. (9/7/93)

Reality check: I asked a mutual friend what had happened to this woman and was told she was in "your part of the world," doing an American lecture tour on the theme of stately homes and gardens. (9/9/93)

Dream #10: I am asked to assist with a healing. Two large white disks are stuck together in the patient's neck or upper back. (11/20/93)

Reality check: Two days later, an active dreamer called to ask me to send "healing energy" to a woman I knew slightly. She had smashed her cranium down into her spine in an accident; disks that had been squashed together now had to be separated by surgery. (11/22/93)

Dream #11: A gap-toothed woman flirts with me in a lobby area. I ask about some historical maps. (2/25/94)

Reality check: The next day, an Irish-American neighbor invited me out for a beer at a neighborhood tavern. A gap-toothed woman at the bar struck up a conversation. An acquaintance came in sporting what looked like a historical map on the lining of his suede jacket. I asked him about it and he said it was a map of Marlboro Country. (2/26/94)

Dream #12: I am horrified to learn that racists in the South African police are planning a massacre in an effort to derail the reform movement. The intended crime will take place in a black neighborhood, but the target audience is white. (3/26/94)

Watching the news: The top story on the TV news the following night was of the death of thirty-one people in factional fighting allegedly incited by police agents provocateurs. (3/27/94)

Dream #13: At a restaurant in a brick-walled courtyard, I am surprised to find moose on the menu. (5/9/94)

Reality check: I went to a new restaurant the following day. I had trouble finding it and asked for directions at the nearby office of an environmental group. They gave me a brochure. It contained a large photo of a bull moose that I was admiring when my lunch guests came into the courtyard. (5/10/94)

Dream #14: I get a call from a man with the same initials as my agent: SK. He is eager to discuss some "game cards" with me. I tell him I am developing a new workshop on the theme that life is a dream. (6/8/94)

Reality check: The next day, I received a letter from Strephon Kaplan-Williams (SK) urging me, inter alia, to experiment with his Dream Cards. (6/9/94)

Dream #15: A close friend in Europe apparently fakes his death. I attend his funeral, but we meet privately afterward and have a long conversation. (8/4/94)

Reality check: Two weeks later, my friend suffered a serious stroke that left him paralyzed on his right side for months. The day this happened, while traveling in a different country, I became violently dizzy and felt my head was about to explode. In later dreams, I seemed to enter the confused consciousness of a stroke survivor who did not recognize his children when he first came round—all examples of telepathy. (8/23/94)

Dream #16: I watch a crowd of people milling around, waiting to take a driver's test. I talk to a young male guitarist who has failed his test. I tell him it's tough luck, but certain standards must be maintained for public safety. (8/9/94)

Reality check: The next day, a new editor drove up from New York City to introduce himself. He looked like an older character in the dream. He told me his son was a guitarist in a rock band and was going to take his driving test at the end of that week. His son failed the test. (8/10/94)

Dream #17: I am with a circle of people who boast about their shamanic accomplishments. I am amused by their instruments, which resemble kitchen appliances. One of the drums looks like a frying pan. Another resembles a toaster oven. "How can you be shamans if you can't drum?" I tease them. (8/28/94)

Reality check: The following week, I attended a seminar on Celtic shamanism. Because of the humidity, the leader used a plastic drum that looked like a frying pan. Another member of the group—an inexperienced drummer!—asked the sponsors if he could dry out a deerskin frame drum in their toaster oven. (8/29 and 8/31/94)

I like to use ho-hum dreams of this kind as teaching examples to underscore the point that dream precognition and telepathy are not gee-whiz phenomena; they are going on all the time. In the next sections, we will look at clear dreams that have distinctly more challenging messages, and some special problems associated with getting those messages right.

DEAD RINGERS

*R*obin, the mother of a teenage boy, came to me with the following dream:

> *I saw my son hit by a car. He was thrown through the air a long way and didn't get up. I think he was killed.*

Robin was worried that this was a literal warning. Her son had recently gotten his driver's license and had already been ticketed for speeding. Robin thought the boy's father was overindulgent, allowing him to take his truck out at all hours.

I had observed that Robin frequently dreamed things before they happened, although she tended to get the players mixed up. She came from an extended family and was often confused (for example) about which of her five sisters had featured in a dream, or whether the sister was actually her mother, one of her daughters, or herself. Such muddles are common in dream reports involving family members, work colleagues, and neighbors. Under these circumstances, a dreamer may report a "clear dream" that accurately describes a future event down to the last detail—except that the identity of one or more of the central characters is mistaken.

I did a guided reentry with Robin, focusing on the location of the apparent accident she had witnessed in her dream. She got the image of an open area with lots of bare earth, perhaps a construction site or new development. The oncoming vehicle was no longer a car. Its size was overpowering. She thought it might be a tractor-trailer. She saw her son thrown into the air when this vehicle struck him. She could not change the ending in a way that seemed convincing. She picked up a couple more details that might be significant. Although she thought her son had been killed, there was no sign of blood. And she could not find the vehicle he might have been driving.

We worked with the notion that the boy might have been on foot. We both had the feeling of confinement in the place where he was struck, as if the road had narrowed. With limited time, we had to leave it at this. Robin undertook to have a serious word with her son about road safety.

The next day, the boy's best friend was struck and killed on a railroad trestle near Saratoga by an Amtrak express train hurtling south from Montreal at 70 mph. Badly shaken, Robin showed me the photograph that ran in her local paper, *The Saratogian*. She told me, "It's the scene from my dream." As in her dream, the boy had been thrown through the air a long way, more than forty feet, and had been killed with few visible signs of injury.

Robin's dream seemed to contain clear precognition of this tragedy, except that she had misidentified the victim. She told me the dead boy was not only her son's best friend, but that they were "dead ringers"— the same gawky height, the same thick-lensed eyeglasses, even the same cowlicks. It was easy to understand how she had confused them in her dream memories. She might have made the identical mistake in waking life, glimpsing the scene on the railroad trestle from a distance.

The problem of confusing a dream character with someone who is more familiar is a constant challenge in working with precognitive dream material. An ancient king of Persia lost his throne and ultimately his life because of this difficulty. The story has been handed down to us by Herodotus. It is a classic cautionary tale about the need to screen dream warnings about future events as carefully as possible:

The Cambyses Problem

While campaigning in Egypt, Cambyses, king of Persia, dreamed that a messenger came to him from his royal capital with the evil news that Smerdis had seized the throne. Smerdis was the name of the king's brother.

Waking, Cambyses concluded that he had received a dream warning of a palace coup being plotted by his brother. He sent his most trusted lieutenant back to Susa with orders to get rid of the possible usurper. The king's brother was secretly murdered.

Unfortunately for Cambyses, there was a second Smerdis in the Persian capital. He was a Magian priest-magician who not only shared the same name as the king's brother but bore a striking physical resemblance to the murdered prince. This second Smerdis, posing as the king's brother, now seized the throne.

"It was Smerdis the Magus, not my brother, of whose rebellion God warned me in my dream," Cambyses lamented as he gathered his army to reclaim his kingdom. He never made it back to Persia. In a final twist of fate, said to fulfill an Egyptian oracle, Cambyses gashed himself with his own sword and died of gangrene.[7]

Cambyses' dream, like Robin's, appears to have contained a quite literal warning about a future event. In both cases, the dreamers misinterpreted the warning because they mistook the identity of the key character in the dream.

By my observation, we tend to substitute familiar names and faces for less familiar ones quite routinely as we process our dreams into dream reports. This is especially likely to happen when we dream about somebody we have not yet met in waking life. In our dream memories, we attach a familiar identity to a person who is known to us only in the dream.

For example, when I was in the throes of financing the purchase of a house, I wondered why I had a series of dreams about a former boss with whom I had had some heavy-duty disagreements many years before. In one of these dreams, we lunched in a restaurant that looked like a greenhouse. I had not seen the ex-boss in fifteen years. Was it possible our paths were going to cross again? Were my dreams telling me I still needed to lay old animosities to rest? Or did the ex-boss in my dreams represent some unacknowledged aspect of myself?

I got my answer a couple of days later when I met a new loan officer from a bank with which I had previously had fairly good relations. The bank official was a dead ringer for my ex-boss. Furthermore, he was unhelpful to the edge of rudeness, and incredibly sexist in his views of women. After an unpleasant interview, he invited me to an expense-account place for lunch to try to smooth things over, and I found myself in the fern restaurant from the dream. I still took my business elsewhere, figuring that the loan officer might resemble my old antagonist in more than his looks.

As this story suggests, in our dream memories we are constantly making analogies between people and situations that are (as yet) unfamiliar to us in waking life and those we know better. This can be more than a case of mistaken identity. Some of these analogies can be quite instructive, helping us to consider how we responded in the past to situations that presented challenges and opportunities similar to those that lie ahead. You might start dreaming of an old flame, for instance, just before you meet a new love interest. The dream might be inviting you to reflect on what went right and wrong last time round, and whether you want to repeat your mistakes or make better choices.

Because dreams have multiple layers of meaning, as mentioned before, we should always be open to more than one way of reading dreams of this type. The fact that the odious bank official resembled my old boss does not preclude the possibility that I was *also* being told by my dream source to forgive old grievances and move forward.

The main point for now is that in screening dreams for precognitive (and other HSP) material, we should be alive to the workings of analogy and alert for the constant risk of switching identities. Though this is unlikely to cause you problems on the Cambyses scale, Robin's story is sobering. Is it remotely possible that the tragedy on the railroad trestle could have been avoided if we had been able to get a more precise fix on the dream location and, above all, if the dreamer had realized that the accident victim in her dream was not her son? I cannot answer this question.

What I can say with conviction is that you are likely to find you achieve higher accuracy and resolution with your dream radar the more you practice and the more familiar you become with the terrain you are covering, the interference patterns, and the variety of moving objects that may show up on the screen.

MEETING YOUR FUTURE SELF

*I*n dreams of the future, we not only glimpse events that have not yet taken place; we see our dream selves acting and responding in ways we may not comprehend in waking life, at the time of the dream. Dreams of this kind may or may not be precognitive. They are often self-fulfilling, in the sense that we may be drawn, more or less consciously, to play out the content of the dream.

These dream encounters with a future self can be extremely valuable, once we recognize what is going on and learn how to work with the process. Here are two examples of dreams in which I saw my future actions but failed to grasp what was unfolding until I found myself playing out the script in ordinary reality:

——— 1. ONSTAGE SIX YEARS EARLY

In March 1987, while vacationing in Mexico, I woke from a vivid dream in which I was both observer and performer in a series of dramatic productions played out on a stage that changed from a forest clearing to a Greek-style amphitheater to a more modern theater. In the last scene, I watched a man in eighteenth-century dress (who was and was not me) performing in front of a big audience. The play seemed to be entitled *The Olive of Lydius.* I woke with lines of blank verse rolling through my mind and wrote down the final couplet.

At the time, I had just hatched a plan to write a historical novel revolving around events in the life of a colorful eighteenth-century figure, Sir William Johnson, a wild Irish tearaway who flourished on the early American frontier as land baron, ladies' man, and friend and protector of the Iroquois Indians. I took my dream glimpse of a big audience in attendance for a performance in colonial dress as a "go" signal for the book, but did not understand the other elements.

Six years later, after writing my book and giving some lectures about its hero, who had by now appeared to me in many other dreams, along with other characters from his world, I decided to go one step further. I decided to craft a one-man show in which I would appear as Johnson and talk about my dream character's life, loves, and Indian intrigues. This ninety-minute production premiered in Johnstown, New York— the city Johnson had founded—in June 1993 before a large audience. As we moved toward opening night, I became aware that I was fulfilling a dream from six years before. At the end of that year, I made the conscious decision to honor the dream by using the title of the dream play as a chapter title in a bigger novel, *The Firekeeper,* that sprang from a new series of dreams that carried me deeper into another time and other countries of the mind.

In my dream in Mexico, I glimpsed a role I would play in waking life in Johnstown, New York, six years later. The trail I followed between these two incidents never ran straight; I explored many different directions. If I had grasped the full meaning of my encounter with a future self in March 1987—which goes far beyond what I have explained here—I believe I would have made better choices, as the next example will confirm.

2. REPAYING THE ADVANCE BEFORE CONTRACTS ARE SIGNED

A couple of years before I walked a physical stage in eighteenth-century dress, I signed a contract to write a murder mystery. Two months before the contracts arrived, I dreamed I was writing checks to repay the advance I had not yet received, in waking reality, from the publisher.

This dream troubled me, but I decided to ignore its message. I had persuaded myself, at that time, that I needed to crank out the mystery to pay my bills.

It took me a full year to realize what my dream had already shown me: that my heart was not in the murder mystery. I decided to abandon the project and return the advance, in order to concentrate on dreamwork and other kinds of writing. As in the dream, I was now obliged to write a series of checks to settle my debt.

The real question is not whether such dream encounters with a future self are self-fulfilling; it is whether we can use them to become more conscious in waking life of where the paths we are walking are likely to lead, and the consequences of choosing a different path.

When you dream of your future self, you have the chance to clarify the natural path of your energy. Are you working with your basic energy or against it? Are you walking the path of soul? So many of our failures and disappointments come from blocking the natural expression of basic energy and creativity.

The two dreams I have just quoted gave me very different messages, conveyed by feelings even more than content. After the theatrical dream, I felt energized, upbeat, full of juice. After the dream of repaying the publisher's advance, I felt anxious and lackluster. If I had honored both dreams, and the feelings attached to them, immediately, I believe I would have saved myself and others a great deal of time and trouble.

These stories underscore the need to pay close attention to how our dream selves part company with our waking selves.

I suspect that spontaneous sleep dreams give all of us glimpses of our future selves, just as they show us future events. If we choose, we can make this a conscious encounter.

Life is full of crossroads. Often we hurtle through them without even pausing to study the signs. Suppose it were possible for you to go forward ten years and take a good look at how you will be living and feeling if you stay on the path you are on—or alternatively, if you change jobs or homes or partners. This is not about making life predictable. Happily, there is a force in the universe that ensures that human affairs will never be that; were it otherwise, life would be deadly dull. This is about exploring a *probable future* and your role within it. When you encounter your future self, you not only learn about your chances of fulfilling your present ambitions; you discover whether you will be content with your present goals and values further down the road. This is another way of getting in touch with your soul.

Are you ready for a conscious encounter with your future self? This is not science fiction. I learned quite a bit about arranging this kind of meeting when I was working with Ginny Black Wolf in a shamanic circle in the Boston area.

I asked Ginny to journey for me during a drumming session to seek guidance on how I could become a better teacher.

Ginny came back grinning from ear to ear. She told me she had met a guide who had words of advice for me.

"He says you need to be more humble."

"Did you tell him I've been working on it? I'm very proud of my humility."

"He says it's not enough."

"Anything else?"

"He said to tell you not to spend a minute of your life worrying about your public image, your persona. He says if you do what you're called to do, people will welcome and accept you because of what you are."

I thought about this. Both pieces of counsel seemed to me right on the money. Ginny proceeded to pass on more specific information, which proved to be both accurate and useful.

I was curious to know where this stuff was coming from. I asked her about the guide she had encountered in her waking dream.

Ginny laughed. "He looks just like you, Robert. Except he's maybe twenty years older. He was wearing a robe and his hair was completely white. By the way, he was holding a huge crystal ball that looked like it was full of electricity. He said to remind you this belongs to you and you ought to use it."

My curiosity was fired up. I decided to check out Ginny's sighting for myself. During another drumming session, I set off in search of this future self. I quite liked what I found: a teacher who lived comfortably but without show, in a house filled with old books and native artifacts, offset by ultramodern communications equipment. I watched him mediate some kind of healing and was glad to see he did not allow the people who came to consult him to treat him as any sort of guru. I liked him better than I liked myself at that time. I noticed some specific things that guided choices I later made.

I did not speak to this older self; I simply observed him. Since then, I have found myself checking in with my future self—in fact, with a variety of possible future selves—both in dreams and in dreamlike states. I have found this the source of many practical insights. I don't attempt it too often. I do not choose to know everything that lies ahead. In any case, the moment you start believing that you know where you're going is the moment that (count on it!) the rug is about to be pulled from under you. The purpose is basically to develop a more generous and humorous perspective on life's ups and downs, on the successes and failures your future self has hopefully survived: to stop taking everything so seriously and relish the game beyond the moves.

If you want to try this for yourself, here is a simple exercise that will get you started:

Tracking Your Future Self

See yourself going along a road. Move forward to the next major crossroads. Examine the road signs carefully. Maybe one is pointing to a new job, a new city, a new relationship. Decide which road you are going to take.

Now go forward to see what lies at the end of that road. Picture yourself five years from now in this new situation. Are you satisfied with your lifestyle, your friends, your achievements?

If not, return to the crossroads and choose another path. Repeat the exercise to see where that one comes out.

Write up a travel report and decide how to act on it in your everyday life.

THE FLIGHT NOT TAKEN

I believe that my life was once saved by a dream that came like a firebell in the night, ripping me from sleep at 3:30 A.M.

In the dream, I was driving an unfamiliar car along unfamiliar roads. The sky was leaden and oppressive. The air seemed to be full of coal dust. I drove under a bridge and got a clear glimpse of a small blue car passing overhead.

Then the action stopped. I was no longer at the wheel. I was on my back. From the corner of my eye, I could see a convenience store. Faces leaned into my circle of vision, peering down at me. I seemed to be rising toward them without moving my limbs.

I woke up in a cold sweat, my heart thudding like an angry judge's gavel.

My first thought was, "I just saw myself killed in a road accident." The felt quality of the dream and the way it had shocked me out of sleep convinced me that what I had seen was not a symbolic death, but a possible physical death.

My schedule made it vital to check the meaning of the dream immediately. I had a reservation on an early flight to Pittsburgh that morning. I was planning to rent a car and drive down to Lancaster County, where I had business. It struck me that this section of Pennsylvania, which I had never previously visited, was coal miners' country, and that I had been driving into coal dust in the dream.

I lay back on my bed and tried to reenter the dream. The images came surprisingly quickly, perhaps because of the urgency of the message. I was able to observe and memorize many more details of the drive: road signs, route numbers, landmarks. I drove under the bridge again and noticed that the small blue car on the overpass was a Honda.

The action stopped, as before. This time, I got a better look at the men who were peering down at me. I saw cops clearing a path for paramedics through a knot of men in work clothes and hunters' camos. I saw an inert form under a sheet on a stretcher.

I felt strange. I was aware I was dreaming, and that my body was in the bed, and here I was inspecting a second body: my dreambody or dream double.

I experienced a powerful tug. Something was pulling me upward, deeper, and higher, into the dream. I felt a radiant, loving presence and allowed myself to rise toward it. I saw myself borne upward on clouds of light. This felt wonderful. Elated, I lost consciousness I was dreaming. I was borne higher, to a point where it was made clear to me that I could not journey further in my present vehicle. I saw myself separate from my astral body. I watched it float down, like a discarded bodysuit. I was perfectly relaxed about leaving it until I noticed a stir of activity. Some rather sinister, vampirelike characters seemed to be taking great interest in what I was leaving behind. I thought I had better go back and make sure they did not meddle with it.

Wait a minute! an inner voice interrupted. *You're not dead! You're dreaming!*

I recollected myself and came back with a thump to ordinary reality. Breathless and excited, I rushed to the family room to check in a road atlas the highway information I had picked up. The details I could confirm from the maps were remarkably accurate. It is entirely possible that in my dream reentry I seized on information that had previously been available to me, but I doubt that accounts for the precision of my dream sightings. I had decided on my trip only the previous day and had not gotten round to studying road maps, figuring that I would have plenty of time to do that on the plane.

In any case, the fact that I had been able to see physical locations so clearly affected me less powerfully than what I had glimpsed of a possible series of after-death experiences. This gave me insight into what shamans mean when they say that we have more than one soul (or sheaths of the spirit), and that these souls go to different destinations, and the mechanics of what Western esotericists describe as the "second death."

On the morning of that dream, I had a practical decision to make. I called the airline and canceled my flight to Pittsburgh. What would you have done?

CHOOSING YOUR FUTURE

*M*y dream of death on the road was a dream about a *possible future.* Many dreams about future events are actually glimpses of possible futures. If we get the message, we can take action to enact or avoid the dream scenario. If we can see into the future, by dream radar or other means, we may also be able to change it.

There is a paradox here, which J. B. Priestley stated elegantly in *Man and Time:*

> The future can be seen, and because it can be seen, it can be changed. But if it can be seen and yet changed, it is neither solidly there, laid out for us to experience moment after moment, nor is it nonexistent. . . . If it does not exist, it cannot be seen; if it is solidly set and fixed, then it cannot be changed. What is this future that is sufficiently established to be observed and perhaps experienced, and yet allow itself to be altered?[8]

Philosophers and physicists have wrestled with this. Some modern physicists have floated the hypothesis that we inhabit one of countless parallel universes, in which all our possible futures are actualized. In one of these parallel universes, Hitler won World War II. In another parallel universe, you married (or divorced) your childhood sweetheart. Yet another parallel universe may be identical to this one apart from the fact that you stood up your dinner date last Tuesday. The number of such parallel universes might be infinite. If you change the future you perceive in dreams by the action you take in waking life, that future will still be played out in some parallel world. It might then be said (to coil the argument into a Möbius strip) that the future you perceived in a dream was your future in a parallel life.[9]

At an intellectual level, these arguments are giddying. But they can be explored and tested through dreaming. How often have you dreamed that you were with your old partner, or in your old job, at your present age? Such dreams may provide instruction through analogy, causing us to reflect on what we did right or wrong in a previous situation in order to distill guidance on present or future challenges. However, there are dreams in which we seem to be walking along *ghost trails*. I have had scores of dreams over the years in which I am still living in London, still married to my ex-wife, still working for a newspaper. I watch myself age, as I do in this reality, and wonder whether there is another Robert, or any number of Roberts, out there, walking the paths from which I turned. If this could be true for the past, it would also be true for the future. In dreaming, there is only *now*.

We will soon get lost in these thickets if we approach them with linear reasoning. Shamans seem to understand these things better, even if they have never heard of quantum mechanics. Shamans believe that in dreaming, we not only scout out the future but may actively *choose* between possible futures that are open to us. The more conscious we become, the greater our ability to choose. Physical events are born inside the dreaming, where it is possible to change them before they are manifested. If we see future events in dreams that are not enacted in waking life, it is because a different possible future has been selected. We observe only part of these processes because, waking or dreaming, we perceive only phenomena that have meaning for us, and we are confined by our belief systems.

To bring this discussion down to earth, where shamans like to be, we could say that the probability that any future event in our lives will take place is constantly changing. Dream radar gives us fairly precise readouts on the probable outcome of our present actions and behavior, and the probable consequences of choices we might make in the future. Active Dreaming gives us tools to rearrange these orders of probability. Through *dream reentry*, we check our messages and make sure we are working with all the pertinent information. Through *dream enactment*, we learn how to steer toward or away from the dream result in waking life. Through *conscious dreaming*, we position ourselves to change the outcome inside the dream itself.

The probability that a possible future event, perceived in a dream, will be enacted depends on a number of factors. These include:

1. Time lapse. Generally, the shorter the interval between the dream and the probable enactment of the event foreseen, the greater the chance that the dream will be played out in waking life unless you are able to take deliberate action to avert the dream fulfillment. *

2. Personal involvement. Is the dream about you or people connected with you whom you may be able to influence? If so, you may have latitude to act to change the dream result. But if the dream is about strangers, a remote situation, or a natural disaster, there is probably little or nothing you can do—except, say, call a friend in Los Angeles to warn about the next earthquake and risk being regarded as a nut or (maybe worse) as merely stating the obvious.

3. Active dreaming. Are you working actively with your dream source? Do you make it a habit not only to read dream messages but do something with them? If so, you may have more room to work around dream results you don't relish.

4. Life burdens. The future events you dream may be the results of disease, old age, past actions, decades of bad habits, or the culmination of a whole lifetime. It might be difficult or impossible to get out from under a big accumulation of personal karma! But even if an unwanted event, perceived in the dream, now proves to be unavoidable in waking life, the lesson brought home by the dream may prepare you for the worst and lay the ground for a fresh start.

There is a wonderful story about such possibilities, reported by Sir Laurens van der Post from his time among the Bushmen of the Kalahari. An explorer was told by native elders that he had angered the spirits of the Tsodilo mountains by violating their sacred space without permission. Bowing to local beliefs, the explorer wrote a formal letter of apology to the mountain spirits, accompanied by appropriate offerings.

* Dreams of the imminent future sometimes turn out to be dreams of things that have already taken place, or are already in process. You dream of receiving a letter that turns up in tomorrow's mail. You dream your aunt is flying, and learn the following day she died during the night.

A shaman of the Bushmen consulted with the spirits and reported back to the explorer, "All is well. The spirits ask me to say to you that from now on all will go well with you." The shaman added that there was one small problem. Misfortune awaited the explorer at his next destination. This trouble could not be avoided; it flowed from the explorer's actions before he wrote his letter of apology. However, he should not lose heart. "The spirits say your bad luck belongs to your past, not your future."[10]

DREAMS OF THE DEPARTED

As long as you do not know how to die and come to life again, you are a sorry traveler on this dark earth.

Goethe

The dimension that separates the living from the dead is exactly as wide as the edge of a maple leaf.

Handsome Lake, the Seneca prophet

THE TABOO SUBJECT

I once taught a philosophy class for nurses at a busy city hospital. To get some idea of what they were thinking about, and what they might be open to exploring, I set them the following exercise on our first evening:

> Suppose you meet a true spiritual master, someone who has the answer to any question you might choose to ask. You might perceive this teacher as Moses or the Goddess, as Buddha or your favorite archangel. You can ask any question, and it will be answered by a spiritual source you trust absolutely. But you can ask only one question. So, what question will you ask, from the beating heart of your life?

The twenty-two nurses in that class wrote their questions, anonymously, on scraps of paper, which I read at home later that night with mounting excitement. The nurses were asking the big questions, like the ones Gauguin daubed on his 1897 triptych: *Who am I? Where do I come from? Where am I going?* Nurses often have to deal with the messy, unpleasant end of life. Quite a few of those women wanted an explanation for pain and suffering and the phenomenon of evil in our world. But by far the most pressing question, the one asked by more than half the class, was, *What happens when I die?* Nurses are highly practical people. They wanted specifics. "What will be expected of me?" "How do I know for sure?" "Will I meet my dead relatives?"

I took these questions as a mandate to do things in that class that not only jumped the fences of the previous curriculum but flattened them. We worked with dreams; we discussed deathbed visions and near-death experiences the nurses had attended; we read visionary accounts of the soul's passage after physical death from the Tibetan Book of the Dead to Swedenborg. We improvised a class in "real philosophy," to borrow Jacob Needleman's phrase. We rediscovered the truth of Plato's insight that real philosophy is *phaedros melete thanatou*, practice and preparation for death.

In a society where we let so many people die in hospitals, among strangers, nurses are frequently the dying person's last companions. Nurses not only check vital signs, switch off respirators, close eyelids; they share the deathwalk. They care for souls as well as bodies. Cast in this role by a society that cast out its soul doctors, nurses are naturally preoccupied with the meaning of death and the facts of the afterlife.

It also is natural for all of us to be curious about the end of life and life after life, because one thing certain in human affairs is that all of us are born to die. Each step we take, after the difficult passage down the birth canal, is a step toward physical extinction. In many sections of our society, we have made this simple truth a taboo subject. Lame Deer, the Lakota holy man, remarked that he could not understand European Americans because they rushed through life as if it was a race to a goal— and all they saw at the end of the race was a gaping black hole.[1]

It is difficult to look at death, just as it is difficult to look at the sun. But you can get viewing equipment that will allow you to monitor solar activity; I remember my father showing me how to make a device for tracking a solar eclipse with the aid of a pin and an old shoebox. Dreams are the shadow box in which we can watch the cycles of death and re-birth. They are also a transceiver through which we can receive and transmit messages to the departed. These matters are too important to be taken on trust. We may delay our explorations until the shadow of our mortality falls across our path, maybe because of a personal health emergency or the loss of a loved one. We may shrink from a dialogue with death and the departed out of raw fear. But that dialogue will take place, on one side of the swing door of physical death or the other. We can join in it any time we choose, because our dead are always with us, even (and sometimes especially) if we do not acknowledge them.

In recent years there has been lively public interest in accounts of near-death experiences reported by people who recovered from major surgery and life-threatening accidents or illness. The description of a typical NDE is brief: a journey through a tunnel, the vision of a wonderful unearthly Light, a glimpse of friends on the other side, the benevolent voice telling the soul to return to the body because it is not yet time. Such experiences have often brought positive changes in the lives of those who have shared them. At the least, a near-death experience tends to make a person far more humorous and relaxed about the ups and downs of everyday life. If you *know* there are larger fields of possibility awaiting you after physical death, and you know this as a matter of personal experience, you are likely to be far less prone to hurry sickness, status-seeking, and other disorders of Western society.[2]

Shamans do not speak of near-death experiences. They speak of "dying and coming back" or of "temporary deaths." Such experiences are common in a shaman's training and initiation. By definition, the shaman must be one of the twice-born. Shamans have died to their former life, journeyed in the realms of the dead, and returned to assist souls on both sides of the divide. How can the shaman be trusted to guide souls on the roads to the afterlife or to bring back lost souls that have strayed among the dead before their time unless he or she has walked those roads and is intimately familiar with their geography?

The shaman may have earned visitation rights to these territories through a crisis, both physical and spiritual, that a Western medical practitioner might describe (in the wake of Dr. Raymond Moody) as an NDE. However, shamans know that it is not necessary to have a heart attack or a bad trip under the surgeon's knife to explore these realms. The shaman returns to them in dreaming. The path is open to any one of us, if we are prepared to walk it and the time is right. Death is a great teacher, as the stories of Yama, the death lord in the *Katha Upanishad*, reflect, but we should not trouble him without reason.

When you are ready to make this journey, you will find that in dreaming, you can not only explore the territory described by NDE survivors, but go far beyond the threshold where they usually stop. You can examine many worlds beyond the physical plane. You can study the soul's transitions after physical death and investigate alternative afterlife possibilities.

You have guidance on these matters available to you tonight, from departed members of your family circle. Our dead are always with us. They speak to us most frequently in dreams, because in dreams we do not draw rigid distinctions between the dead and the living. In dreams, released from the body, our condition is also that of spirits.

I have been receiving dream messages from dead people since my earliest childhood, when, as a function of that recurring cycle of life-threatening illness, I seemed to spend as much time with disembodied spirits as with people who owned regular bodies. Dreams of the departed, like other kinds of dreams, are susceptible to many explanations, to which the dreamer's cultural tradition, personal belief system, and practice and experience of dreaming are all relevant. In some dreams, a dead person may represent an aspect of the dreamer's own identity, a dramatization of hopes and fears, a long-buried trauma that is now fighting its way to the surface. In some cases, the appearance of a dead person in a dream may indicate a transpersonal source that goes beyond the individuality of the dead person herself. Other dreams of the departed strongly suggest a literal visitation, a theme that may be underscored by a knock on the door; a ringing phone; a bell; a voice calling out, "Your mother's here!"; a car pulling up; even a spaceship landing. Though we can debate the transpersonal nature of individual dreams of the departed, we can surely agree (as Patricia Garfield puts it) that "the dead live on in our dreams" and that dead people often appear in dreams as messengers.[3]

Of the many gifts of dreaming, dream messages from the departed and dream insights into the nature of death rank with the highest and most empowering. They challenge us to serve the purpose of soul and spirit in our everyday lives. They bring the following tools and insights:

1. The soul's survival of physical death. Belief in the immortality of the soul is perhaps the oldest shared belief of our species, and one of its defining characteristics. Dreams provide constant instruction in the reality of the soul. Dreams in which we realize we are journeying outside the body, as well as dreams in which we encounter spiritual beings and glimpse possible destinations of the soul after physical death, provide personal confirmation of life after life.

There is an enlightening story about this in the *Jesuit Relations,* from the early American frontier. A blackrobe missionary in the little stone church at Tadoussac, near the mouth of the Saguenay River in Canada, sermonized to the Indians he was seeking to convert about the immortality of the soul and how it would be judged after death. Usually the Indians said nothing after hearing these homilies; they just took their little gifts of beads and mirrors and went home. But one day a stranger stood up in church, a shaman, to judge from his bones and feathers. He told the priest, "We already know that the soul is immortal because at our choosing, in dreams and visions, our soul may leave our bodies and visit other worlds and see things that are half a world away."[4]

2. Communication with the departed. Our dead return to us in dreams, when it is easier for us to hear them. The dialogue initiated in dreams may be resumed in waking states. The reasons the departed come to us in dreams are manifold. Our lost loved ones may come to give us closure and reassure us that all is well with them on the other side. They may be trying to give us counsel and information relevant to our current health and well-being. They may be seeking to tie up unfinished business. They may wish to express praise or blame or simply vent their feelings. They may be trying to prepare us for our own deaths, to coach us through dying and to remind us we have friendly guides on the other side of the swinging door.

The departed person who appears in dreams may be a stranger, with a separate agenda.* Maybe he or she is trying to send a message to another person, speaking through us because we may be more receptive than the person for whom the message is intended.

Maybe the dream visitor is a departed teacher, calling us to follow in his or her path, as dead shamans appear to shamans-to-be to summon them to their calling.

3. Boundary issues. Contact with the dead, dreaming or waking, is not always positive. Spirits can be jealous, vindictive, or deceptive, just like living people. Spirits are not necessarily repositories of universal wisdom or cosmic love; some dead people seem to remain stuck in the hatreds and prejudices with which they lived. Some people get lost after they die and remain attached to the earth sphere, a burden to the living. There are even discarnate entities, called *criminal souls* by some shamanic practitioners, who infest or seek to possess the living for malevolent purposes. In such cases, the afflicted person may need special help (help that shamans know how to provide) to separate herself from these unhealthy intrusions.

Dreams expose problems of this kind. Through dreams, we learn about the need not only to honor our dead but to ensure that we observe proper boundaries in our relations with the departed.

---

* Under these circumstances, it may not be clear initially whether the dream visitor is a living person, or someone who has passed on. Active dreamers develop an intuitive feel for these things. Follow-up research, as well as waking dialogues with the dream visitor, are often appropriate.

4. Making death an ally. To go beyond the gates of death, this side of physical death, is true initiation. To dialogue with one's own death and transform it from a lurking fear into a recognized teacher is to empower oneself to live life with new courage and generosity of spirit. If you believe that there is life after life—not as a received article of faith but because of what you have seen and lived in the orders of reality that lie beyond the surface world—then you are likely to roll with the punches of everyday life with unusual grace, because you know there is a larger purpose.

DIALOGUES WITH THE DEAD

*I*n the year after my father's death, he often appeared to me and to other members of my family in dreams. In some of these dreams, he offered practical advice, including information that was previously unknown to us. In one dream, he was extremely agitated and had speech difficulties similar to those he had suffered after a stroke. As best I could understand him, he wanted my mother to move out of her apartment immediately. He goaded all of us into a moving truck that took off along Queensland's Gold Coast highway. He kept repeating a Spanish name, something like Rodriguez. This meant nothing to me. But the force of my father's feelings was so strong that I phoned my mother in Australia when I woke from this dream. She not only knew someone called Rodriguez; she told me this was the name of the realtor who had sold my parents the last apartment they had shared together. Because of my dream, she agreed to call the realtor. Things came together for her with remarkable speed and grace. Within the week, with the aid of the realtor, she had sold her apartment and arranged to move up the Gold Coast highway to the retirement community in Southport where she spent the happiest years of her later life.

My father appeared to my middle daughter, Candida, in a series of dreams that same year. After the first of these dreams, Candida asked if I had a photograph of my father as a young man. I found one that showed him as a junior Army officer, his hair and mustache still dark. "That's him," my daughter told me with deep certainty. Born and raised in England, Candida had never met her grandfather in waking life and had seen photos of him only as an elderly man with silver hair. In her dream, she had been visited by a robust young man in the prime of life. He had taken her horseback riding; they both loved horses and my father had once been the equestrian champion of the Australian Army. At the end of their ride, they came to a fence where my father bade farewell to his granddaughter. When his horse jumped the fence, Candida started to ride after him, then realized that an invisible barrier was between them. She was saddened by this separation. But her conviction that the grandfather she had never known in ordinary life had been able to visit her and share knowledge and simple pleasures after death brought her a blessed sense of closure and deep happiness.

Doubters may choose to dismiss individual accounts of this sort as "anecdotal" and psychologize their contents away as "wish fulfillment" or the workings of tacit memory. We certainly need to learn to distinguish projection from genuine visitations. But my personal experience in hundreds of dreams and dreamlike encounters with the dead, confirmed by my work with many other dreamers, leaves me in no doubt that many of these dialogues are quite real, and that Edgar Cayce was entirely accurate when he said that the "thread of love" stretches beyond the grave. Our departed loved ones want to be known and recognized as still living, on another plane. They may wish to settle unfinished business. They may be asking to be honored by us, in appropriate ways. Sometimes they are seeking to communicate specific information that may be vital to our well-being. In cases of bereavement, such encounters sometimes seem to give survivors permission to get on with life.

— TOM GETS PERMISSION

Tom was a stocky, white-haired retiree in his late sixties. He had lost his wife three years before, and he had not managed to fill the hole this had left in him. I could feel his pain. He had been with the same partner for almost all of his adult life, and he had spent two of the three years since her death on a kind of pilgrimage. He had crisscrossed the United

States, consulting spiritualists and psychics, shamans and psychologists, attending workshops and séances. His purpose was single-minded: he wanted direct communication with his deceased wife. He wanted closure. He wanted her counsel on how he should live.

Tom was sad, even desperate, when he came to one of my workshops. Some of the psychics he had visited claimed to have spoken with his wife, he reported, but their messages were conflicting. And nobody had been able to put him in touch with her directly.

I asked Tom if he had looked for his wife in dreams. He sometimes remembered dreams, but his wife had not come to him. "Maybe she's mad at me. You see, I met this girl in a church group. She made it known she's interested. I didn't get into anything because I felt it would be like being unfaithful." Tom actually blushed. His "girl," incidentally, was in her sixties.

I felt little shivers as Tom talked about this. I had a strong feeling that his wife wanted to speak to him and might come through that day if the door was opened.

We opened the door that afternoon. Within a protected circle, we asked if there were departed relatives or ancestors who wished to communicate with individual members of the group at that time. As I circled the group with the rattle I use to lay a path for the spirits, I felt a sense of overwhelming love as I approached Tom. It brought tears to my eyes.

After the drumming, Tom's eyes were glistening, too. "I found her," he told us. "She didn't want to give me a lot of time. I guess she's pretty busy in her new job. I asked her if she missed me. She told me no. She says she's been assigned to help people with adjustment problems on the way up. She says she's got lots to do and that I should keep busy, too. She told me to enjoy the rest of my life—she thinks I've got quite a few years left—and not feel bounden to her. She says she'll see me when I'm ready and that everything will be different."

Beyond the simple words, everyone was moved by the raw power of emotion at work in that space. At the end of the day, Tom's eyes were brighter, his step lighter. He said he felt like a new man.

Skeptics can of course say that Tom found what he wanted to find, though he was far from pleased when his wife told him she did not miss him! What is not in doubt is the liberating effect of this experience. He had plugged that gaping hole.

I wondered afterward what effect this might have on Tom's subsequent life. I got my answer a few months later, when I ran into Tom, near the pineapples, in the produce section of a supermarket a few miles from my home. Tom looked terrific, tanned and fit.

"What happened to you?" I demanded as he gave me a big hug.

"I got married."

"The girl from the church group?"

"Yup. We just got back from our honeymoon in Jamaica. I couldn't have done it, you know, without checking in on my first wife. I guess that set me free."

Tom's dialogue with his dead wife took place in a waking dream, incubated within a supportive circle. The next encounters involve spontaneous sleep dreams, as well as what flowed from these in waking life.

— COMING BACK TO EXPLAIN—AND PROTECT

Cathy's world fell in when her farmer husband died in a freak accident. He had gone to help a neighbor. He was working on top of a big silo used to store cattle feed when he somehow fell into thirty feet of corn. He never came out alive. Nobody saw the accident. No one could explain it to Cathy's satisfaction. The coroner said her husband must have been overcome by toxic "off-gases" pent up inside the silo.

Cathy's grieving flowed on a riptide of anger. It had been a long struggle to hold on to the family farm. Now she risked losing everything. She had been left to support four small children, and she could not even give them a clear explanation of how their father had died, let alone why.

A few nights after his death, Cathy's husband appeared to her in a dream. "I was mad at him," she recalled. "I did not want to listen to him. He kept trying to tell me exactly how he had died. He dragged me down to that silo, in the dream. He was trying to point out something that caused the accident. He kept saying it wasn't his fault. I wouldn't listen. I was just too angry at him for leaving us."

For a while after that, Cathy tried to shut out her dreams. Then her three-year-old son, Brian, said to her accusingly, "Why didn't you tell me I can talk to dead people in my dreams?"

Cathy questioned her son. He told her his father had been coming to him in dreams nearly every night. "Dad says what happened didn't need to happen."

Cathy began to get the message. She insisted on a new investigation of the circumstances of her husband's death. When the locals dragged their heels, she hired an out-of-town attorney. It was discovered that the company that manufactured the silo had been required to supply a certain part designed to prevent the type of accident that had just taken place. In this case, the company had failed to do so. When this fact was established in court, Cathy was awarded a large cash settlement that saved the family farm.

Now Cathy's husband appeared to her in a new dream that helped her get through her emotional conflicts over his death. In this dream, he took her on a motorbike ride down country roads, as in the days of their courtship. "Then somehow the earth opened and we went down into it," Cathy recalled. "We came to a simple village, thatched huts with hearth fires burning. He told me, 'This is where I'll be.' We kissed good-bye tenderly. I woke with a feeling of overwhelming love."

Meanwhile, Cathy's small son Brian continued to dream of his father. Two years later, Brian claimed that his father had intervened, in waking life, to save him from a near-fatal accident on the road.

An older female cousin was driving Brian home that night, along a winding back road. I know that stretch of road; its blind corners are treacherous in the dark. Brian's cousin was nervous and inexperienced. Rounding a sharp bend, they were confronted by a tractor-trailer, jack-knifed across the road directly ahead of them. By a spectacular feat of driving, the cousin managed to land them in a ditch rather than a head-on collision.

In the emergency room where he was taken for stitches, Brian announced to the people who congratulated his cousin on her smart driving, "It wasn't her. Dad took over the wheel and put his other arm round my shoulder. He told me it wasn't my time yet."

~ GUIDANCE AND CONFIRMATION

Evan, a troubled teenager, was going through a rough patch at school when his grandfather appeared to him in a dream and gave him some reasons for trying harder:

> *Grandpa showed me many scenes and problems from my future life. I saw my wedding. It seemed to be somewhere in the Southwest. I was twenty-six or twenty-seven, wearing a tuxedo. I was marrying a beautiful dark-skinned girl. I don't remember the rest because Grandpa erased it. He literally rubbed it off the blackboard. He said I didn't need to know too much, just enough to keep my spirits up.*

In checking my dream messages from the dead, I find that people to whom I was especially close quite often appear to confirm a certain course of action (or alternatively to caution against it). For example, when I was considering returning to historical fiction, I dreamed I was exploring a rambling but somewhat run-down rooming house by a river. As I explored an apartment upstairs, I was surprised and delighted to find stacks and stacks of material for my historical novel arranged in folders and boxes of index cards by an unmistakable hand—that of my favorite history professor, who had died many years before. Inside the dream, I was elated to discover that he had been working for all these years on my own project.

⮕ SHARING THE FUN

Dream reunions with the departed sometimes feel like shared entertainments, as in Candida's dream of the horseback ride. Such dreams may replay scenes from the past, as in my dreams in which I wage miniature wars with my father with armies of model soldiers, as I did as a boy.

In dreams, the dead are not only sources of information; sometimes they seem to be seeking information from us. Jung reported in his memoirs on several powerful dreams in which departed sages and priests appeared to be asking him for guidance. Edgar Cayce, the renowned psychic, spoke of our need to recognize that dead people like to be brought up-to-date.

When I was first experimenting with shamanic techniques, I not only received extensive instruction from past practitioners in dreams, but occasionally dreamed that shamans of earlier times were seeking knowledge from me, as in the following dream:

> *I am in a hill country, possibly the Balkans, many centuries ago. Two neighboring villages are at war. Each has its warrior shamans, some of*

whom are associated with the power of the Taurs. These shamans come to me for help and advice. I am disgusted by their cruelty and greed; they really seem to be exploiting people. I tell them I will have nothing to do with them unless they pursue a more spiritual path.

This dream certainly contained a teaching parable. In following a shamanic path, it is vitally important to serve the purposes of soul and spirit: to follow the inner Light and not allow oneself to become fascinated by psychic abilities and paranormal phenomena on their own account. However, I also felt that my "Balkan shamans," like other past practitioners who have figured in my dreams—a Seneca medicine man, a Papuan sorcerer, a druid oak-priest, a Renaissance magus—were not aspects of my present personality, but people who lived separate lives in another time and place.

➤ DEMANDING JUSTICE

The dead appear in dreams not only to counsel and protect but to demand justice or revenge. One of my favorite stories about this involves a court case in seventeenth-century Rhode Island. Dreams were not only admitted into the court record, they inspired the prosecution that led to the conviction of Thomas Cornell, who stood accused of murdering his mother.

The old woman had absented herself from the family's midday meal, declaring that she could not abide the taste of salt fish and would smoke her pipe by the fire in the next room. Thomas left the table during the meal, saying he would check on her. After lunch, they all went in to the next room and found the old lady dead. Although her skirts were charred, her death was ascribed to natural causes—until she appeared to another of her sons in a powerful dream, insisting that he should investigate how her skirts came to be burned. It was eventually concluded that Thomas had pushed his mother into the fireplace and smothered her in the smoke. He was found guilty in court and hanged.

➤ FRIENDS ON THE OTHER SIDE

Departed friends and relatives often appear in dreams to prepare us for physical death and guide us through the transition to the next life. Such dreams provide reassurance that the dying person has friends on the other side who will help her make the transition to life after life.

Alice had entered her mideighties when she started receiving dream visits from her sister Dorothy, who had died several years before.

"Are you ready to move on?" Dorothy asked her in the first of these dreams.

"Certainly not!" Alice countered indignantly.

"Very well. Just remember I'll be back when you're ready."

Alice reported that after that first dream, her sister took to "dropping in" on her every six months or so. This annoyed Alice at the outset. She was still full of beans and had no intention of being hurried into her grave. But as time passed and her health deteriorated, it was a comfort to her to know that, when her time came, she would have a familiar guide waiting for her.

When we shut out our dreams, a message of this kind may be picked up by someone who is more receptive.

Peter, a college librarian, was a mediocre dream recaller and an agnostic on the subject of life after death until he had the following dream:

The Doorbell That Shouldn't Ring

I'm doing household chores, cleaning up the mess in my living room. It's a boring, everyday situation. I have no idea I'm dreaming until the doorbell rings. I know there's something strange going on, because I had that bell disconnected months before. When I try to figure this out, I wake up to the fact that I'm dreaming.

I open the door and find a pleasant, smiling woman. She's wearing a lacy white dress, as if she's going to a wedding. She introduces herself as Sarah W. The name means nothing to me. She tells me, "I have a message for your mother."

I explain that my mother doesn't live with me; she has her own place. "I know that," Sarah says patiently. "I want you to tell your mother that everything is going to be fine. Tell her I'll be waiting for her."

Peter was excited by this dream. He wasn't sure what it was telling him, but he felt certain it was important. The doorbell that was not supposed to ring had made him conscious he was dreaming inside the dream, a novel experience that helped to ensure he did not forget.

Peter went to his mother's house for Sunday lunch. They were washing the dishes when he started to pass on the dream message. When he mentioned Sarah W.'s name, his mother turned white and dropped one of the plates. She would not explain why.

The next day, Peter's mother died from a massive heart attack.

Peter did not understand the whole story until several years later, when his father also passed on and Peter started sorting out family papers. He came upon a journal his mother had kept in her teens, written in the "Dear Diary" style of a previous era. His mother described people she liked as "peachy."

To his astonishment, Peter found that one of the "peachy" people mentioned in the diary was the Sarah W. who had rung his doorbell in the dream. There was her full name, spelled out in his mother's adolescent copperplate. The 1930s entry recorded that Sarah had died at a relatively early age. "She was a wonderful soul," Peter's mother had written. "I hope someday I'll see her again."

Peter had no doubt his mother's wish came true.

A LOVE STRONGER THAN DEATH

*J*ohn Hotchin was deeply in love with Lois. He had left his first wife for her, overcoming wrenching feelings of guilt. For many years, John and Lois were colleagues as well as lovers, working together in a medical research laboratory. When Lois, who had never been a smoker, was diagnosed with lung cancer, they both felt betrayed. In the face of this killer, all their medical knowledge proved useless.

A week after Lois died, John woke on a bitterly cold midwinter morning in a state of crawling dread, not sure if he was truly awake or still dreaming. Beside his bed, in the half-light, he could still see his dead wife as she had appeared to him during the night. Lois was wearing a red dress with a ruff at the neck, the one he had called her "Queen Elizabeth dress"; he had never liked it. John recalled:

> *Lois just stood there. She either said to me or simply transmitted the thought, "You must kill yourself." She very badly wanted me to commit suicide. I could not tell whether I was still asleep, or whether she was actually there next to the bed although I had woken up. I felt terribly afraid of her. It seemed she had an evil power to make me do what she wanted. I felt that unless I got help at once, I might be driven to kill myself.*

Anyone who has lost a loved one will empathize with John's pain and rage. Anger toward the person who has departed is a common emotion in early stages of bereavement, as the work of Elisabeth Kübler-Ross has confirmed.[5] John was familiar with such studies. He tried to persuade himself that he had simply projected his own despair onto the image of his dead wife. Yet, even after he regained his balance, he was not satisfied with these rationalizations. In part of himself, he was convinced that he had received a real visitation.

John was an M.D. and a Ph.D., for many years an assistant director of the New York health department, in charge of critical research into viral diseases. As a genuine man of science, John was open to experiential data that might provide evidence of transpersonal encounters and the soul's survival of physical death. Now he faced a quandary. He was unwilling to believe that the woman he had regarded as his soul mate would come to him in the guise of the "evil dead." Yet the felt quality of his experience led him to believe that it was more than one of his own projections.

Though Lois did not appear in another suicide dream, John's nights continued to be troubled:

> *I dreamed I had to save an important man who was dying. He became smaller and smaller, while I desperately worked to save him. Finally he got so small I lost him. This dream was very distressing to me.*

John decided to get out of the oppressive atmosphere of the home he had shared with his dead wife. He booked himself on a group tour of the Southwest.

He was feeling sullen and out of sorts when the group arrived at the beautiful old mission church of San Xavier del Bac in Arizona. He dawdled behind the group, not feeling like looking at churches. When he finally stepped inside the mission church, his mood was transformed. He was awed by the beauty of the interior, by the haunting strains of a native guitar, by the lights of hundreds of votive candles. As he tells it:

Vision in the Mission Church

I began to feel a strange warmth, not heat from the candles but a warmth in my brain, in my heart. It was a comforting feeling that grew stronger and stronger. I became incredibly happy.

I had a strong impression that some important person had entered the church. I turned to look toward the door, but nobody was there. Then a conviction began to dawn in me that was totally definite and final. I knew beyond all doubt that my wife had entered that church and was there beside me. She was with somebody else, a veiled presence. This was someone she loved, in whose love she was held and embraced. It was God, or some part of God. This knowledge did not originate in me. It came to me from a higher place. It moved through me like music.

Tears streamed down my face. I was deeply moved and immeasurably happy. I believe I was granted some kind of grace or gift from God.

This settled one thing that had been worrying me. Because we had been so much in love, I had felt that even if my wife was in heaven, she could not be happy, because she would miss me as I missed her. In that church, I knew not only that she was with me but that, with God, she was happy and complete. This was comforting knowledge.

When he returned home after this waking vision in the mission church, John's dreams of his dead wife were less troubled.

A new theme emerged, as he found himself experimenting in dreams with various ways of communicating with Lois. Frequently, he found himself talking to Lois on the telephone during his dreams. He began to associate phone calls in dreams with communication with the spirit world. Waking or sleeping, he decided, "we need a type of telephone that can place calls to heaven."

In one dream, he inspected a novel device for journeying to the spirit world:

A Submarine for Visiting Spirits

I was with an important man, who was demonstrating how to install a device in the roof of a ship that was capable of special travel. The ship looked a bit like a submarine. The device was a two-foot cube of heavy metal. I fitted it into a slot on the roof. The great man was surprised. He asked, "How are you strong enough to do this?" I told him I did exercises every day and proved this by swinging from pipes on the ceiling. Then I led the way up through the hatch, into another world. The great man and other people followed. We came out into an open field. The scene was beautiful. The grass was quite different from normal grass, and very long. I saw Lois in the distance, at a picnic table.

John was excited by the idea that, as in the dream, he could perfect his ability to communicate with other planes of existence through regular "exercises." But despite these promising dreams and his moment of grace in the mission church, he was often wretchedly lonely. Sometimes he had vivid sexual fantasies in which his dead wife was always his partner. These brought him some transient consolation but also guilty fears—bubbling up, in part, from his strict Methodist upbringing—that he was engaging in something immoral, or consorting with "low" spirits. He also wondered whether, in some obscure way, these diversions might be unhealthy for his departed wife.

When he blocked out sexual thoughts of Lois for a couple of weeks, he worried about her, night after night, in dreams with a new and recurring theme:

Lost Address

I realize I haven't seen Lois for a year or two. I am horrified I don't even have her address. I feel I must get in touch with her and marry her. This is a life-and-death matter. I wake up intensely anxious, to the point of panic, about the risk of losing her.

About this time, John came to one of my workshops, where he experimented with active-dreaming techniques. He found he could use the "special submarine" from one of his dreams quite successfully as a vehicle for exploring nonordinary reality. He had encounters with Lois and with a spiritual guide who introduced himself as Zeke. He was told, lovingly but firmly, that his departed wife had moved on to a higher plane, and he must let her go on with her journey alone.

After these experiences, John had another powerful dream about his dead wife:

Spirit in Two Containers

I am driving with Lois in an open car along a concrete beachfront. We come to the end of the concrete and park on a slope that goes down to sand and mud. I ask some workmen if it is okay to go on. They do not respond. I park round a corner, near a house that seems familiar. We both get out. The owner of the house is a scientist. I want to question him, but he avoids me. I get back in the car and drive off.

I am horrified to realize I have forgotten my wife.

I go back and find Lois is still there, talking to some people. She seems weak and unsteady, but smiles and says she is fine. I get her in the car. When I turn around, I see that somehow she has put herself inside two Coke bottles. The bottles contain clear spirit. One is full, the other part full. I carry both bottles, hurrying now to get home.

We arrive at a huge cathedral-like place, maybe a university, with many buildings—I have dreamed of this place several times before. I carry the spirit bottles along many passages, then up some stairs, trying to find the way home. I ask a caretaker for directions. He tells me, "Keep to the right and straight on" at the foot of another flight of stairs.

I enter a glass-sided elevator that shoots up at terrific speed. Inside are a college professor and a scientist. I remark that we must have gone up at least four floors. "Fifty-four floors," they correct me.

I get out of the elevator and speak into the mouth of the full Coke bottle. "Are you all right, honey?"

"Yes, I'm fine," I hear Lois speak from inside the bottle. Her voice is warm and vibrant. I am very relieved.

I arrive at a hospice-type room; Lois comes out of the bottle. I am impressed and amazed. I think, inside the dream, This is a supernatural psychic event, like the one in the mission church. *I know Lois is telling me her spirit is alive and well.*

John was elated when he woke from this last dream. As with his terrifying suicide dream, it took him some time to realize he had been dreaming. The experience seemed hyperreal. This time, however, the experience was wholly positive. And it brought him—finally!—a sense of closure.

What is going on here? In psychological terms, John's dreams and visions are phases in a challenging and moving journey through loss and grieving. From this perspective, the changing images of his dead wife may be seen to mirror the dreamer's changing emotions and movement toward integration. From a shamanic viewpoint, however, the dreamer's sense that his experiences were "real"—i.e., transpersonal—would be taken quite literally. Shamans know that the spirits of our dead communicate with us through dreams, and that such dreams sometimes indicate the need to draw boundary lines between the dead and the living. Shamans also believe that more than one aspect of a dead person may appear to the living in dreams or in other kinds of visitations.

This story of John and Lois provides rich experiential insights, from the dreams of a contemporary Western scientist, into the possible transitions of the soul after physical death, and the possible validity of the shaman's perception that the soul has several distinct aspects, containers, and destinations.

In the suicide dream, John's dead wife appears to be both lost and voracious. Instead of following the Light, she is urging her husband to join her in some in-between state by killing himself. I have worked with quite a number of dreams, some more terrifying or more desolate, in which recently deceased people seem to have lost their way. Dreams in which dead people urge their survivors to join them are commonly reported by those who have lost loved ones to suicide or sudden death, as well as by those who might (rightly or wrongly) consider themselves responsible for a death. In the case of John and Lois, it seems possible that the dead person's resentment of the unfairness of her death sentence (lung cancer) and the force and sexual vibrancy of her love for her partner might have caused her to lose her way, for a time.

There is a complete change of quality in the inspiriting vision in the mission church. Now John feels his wife is accompanied by a sacred guide and is caught up in an oceanic communion with the divine. From this point forward, it seems to be John who is calling his loved one back to the earth sphere—or questing after her on the higher planes.

His dream of the two "spirit bottles" is the most revealing and provocative in the whole series. This dream opens up territory that is not much explored in our contemporary mainstream religions, but may be fundamental to the care and guidance of souls after physical death. John sees his dead wife transferred to twin bottles of "spirit," one full, one only partially filled. He sees her reemerge, on a much higher level, from the full bottle. In his dream, the scientist and the workers, masters of external reality, cannot or will not explain what is going on.

Shamans have a possible explanation, as do esoteric practitioners in both Western and Eastern traditions. All recognize that the spirit has vehicles in addition to the physical body.[6] There is, at the least, a "subtle body" or astral vehicle that separates from the physical body after death and will eventually disintegrate once abandoned by the enduring spirit. However, this "second self" may survive for a lengthy period. A soul that is lost or confused after death may believe that this vehicle is its home. Since the astral vehicle initially resembles the physical self, a lost soul may not even realize it is dead. The comedy film *Ghost* gives a colloquial, but probably fairly accurate, picture of the confusion that can result.

People get lost, after physical death, for various reasons. They may not be ready to release desires or fears or addictions and may be bound by these to the earth sphere. During physical life, they may consistently have denied the possibility of life outside the body and are therefore confused about the new state of existence in which they find themselves. Alternatively, they may be terrified by horror tales about hellfire and damnation. For whatever reasons they get stuck, earthbound spirits cause all manner of complications for the living, among which classic hauntings are less frequent and troublesome than what the church used to call "obsession": the transfer of cravings, appetites, and even physical symptoms from the dead to the living.

John's suicide dream may exemplify this problem; more troubling examples are in the next section. If John's departed wife experienced some transit problems on the other side, they seem to have been resolved fairly quickly, thanks to guidance from higher levels.

The spirit-bottles dream seemed to suggest that John was dealing with *two* aspects of his departed wife. The spirit is contained in two vessels; it is reborn on the higher plane from only the one that is full of clear spirit.

Dreams of this kind have given rise to the oldest belief of the human species: that a part of our larger identity survives physical death. As John's experiences suggest, we should never take statements of this sort on trust. We should dream on them.

LOST SOULS

Spirits linger. For many years after her mother's death, Bonnie dreamed of her and felt sure she was still with her. This was not an uncomfortable relationship at the outset, though Bonnie's mother tended, as in life, to be opinionated and interfering. In dreams, she was constantly meddling in Bonnie's love life, cautioning her that all men were cheats and that she ought to get rid of her current boyfriend. Bonnie's mother was just as outspoken with advice on diet, clothes, and even her daughter's latest hairstyle.

"I started to feel suffocated," Bonnie recalled. "My mom was always that kind of engulfing mother. Now it seemed I couldn't get away from her. She was around all the time, telling me how I was screwing up. I couldn't enjoy sex anymore. It was like I was doing it in public."

Bonnie also noticed that she was developing a new set of physical symptoms—sudden energy dips, arthritis pains, even embarrassing bouts of incontinence—that she did not feel belonged to her. These, in addition to increasingly troubling dreams, persuaded her that she might be dealing with something more than an internalized mother figure. She sought counsel from a spiritual practitioner, who advised her that her mother had remained attached to the earth plane. Bonnie's mother was confused after her death in a car accident. For a considerable period, she had apparently not understood she was dead. More recently she had avoided moving into the Light because she truly believed that her daughter would not be able to hack it on her own.

The spiritual practitioner told Bonnie it was time for her mother to move on. Bonnie agreed with relief to allow the practitioner to dialogue directly with her dead mother. He explained to her, gently but firmly, that she was dead and had more important things to do than to hang around her daughter attempting to dictate her hairstyle. After some discussion, he assisted Bonnie's mother in moving on to the next stage of her soul's journey, where another guide was waiting to escort her.

Bonnie's story is typical of problems that arise when spirits of the dead remain earthbound. Dreams and unfamiliar physical symptoms associated with the dead person helped Bonnie to recognize the nature of what was burdening her. Releasing that burden required a conversation with Bonnie's deceased mother, as well as certain cleansing procedures. In such cases, any genuine spiritual practitioner will regard the dead person as the client, just as much as the living. A serious limitation of psychotherapy is that, just as the therapist may fail to appreciate that her client is not all there (because of soul-loss), she may also fail to perceive that she has more than one client, in the most literal sense.

Edith Fiore, a psychologist who dialogues with the dead and conducts "depossessions" routinely as part of her practice, has produced a valuable corrective in her book *The Unquiet Dead*. Fiore maintains that lowered energy and major fatigue are often associated with the presence of earthbound dead, who are trying to feed on the energy of the living. She states that in her practice she has *always* detected the presence of earthbound spirits—dead drunks and junkies, trying to get another snort—in people with serious cases of alcoholism and drug addiction.[7]

It may be passing the buck to attribute the addictions or vicious habits of a living person to someone who lived before. But I certainly agree with Fiore that our bad habits and addictions, and the environments where we give them rein, greatly increase our vulnerability to negative encounters with the dead, as in the following case.

⌐ DEATH ON THE THIRD RAIL

Sober, Alan was an intellectually brilliant and often charming business consultant, popular with colleagues, devoted to his wife and daughter. He was also a binge drinker who could not seem to leave a bottle unfinished once he had opened it. Drunk, he degenerated into a brutal, leering hooligan, capable of any degree of psychological violence, and sometimes physical violence as well, against those who most loved him.

Alan was haunted by two recurring dreams. In one of these dreams, he saw himself killed when he fell on the third rail of a train line. He was not sure, in the dream, whether he jumped or simply fell—or was pushed. But the scene was played out again and again. It had gotten to the point where he hardly trusted himself to go near the edge of a railroad platform, for fear he would act out the dream in waking life.

In the other recurring dream, Alan kept trying to squeeze his large, meaty body through a tight opening. "I am like a bird trapped in an angle of the roof, trying to get through a crack."

The morning Alan told me this second dream, by a grim synchronicity a bird flew inside his house and was torn apart by one of his cats. He did not share his dream of death on the third rail with me until after the events I am about to recount.

With some misgivings, I had agreed to spend a weekend at his house. The day I arrived, he was drinking ferociously, quadruple gins with just a splash of tonic, followed by tumblers of neat whiskey. He became violently abusive toward his wife, who retreated in tears. I considered leaving the house, but decided to see what the night would bring. I left him drinking alone and went up to the guest room, pursued by foul curses and threats, bawled in a voice that was unrecognizable as Alan's.

It was a curious night. The atmosphere in the house was dark and oppressive. When I turned off the light, the air in the guest room seemed clotted. A swirling black mass leaped toward me, almost a physical thing. I felt my energy field pulsating violently with the force of its attack. The lamp rattled on the table. A closet door swung open and slammed shut.

It was clear to me now that while Alan's problems were obviously self-invited, they might not be wholly self-generated.

I kept vigil that night. I did some simple cleansing operations. I invoked spiritual protection, for Alan and his family as well as myself. Alan was now snoring loudly, blacked out on the living room floor. I tried to channel light energy toward him. I focused on the only happy moment the previous day, the moment when he had expressed delight over the smell of honeysuckle during a walk past a neighbor's garden.

I shifted consciousness, scanning for clues to the source of the menacing psychic turmoil in that house.

The name George came to me immediately and distinctly. I saw a slim young man, good-looking but somewhat shifty. An alcoholic like

Alan. He tried to avoid me, but I stalked him. He was tricky, changing forms. I saw him running along railroad tracks and suddenly I *knew* this person had killed himself by throwing himself in front of a train or by touching the third rail.

I told him he had to move on. I saw a possible guide waiting for him. But George fled the opposite way. He seemed to fear punishment for his suicide and was still in the grip of his addiction.

I was diverted by a hoarse call for help from Alan, inside this conscious dream. I turned toward the source of this call and saw a huge truck smashing through buildings, bystanders, and parked cars, seemingly unstoppable. I tried to halt its crazy progress, but it went hurtling on toward a cliff. I tried to see it in a different way. I went to a greater height and reenvisioned the behemoth as a child's toy I could contain in a box and pack away in a closet.

In the morning, Alan was mild and subdued. He told me, "I dreamed about a truck." He did not remember the details, but the dream had a happy ending. "I almost feel like a new man."

I asked him if he knew someone called George.

"It was my father's name."

"Do you know any other George?"

Alan blinked. After a long pause, he told me one of his closest friends was called George. This George, a radio producer, had died suddenly about six months before. Alan conceded his friend might have been drinking "a bit too much."

I asked if it was possible that George had committed suicide.

Alan stared as if he had just been shot between the eyes. He did not know the details, he confessed. George had died in another country. Alan had only heard about it after the funeral.

Alan excused himself to make a phone call.

He returned visibly shaken. He had just learned that his friend George had killed himself by throwing himself on the third rail. Now Alan broke down and told me his recurring dream, and waking fantasies, about killing himself the same way.

"I need a drink," he announced, reaching for a beer.

"Are you sure it's you who needs it?"

"I guess not."

Alan stayed dry that day, and for a good while afterward.

⟶ BUGFESTS

In many traditions, it is believed that a suicide will be required to serve out his or her appointed time in a limbo close to the living. Among indigenous peoples, it is widely recognized that there may be a risk that out of loneliness, despair, or feelings of revenge, a suicide may call on survivors to end their lives prematurely. Small epidemics of suicide among the Iroquois—frequently committed with the aid of water hemlock *(Cicuta maculata),* not an easy way to go out, since the victim basically drowns in her own blood—were attributed to this phenomenon. Religious traditions that teach that suicides will be subjected to eternities of torment or damnation exacerbate the problem; in such cases, spirits of the departed may remain earthbound for fear of punishment.

Spirits of the dead get stuck for other reasons. Victims of sudden death, like Bonnie's mother, may be confused. "There are many people out there who do not even know they are dead," observes Michael Harner, a leading shamanic teacher. People who were adamant, during physical life, that there is no such thing as life after death may be especially prone to this kind of confusion about their new estate.

Criminal souls may choose to remain earthbound, not only in hopes of escaping punishment and retraining on the other side, but in the belief that they can manipulate the living. Some of these entities are quite ancient and delude themselves that they are master sorcerers with demoniac powers. One of the most unpleasant entities of this kind I was ever called on to help separate from the living claimed to have been a medieval pope, a notorious prelate who dabbled in sorcery and poison and had numerous sexual liaisons. In cases of this kind, the afflicted person will probably need specialist help, of a kind that is sometimes still available from Catholic or Episcopalian priests, and from Orthodox rabbis, as well as from shamans, though I would caution that we should not make the mistake of demonizing lost souls. In the overwhelming majority of cases, boundary problems between the living and the earthbound dead call for open dialogue and a simple cleansing, not an old-fashioned exorcism.

Just as the need for cleansing is reflected in dreams, the most important part of a cleansing may take place in the dreamstate itself. The presence of the earthbound dead is frequently suggested in dreams by an infestation of bugs. Clairvoyants and shamans often perceive a "hitchhiker" of this kind as a large bug, attached to its living host at the back of the neck or between the shoulder blades. Significantly, persistent neck pains and upper-back pains are traditionally analyzed by shamans as possible symptoms of "ghost sickness," as are serious depression and chronic fatigue syndrome. Some of these themes and images surfaced in a woman's dream that also appeared to contain a liberating resolution:

Rachel's Bath

I am coming back from outer space. I am covered with bugs. They are quite colorful, green and gold. Jason, a spirit guide I had met before and have come to trust, tells me I need to be cleansed. He helps me pour a special bath. All the bugs I can see are washed away.

"We're not finished," Jason cautions. He makes me aware that three enormous bugs I had not noticed are attached to my upper back, around the base of my neck. He tells me he is going to get them off. He uses a tool I can't see. It makes a clicking sound; I think of someone cutting clothes off a body.

When he removes the bugs and arranges them in a circle in front of me, they are no longer bugs. They are metallic objects. I don't know how to describe them. They made me think of staplers. Also of ballast. I was glad they were off me. I woke feeling charged with energy.

Not all insect life in dreams—be it noted!—is negative. A scarab is very different from a cockroach. Bees are also messengers of the *melissa,* the priestess of the Mysteries. Souls that are far from lost are sometimes perceived in modern dreams, as in the shaman's dreaming, as fireflies or butterflies. As with any dream vocabulary, what you make of these elements will depend on your personal associations and intuition. Rachel had had many dreams of bugs, which often left her with "creepy" sensations, before her dream guide helped her to conduct a cleansing. It is sufficient to observe that her dreams signaled her need to separate her energy from something that did not belong within her field.* The necessary separation appears to have been accomplished inside the dreaming, at a time when Rachel had become an active dreamer, open to guidance from spiritual sources.

DIFFERING AGENDAS

*E*verything in our universe depends on the exchange of energies. If you choose to work with spirit guides, you will soon realize that you are expected to give something in return for the help you receive. A departed loved one may wish only to help you achieve the best that is possible for you. Higher beings may ask only that you lead a better life and use the gifts you receive for purposes of soul and the benefit of others. By committing to that, you will become a clearer channel for their energy and insight.

But you are likely to encounter other personalities on the inner planes who have their own agendas. We have already looked at the problem of the earthbound dead. Some spirit entities ask for offerings. Some ask simply to be remembered with love and respect. To work with the spirits, you must learn to discriminate. You will need to screen the entities with whom you establish contact and determine their nature and motives; remember that spirits can be deceptive, just like people! You will want to think carefully about what you are ready to give to these relationships. You will certainly wish to avoid any Faustian bargains. As a rule of thumb, you should avoid contact with any spirit beings who

* Interestingly, the night Rachel dreamed of her cleansing bath I had a dream in which I was counseled by a dead physician on several washes that might be used in treating rickettsia, a condition associated with microorganisms that are parasitical on "bugs" such as centipedes and spiders, and pathogenic in humans and animals. I could not comprehend why this information came through to me until Rachel shared her dream.

communicate with you in the language of either submission or domination.

I learned a great deal about differing agendas when I was approached for help by a couple in the Midwest. The husband was a personal-injury attorney. He had made some powerful enemies, some of them Mob connected, and was caught up in a grueling personal and legal battle. Before they came to me, I dreamed I received counsel from the chief justice of a Midwest state. I found his advice confusing, inside the dream; waking, I had no idea what it meant.

I soon learned that, as so often, a departed person with a message to deliver had rung the doorbell in a dream.

After the Midwest couple asked me for guidance on their troubles, I contacted the spirit of a departed person I know and trust. She told me that someone called Michael had information on the case. I dialogued directly with Michael, in a relaxed state. His last name was Italian and began with *M;* it was hard for me to get it straight. He seemed extremely knowledgeable about the law. He gave me detailed advice on legal problems facing the Midwest attorney, referring to possible tampering with evidence and to the role of a private investigator wholly unknown to me.

All of this checked out with the attorney who had consulted me, and some of it proved helpful.

"By the way," I asked him, "do you know anyone of Italian extraction called Michael?"

This drew a blank.

"This might have been a while back," I pursued. "A Michael whose last name began with *M?*"

After a long pause, the lawyer made a connection. "Oh, my God. Michael M. But he's dead."

"That could be the one." I passed on a personal message from Michael to the attorney's wife, involving a ballgown that had been considered risqué at the time that she had worn it to a party decades before. This confirmed the link.

The attorney explained that Michael had been chief justice of the state where he taken his bar exams and begun his practice. He had looked up to Michael as a mentor, but they had not been particularly close. There was now no doubt in my mind that Michael was the chief justice who had announced himself in my dream. But I was puzzled as to why he was involving himself in this couple's affairs, many years after his death, since the personal connection did not seem to be especially strong.

The answer emerged from my subsequent dialogues with Michael. He had a passion for justice. He was outraged by the case of a black woman who had apparently been hacked to death in a car by a boyfriend who was involved with a criminal organization. The boyfriend had never been prosecuted. The woman's children had been neglected, and it seemed she had not even received a decent burial. Michael wanted posthumous justice for this woman and insisted that I pass on the message to the attorney that he should make this his cause. He introduced me to the murdered woman, on the inner planes. I was haunted by the depth of her grief and her love for her children.

I called the lawyer and passed on the information I had received. He remembered a corresponding case, a horrific murder in which a black woman had been stabbed more than forty times in the backseat of a car. There had been only a cursory investigation; it was suspected that this had been due to payoffs from the boyfriend's criminal employers, as well as racism in the local police department. The case had been brought to the attorney by one of the murdered woman's relatives, but he had failed to pursue it at the time, pleading the pressure of other work. Now he promised to go back into the files and see if anything could be done.

My role in all this was merely that of a messenger. Three things impressed me about the case. As already noted, a dead person first appeared in a dream to announce he was ready to offer guidance. His information proved both accurate and helpful, going far beyond my skimpy knowledge of the situation, and often far beyond that of the attorney, too. And finally, Michael had his own agenda, which in this instance seemed wholly positive: justice for a dead mother, in exchange for advice to the living.

GLIMPSES OF LIFE AFTER LIFE

I once received a cry for help from a Catholic priest. "It's like this," he told me. "For thirty years, I've been sending dying people out into the void with the sign of the cross and the sign of crossed fingers. I don't know whether there's anything out there." He wanted to know if there was a way he could satisfy his doubts about life after physical death.

I admired his honesty. I encouraged him to work with his dreams and to carry his questions into the dreaming with the aid of the drum. Sadly, fear soon overtook him. He had ceased to believe in heaven, but in part of himself he still believed in hell. He feared he might be damned because he was gay and had failed to honor his vows.

Churches are founded on teachings about the soul's survival of physical death. Yet in the West the churches are not much in the business of encouraging personal exploration of the Beyond. When we are still issued road maps to the Otherworld, we are asked to trust them without testing them. Ironically, however much they may have been revised and prettied up, such road maps derive from travelers' tales: from dreams and trance journeys and little deaths.

In the sixth century, Pope Gregory the Great made a personal investigation of such glimpses of life after life. Gregory was especially interested in the case of a soldier who "died and revived" during a plague. "He was drawn out of his body and lay lifeless, but he soon returned and described what befell him." The soldier claimed to have journeyed as far as a bridge over a black river. Radiant people dressed in white waited in a meadow on the far side; their houses were all filled with light. But the dangerous bridge had to be tackled first. The traveler was challenged by threatening figures who tried to drag him down into the black waters. They did battle for his soul with "splendid men in white," who tried to pull him up by the arms. The soldier returned to his body before the contest was decided.[8]

Carol Zaleski has written a splendid study comparing such medieval accounts to contemporary reports of near-death experiences. Prior to his early death, I. P. Couliano published a wonderful cross-cultural survey of visionary narratives of Otherworld journeys.[9] Emanuel Swedenborg, a methodical man of science who became a dedicated spiritual explorer after a mystical awakening in his fifties, visited numerous heavens and hells and found them rather different from the ones the churches described. He saw dead people throwing themselves headfirst into the hells in their eagerness to get to environments that reminded them of the ones they had frequented on earth, and fleeing from the Light as if it were hellfire.[10] Swedenborg concluded that after death, the soul follows its ruling thoughts and desires, a view endorsed by many spiritual practitioners, including the seers who left us the Tibetan Book of the Dead and the shamans of Puka Puka, in the South Pacific, who say there are as many locations in the afterlife as there are individual spirits.

Shamans are not academic geographers. They go to the Otherworld in dreaming to retrieve and relocate lost souls and make peace with the dead. Shamanic expeditions to the afterlife suggest, as Holger Kalweit puts it, that there may be "no realm of death as such. Instead, the Beyond consists of all those properties particular to our consciousness once it is independent of the body.[11] Put simply, this means that after physical death we encounter the shapes of our fears and desires, and we see what we are open to seeing. We have a similar experience in dreams. The difference is that, when we get scared in dreams, we can flee back to the body. This option is no longer available after physical death, although souls that are lost or frightened sometimes try to cling to familiar people and places.

Books of the Dead, both written and oral, have emerged from many religious traditions. Their purpose is to reassure the living that the paths to the Otherworld have been mapped and at least partially explored by others, and to provide road signs for the soul's journey after death. Tom Cowan notes that the Celtic equivalent of the Tibetan or Egyptian Books of the Dead may be found in the "voyage tales" *(immrama)*. These not only provide the journeyer with familiar maps, but prepare him for what may await him beyond the known charts; a faery woman tells Bran there are one hundred and fifty islands of the Dead, but he only manages to visit two of them in the story.[12]

Where organized religion has ossified into a corpus of received teachings and discourages spiritual experience, the soul's condition after death is limited to a few standard options. There are manufactured heavens and hells—"creations of the created," to borrow Dion Fortune's phrase—sustained by the collective beliefs and fears of generations of the faithful. Spiritual explorers encounter these locales in dreaming. Here is an active dreamer's account of a visit to a possible "hell," during a conscious dream:

A Manufactured Hell

The images were extremely vivid and brightly colored, but they seemed unreal to me. I felt I was on a movie set. I saw the entrance to a dark tunnel. A group of hooded figures, priests or monks, were watching with keen interest to see whether someone would descend. I decided to go down and take a look. In the inner chamber, I found a humongous demon, red-eyed and all. He was so gross a parody of the genre I had to laugh. He was putting some poor man through all kinds of torment. I felt his victim would be able to get out of there as soon as he stopped giving the energy of his fear to this cartoonish demon. I wondered where a thing like that came from. I sailed straight up through the roof. I found myself inside an enormous cathedral. I realized that the priests had created the terror down below. I got the feeling these priests were crooked and responsible for all sorts of unclean practices. There was an icon of the Virgin, the kind of thing you might see in an Orthodox church, that opened up to expose her breasts and vulva. All this made me quite angry. I guess there are people I'd want to see punished in the afterlife, but not in this way, on the say-so of crooked priests.

This dream was a powerful teaching experience. It led the dreamer to make subsequent explorations, which drew him to the tentative conclusion that *all* Otherworld locations that conform to human expectations of structure and form may be transitional locales, way stations on a journey that may result in rebirth or the transcendence of forms.

Similar insight was the gift of a woman's spontaneous sleep dream, the last I will include in this section:

The Café Noir

In my dream, I am writing a book called Mysterious Realities. *Then I am drawn into a dream within the dream, in which a physician is treating a young soldier who has tried to kill himself. This is taking place on a field of battle.*

To comfort or educate the young soldier, the doctor recounts an experience from his own youth. So now this is a story within a dream, within a dream. The doctor's story goes like this:

"I once suffered a severe illness and was hospitalized. I died and came back.

"While I was out of my body, I was joined by a luminous guide. I perceived him simply as a being of light, without specific form. He escorted me to a narrow, dingy bar in a downtown area, called the Café Noir. The Café Noir was inhabited by both the dead and the living. However, the living people in the bar were oblivious to the dead, who were all around them. These dead people kept trying to join in the pleasures of the living, reaching over them to get to the drinks. The dead couldn't swallow, but they were consumed with thirst. Their other appetites were also voracious.

"These dead people in the Café Noir seemed to be stuck there. They were observed by their guides, whom I again perceived as beings of light, but were as oblivious to these guides as the live people were to them. The dead in the bar engaged in repetitive actions. A couple would go thrashing at each other in a violent argument, finish, then start over from the beginning. Two men replayed the same fistfight, over and over. Outside the bar, a murderer stabbed his victim to death over and over again.

"We eventually got out of that place. My guide took me up to a higher level, to a place that looked like an enormous library. I saw more dead people, working on books that had not yet been written or published in ordinary reality. They seemed to be part of a transmission process. At the proper times, they helped to convey the contents of the new books, as well as vital knowledge about cures for disease and new forms of energy, to the living. These people, also supervised by guides, were operating at a much higher level than the denizens of the Café Noir. But they had not yet escaped their limitations.

"I was shown that there were many higher levels beyond this library, but I was not permitted to enter them fully.

"I was also shown the fate of suicides, and you might be especially interested in this. The suicides I observed were bound to the people whom they had most hurt by killing themselves. They were wretchedly aware of their guilt and obligation.

"I returned to my body and got well. When I left the hospital, I noticed a tavern at the corner. It was called the Café Noir."

The dreamer really enjoyed sharing this experience, which is a reminder that one of the great gifts of dreaming is the gift of story. Listening to her, I had no doubt I was receiving a report from the front. I felt I was listening to someone who had recently visited one of my old haunts, maybe Paris, keenly interested in learning what had changed and to see familiar locales from a new perspective.

In dreaming traditions, travelers' tales about life on the other side of death are often shared in the same spirit, as I have described in a study of traditional Iroquoian dream-telling.[13]

Such glimpses of life after life must be tested and evaluated through experience on the inner planes. In these areas, as Plotinus taught, "the soul understands that which it resembles."

MAKING DEATH YOUR ALLY

*W*hen we dream of our own deaths and do not flee from the experience, we are given glimpses of continuing life.

I was traveling and everything was in black and white except me. I was glowing. I was in Africa. Then I was in the Revolutionary War. There were soldiers on horseback, a battle. All of it was completely real. Then I was swallowed by something. I guess I died. When I came back, everything was glowing but me. I saw a beautiful light. I became one with the light and it became one with me.

This dream was recounted, with great dramatic effect, by a ten-year-old girl in an elementary-school room. The kids all enjoyed the "glow-worm" effects and the stuff about being swallowed. It was great entertainment. It might also have been recognized, in a dreaming culture, as a big dream, one that singles out someone as a person who may have special gifts as a dreamer, including the ability to see and to journey by inner light.

An adult group was no less excited by the following dream, shared by a forty-year-old female secretary:

Because I Did Not Wait for Death

In my dream, I am a man. My male friend is abandoning the mother of his child. We leave his house and climb a dark hill.

Death is coming after us. He is a stooped old man with white hair and beard, leaning on a cane. He moves slowly, but his advance is inevitable. As he mounts the hill, drawing closer to us, I see that his appearance is not fixed. I see him now as a painted figure, mounted on a stick like a child's cardboard cutout. All the same, I know his power is real.

My friend is going to wait for him. I am not afraid of Death, but I don't want to stay there and wait for him. I fly off into the night.

I fly through the house of a dark woman who is talking on the phone. She watches me like I'm a cute little lightning bug, and I realize that must be how I look to her; somehow I have shrunk to that size, and I am glowing in the dark.

I fly out of that house, high up into the sky. Then I land in the attic bedroom of a young Mexican girl. It seems to me this is the girl I used to dream about when I was sick in my childhood. She looks at me like I'm a new cat that's just jumped onto her bed. She gets her father. He looks at me real close. He cuts open a grapefruit in front of me, watching to see how I will react. He seems satisfied and leaves me there for a while.

Then I am me. I am in a white room where the windows have no panes. This room is up in the sky. My male friend is there. He tells me that when he comes back, he is going to invent a car driven by solar energy. I realize he must have died.

This dream led the dreamer on a long journey of exploration. There was a possible message involving her then boyfriend, who was a part-time inventor fascinated by solar energy. There were even stronger messages for the dreamer herself. Eventually, she was able to confront the Death figure she had avoided on the hill and to dialogue with him. This brought many powerful insights, including the following: "I felt very close to Death, close enough to feel sadness as I watched flowers wilt at my touch. I wondered who could possibly be his friends. Then it came to me it must be the shamans of the world, who know Death and honor him."

Dreams that guide us through death and rebirth, within one life experience or beyond it, are an extraordinary gift when we develop the courage to recognize death for what it is. By working with such dreams, we find personal meaning in death. If you have journeyed beyond the swinging door—in a powerful dream, in a crisis of illness, or in the ecstatic trance of the shaman—you will no longer regard death as a rattling horror to be locked away in a crypt, or a black hole you don't want to look into.

Death now becomes your ally. You can now cope with the upsets and embarrassments of ordinary life with grace and humor because you see them from a different height. You can survey the terrain with the dragon's eye.

Shamans, like all true initiates, know that the path of death and the path of rebirth are the same. We die to another world to be born into this one. When we die to this life, we are born to another.

This open secret is beautifully depicted in two modern tarot decks. In Crowley's Thoth deck, Death—the thirteenth trump—is shown as a skeleton, wielding his scythe. But he wears the crown of Osiris, a symbol of resurrection, and beneath the fearful sweep of his blade, bubbles are rising, bearing the seeds of new life. In Vicki Noble's Motherpeace deck, Death is again a skeleton, but he is shown folded like a fetus in the womb, among the roots of a silver birch. When the bones are stripped of everything that decays, they become the seeds of new birth.

Think of your death now. See it where it hovers, at your left shoulder. It could tap you at any moment. In its presence, do you really have time for negative thoughts and feelings, for the nonsense of ego battles and striving to keep up social appearances?

"We should be living every day as our last," concluded a nurse in one of my classes. "If you knew you were dying, you'd take time to smell the roses."

8

DREAM GUIDES
AND GUARDIAN ANGELS

It is a difficult thing, Goddess, for a mortal man
to know you at sight, even a man of experience;
you turn yourself into all sorts of shapes.

Odysseus to Athena, in Homer's Odyssey

I know what you desire and I am with you everywhere.
Hold in your mind all you wish to know, and
I will teach you.

Poimandres

Don't cry, little one.
The Bear is coming to dance for you.
The Bear is coming to dance for you.

Mohawk cradle song

WORKING WITH DREAM GUIDES

*D*ream guides appear in many guises, from departed loved ones to godlike beings of light. The forms assumed by inner teachers, and our ability to communicate with them, are largely determined by what we are open to seeing. As Plotinus said, "We behold what we are."[1] The ancient axiom holds true: "When the student is ready, the teacher will appear."

Being ready involves clearing a space, free from the ego's agendas and the chatter of the monkey mind, where the encounter can take place. I have had numerous dreams that were highly instructive about the need to clear this space. In one of my dreams, I watched an elite commando force parachute into the midst of a forest grove, where its members proceeded to establish a defensive perimeter within which it would be safe for luminous beings from another world to land. I received another revealing message about this scenario in a dream within a dream. Early in this dream, I boarded an aircraft and settled down to watch an in-flight movie. As the action unfolded on the screen, I was drawn into this inner dream:

In-Flight Movie

The hero is sent exploring into an immense cave. He has a guide on a higher level of whose existence he seems to be unaware. The guide watches him from an alcove high up in the cave wall.

From time to time, this unseen guide tosses down tools and weapons. In a light that flickers on and off, the hero works with the tools thrown down by his benefactor. He uses them to clear a space from the huge piles of trash and rubble inside the cavern. The guide smiles as the cleared area slowly grows. I sense that when enough space has been cleared, he will give the hero further gifts.

I am watching all this from the aerie of the unseen guide, wishing that the hero would look up.

Being ready also means being tested and confirmed in your basic purpose. This is especially important to understand if you are following a path, like the way of the *dreamer,* that is likely to increase your ability to influence people and events through the power of focused intention. There is no greater abuse of power than the abuse of psychospiritual power. Look into yourself at this moment and ask, Is it my purpose to follow the path of heart, to live more creatively and to share my blessings with others? Or am I trying to control other people and make myself rich and famous? In dreams as in waking life, the energies and guides you attract are likely to correspond to your purpose. As Gary Zukav observes in *The Seat of the Soul,* "Souls that take upon themselves projects of more magnitude bring to themselves more assistance."[2]

MASKS OF THE MESSENGER

Perhaps you have noticed that in some of your dreams you have a mysterious companion, usually a person of the same sex you cannot identify. In my dreams, I frequently become conscious of this companion when I find myself in some kind of jam, and he intervenes to lend me a helping hand. Sometimes I am faced with a difficult climb (or descent) and am ready to give up hope of finishing the journey when he intervenes to remind me that in my dreambody, I can fly. Sometimes I am facing powerful opposition and he steps in to even the odds. I remember a dream in which a brutish antagonist had gotten a choke hold around my throat, and a companion I had not previously noticed fired a dart into my attacker's shoulder, setting me free. Sometimes the role of this anonymous companion is simply to make me conscious that I am dreaming and outside my body. In my dreams, he is a personal guardian. You can probably find one of your own, rather like him, if you are watchful. I suspect that his influence is not confined to dreams. If he (or she) has helped you out as often as my companion has helped me, you will probably not be embarrassed to call him your guardian angel.

The Greek word *angelos* means "messenger." We have seen how departed friends and family members often appear as messengers in dreams. But dream messengers come in a dazzling variety of costumes, as if there is a marvelous dress-up party going on somewhere backstage. Here are some of the other masks of the messenger I have noticed in dreaming and sharing dreams with other people:

➤ EARTHKEEPERS

Valerie, a legal secretary in New Mexico, was in her early forties when she reported the following dream:

Visit from Raven

I am in my sewing room, which is the spare bedroom of my house. I love to sew and this is my private space. Everything is normal until I feel a pricking at the back of my neck.

I turn around and am startled to find a tall Native American man standing right behind me. He has a mask of black paint around his eyes. I look down and I'm amazed to see that there is a hollow in his body in the area of the solar plexus. A big raven is nesting in this cavity. The raven stares at me with his glinty eyes. The Indian man doesn't say anything. He seems to be just letting me know he's there if I want him. Just thinking about this gives me goose bumps.

Valerie shared this dream with a circle in Santa Fe. I suggested she read up on Raven, who often turns up as Trickster and as the companion of shape-shifting sorcerers in the native mythologies of the Southwest. We took a stroll together to look for a bookstore. On a Santa Fe street neither of us had ever visited before, we paused outside an art gallery. In the window was a clay sculpture of an American Indian with a nesting bird in a cavity below his rib cage. The sculpted bird was not a raven, but the synchronicity was so striking that Valerie took it as a strong signal to find out more about her dream visitor.

With the aid of shamanic drumming, she journeyed back inside her dream to dialogue with the bird-man. She found he was waiting for her. He identified himself as a Menominee shaman, dictated the verses of a power song, and in later journeys, showed her how to bring the humor and foraging skills of the Raven into her everyday life. Though Valerie never entirely trusted her Menominee sorcerer (he was a tricky character, like his bird ally) and eventually broke off contact, she trusted the authenticity of her experience and found it rewarding in many ways.

Her dream adventures helped her to open up a new creative flow in her life. She returned to painting, to honor Raven and other dream visitors. By this route, she moved toward a second career in book illustration and animation. And she found new dream guides, now that she had put out a welcome mat by honoring her dreams.

As already noted, if you are receptive, you are quite likely to have dream encounters with the spirits of the land where you are living. A woman lawyer who had worked as an assistant district attorney in a gritty rust-belt town was startled by the following dream:

Call to the Southwest

An Indian horse warrior appeared in an eagle robe. He showed me a place in the Southwest, far from my present home. He led me all through the house. He showed me how the kitchen worked, and the room where I could do some writing. He escorted me to a spiritual community nearby where I felt completely at home and joined in the singing and dancing. Finally, he led me to a gravesite. It seemed to be my own. I felt he was telling me this is a place where I could live happily for the rest of my life.

While the lawyer was trying to figure out how to honor this dream, synchronicity again came into play. Unexpectedly, she was offered the chance to visit New Mexico on a business trip; she had never been to the Southwest before.

One of my Iroquois friends—the elder who had told me, "I guess you had some visits," when I shared my dreams of native shamans of long ago—offered a note of caution on this theme. He suggested that "white folks ought to be careful what they are getting into" when they start having contact with the spirits of the First Peoples of America. One reason he gave is that dark sorcerers and "hungry ghosts" also stay close to the living, often with murky agendas. Another is that many Native Americans died as a result of an undeclared holocaust, the effect of imported disease and alcohol and deliberate acts of genocide, and may still harbor feelings of revenge. A West African shaman, Yaya Diallo, who now makes his home in Canada, underscores this caution: "The present population of North America does not sufficiently take into account the many ghosts and wandering spirits here. There have been many massacres and injustices that have never been dealt with ritually. . . . This is a disturbing influence."[3]

On a positive note, the appearance of native visitors in the dreams of modern Americans often serves to awaken a sense of responsibility toward the environment and toward other species and a deeper respect for the beauty and wisdom of Native American spiritual traditions. The clanmother who appeared in my dreams impressed on me the vital importance of the Iroquois belief that we should consider the consequences of our actions "down to the seventh generation after ourselves" and that those we choose as leaders should be "walking sticks for the community"—people we can lean on, rather than people who lean on us. Dream guides of this character are truly "earthkeepers," who recall us to live in balance with the earth that supports us.

— RELIGIOUS FIGURES

In dreams, as in prayer and meditation, spiritual teachers reveal themselves in the forms we are open to seeing.

In medieval Japan, pilgrims journeyed from all over the country to three Buddhist temples consecrated to the bodhisattva Kannon, in hopes of receiving help or healing through dreams incubated on holy ground. Some of their stories are told in the *Hasedera Reigenki,* a fifteenth-century collection of miracle tales comparable to the Greek stelae recording dream healings in the ancient temples of Asklepios.

At the Japanese shrines, pilgrims hoped for a dream encounter with a numinous being who might assume one of three recognized forms. The dream visitor might appear as a noble and beautiful lady believed to be Kannon herself; an aristocratic woman reported she had received the dream gift of a jewel from the bodhisattva in this form and was afterward able to conceive a child. Alternatively, the dream visitor might come in the form of a radiant boy (who specialized in curing skin diseases) or as an elderly Buddhist monk in a dark robe, bringing insight into the karmic meaning of suffering and life trials.[4]

Anthropologists call dreams of this type "culture-pattern dreams," reflecting that, dreaming or waking, people frequently see what their cultural or religious tradition has schooled them to see. If you are a pious Catholic, you might hope to receive a dream visitation from your guardian angel, your patron saint, or even the Blessed Virgin. If you are a Japanese Buddhist, you will readily accept a dream guide who appears in the robe of a Buddhist monk. To say this is not to dismiss such night visions as pious projections, or to suggest that genuine healings did not flow from these encounters. It is simply to underscore that the visions we receive are "adapted to the nature of the seer," a quote from Dionysius the Areopagite, who knew a thing or two about angels.[5]

The masks are changeable. The archetypal energies behind them are real.

I am fascinated by the way that spiritual beings present themselves in unexpected forms, especially during periods of major life changes and spiritual emergence. A Methodist woman in one of my groups was astonished when Shakti, the divine consort of Shiva and the personification of female sexual energy in Hindu belief, presented herself in a dream (in her most sensual and alluring form) as a source of guidance. In her dream of the Turning Stair, Diane encountered a guide who evoked both the Trickster, the symbolism of energy, and Key IX, the Hermit, in the tarot.

Sometimes the unexpected visitor seems to be calling the dreamer to a new path; sometimes quite the reverse. A successful businessman in his forties received a dream visitor who seemed to be re-calling him to a path he had forsaken:

The Simple Christian

A stranger knocks at the door of my house. I let him in, although I'm not too impressed by him, to begin with. He seems a bit simple, almost goofy. He reminds me of a born-again Christian I know who drives around with a happy-face sticker on the side of his truck. He tells me his name is Douglas. He says, "I come from my father's house." These words give me chills.

He wanders around my house like he's at home. He looks at the bar, at the books on Eastern philosophy and esoteric stuff I was into a few years ago. He nods, indicating everything is okay. I'm thinking, "Wait a minute. Who's this guy to come in here acting like I need his approval?"

Then he says quietly, "What is your pact with God?"

I am absolutely floored. I don't know what to tell him. It's like I have a pact with God but I've forgotten what it is. I wake up trembling.

The dreamer did a lot of soul-searching on the question of that possible pact with God. The power of the dream, he noticed, was in the simplicity of the message and of the messenger. "We make things so complicated for ourselves," the businessman told me later. "A few years back, I was trying to find the secrets of the universe in some Eastern systems. Douglas was reminding me the secret was right at home." This reading of the dream message was reinforced by the fact that Douglas was an old family name, on the father's side. At the time of the dream, the businessman was a lapsed Christian. The visit from Douglas led him to recognize that Jesus was a personal teacher, and to apply more of his considerable energy and resources to community service in this spirit.

⟶ ANCESTRAL FIGURES

Dreams of departed family members are not confined to recognizable figures from recent generations. Sometimes dream visitors seem to come from the earliest ranks of our ancestry. Soon after I took up shamanic practice, I started dreaming of a man who appeared to be one of my Scottish ancestors. He sometimes appeared in a feathered robe. He was a druid, an "oak-seer," and his appearances—first in a spontaneous sleep dream, later in conscious dream encounters—led me to devote more waking attention not only to the ways of my Celtic ancestors but to the theme of *sacrifice* in life and spiritual practice. I learned that in Celtic societies, in time of great danger, the chief druid would sometimes offer himself as a sacrifice on behalf of his people. He would submit himself to a triple death—by cutting, strangling, and either burning or drowning—in the belief that his personal energy would be released to aid the whole community, while his spirit would be loosed to intercede with the gods on their behalf.[6]

My research helped me to understand the cloud that seemed to hang over my Scottish dream visitor. In one especially vivid dream journey, I learned that he had refused to become the carlin, the willing sacrifice, in a time when his people were threatened by war and disease. He had fled from his native country, fought for a foreign king, and been killed in battle by a spear.

This conscious dream resonated with me on a deep level. It reminded me of all the occasions in my own life when I had refused to sacrifice money or status or settled habits in order to follow a deeper calling and be of service to others.

I was not sure then—or now—that I believed in the Celtic idea of "ancestral karma": that we are in some way responsible for the actions of *everyone* in our bloodlines. I was also disinclined to regard the druid as a previous incarnation of myself. If anything, I felt that, in some mysterious way, his life was being lived *now,* in parallel with my own, and that the choices each of us made might affect the other.

I knew there were issues here that needed to be resolved. With the support of a shamanic drumming circle, I embarked on a conscious dream journey:

The Willing Sacrifice

I see the moon as a pale disk in a midnight sky. I fly through the moon and come out in a sacred grove.

Men in animal headdresses move around the clearing. A priestess stands at the center of the circle. I am wearing the horns of a bull.

I am stripped naked. I have intercourse with the priestess. Then I am crowned with holly and go willingly to the place of sacrifice. I feel the sting of the blade. The garrote bites deep into my throat. My skin is flayed and I am wrapped in a bull's hide and tied to an oak.

After a time, I am released from the tree. Something like gold dust is blown over me. Now I have a new skin.

I am bathed and cleansed in a pool that glows like blue fire. My skin glows like gold.

I am drawn upward. I sail through the sun to a lion throne where a magnificent golden woman, perhaps the Goddess, is seated in state. She motions me to the place beside her. Now I am dressed in lion and leopard skins. A circle of children forms around us.

I feel immense power streaming through my body. It rises from my root center, up to the crown of my head. I am told that I am now able to work with healing energy, and with fire and water. I can work with what flows or needs to be checked; and with what needs to be cleansed or purified.

I am told, "Take neither the right-hand nor the left-hand path. Be the middle pillar of the Temple."

This was one of a powerful series of inner experiences triggered by the spontaneous appearance, in my dreams, of a figure from long ago who seemed to be part of my family. After my conscious dream of making myself the willing sacrifice, the cloud that had hung over him seemed to lift; he became a confident and helpful companion in subsequent dreams.

You will have noticed that in this case, an ancestral dream visitor was not an unambiguous guide; he seemed to be as much in search of help and counsel as I was. In his memoirs, Jung reported dreams and visions in which the dead seemed to be seeking his advice. Edgar Cayce, the renowned psychic, also had many experiences of this kind. In dreaming, where we escape linear time, everything is happening *now;* perhaps that is the key.[7]

➤ ARCHETYPAL FIGURES

For Jung, who gave us the word, archetypes are common themes of mythic force that spring from the collective unconscious and recur again and again in the dreams of individuals and the shared dreams of humanity: our enduring stories, folklore, and art. James Hillman, the American founder of archetypal psychology, describes archetypes as "the deepest patterns of psychic functioning." Archetypal dream figures, from these perspectives, might include the Great Mother, the Wise Old Man (or Woman), the Divine Child, the Shadow, the Anima/Animus, and of course our old friend the Trickster. How do you know if you are having an archetypal dream? The hallmarks, according to some Jungian analysts, are dream encounters that (1) confront us with situations that are impossible in everyday life; (2) carry us into "the realms of myth and magic"; and (3) possess a "cosmic quality" and numinous power that inspires awe.[8]

This is all great fun, as long as we do not allow the Jungian vocabulary to blur the factual content and vital originality of the dream experience.

Take the case of Suzanne's dream, whose title alone is probably enough to set archetypalists aquiver:

The Wise Woman and the Whale

I am in a beautiful rural setting. I notice a white cottage among flowerbeds. An older woman welcomes me inside. She is not that much older than me but I sense she is immensely wise. I feel she is related to me.

She shows me her herb garden and says I am welcome to take anything I need from it. She says I can stay as long as I like, but there is something she needs to show me.

She leads me to the top of the hill. Something monstrous is happening on the other side. A river is running red with blood and body parts. I look for the source of all this carnage and I see that a huge whale is jammed into a narrow space between concrete building foundations. It doesn't belong there. I realize that if something is not done, it will bust up the whole neighborhood and people will die.

We could all have a field day with the symbolism of the whale, invoking everything from the story of Jonah to the Medicine Cards, and the numinous quality of the Wise Woman in the country cottage. But it would be inadvisable to hare off down those trails before checking for a possible warning about a situation in the dreamer's external life (however improbable that may seem at first glance) and without investigating the *specific* identity of the older woman.

As we explored Suzanne's dream within a circle, she made a connection with a construction site not far from her home, where foundations were being laid for a multistory building. Several years before, an accident at a similar site, which she attributed to the contractors' violations of the building code, had resulted in several deaths. Suzanne acted on her dream message by initiating an inquiry into safety practices at the new site, which was easy for her to do because of her job in local government.

Now we could go to work on the rich symbolic associations of the bleeding whale and, most important, the nature of the guide Suzanne had discovered in the country cottage.

She now felt certain that her "wise woman" was a genuine guide. Her white cottage became a special place for Suzanne, who returned to it in conscious dreams to seek further advice.

Suzanne's "wise woman" might be an archetype; she might also be (as Suzanne suspected) a great-grandmother in the old country. Diane's guide with the lantern and baton (in her dream of the Turning Stair) might be an archetype; he might also be a demigod. If Jung were still with us, he would still be revising his terms, to adapt to the ever-changing productions of the dream source.

— GENERIC GUIDES

The well-known psychic Alice Bailey believed that both anonymous companions and other generic dream figures—the train conductor, the taxi driver, the telephone operator—may all be angels in disguise. Maybe you have noticed how such characters sometimes play the role of guardians or guides in your dreams. Here are a few cases from my own dream journals:

• *The telephone operator.* In one dream, I found a message on my telephone answering machine from a troubled woman who had caused a good deal of confusion in my life. As I listened to the message, which was an appeal for a meeting, the voice of the operator came through. The operator explained that she did not want to let calls from this person come through because her intentions were harmful. In my dream, I was able to print out the message, which I then destroyed by putting it through a trash compactor. I often find that the telephone operator in my dreams helps me to screen communications on the inner planes. The telephone operator or switchboard also helps to route calls to higher sources of guidance.

• *The immigration or customs official.* Since I do a lot of traveling around the world, these figures frequently appear in waking life. But in dreams, they usually play a deeper role. Customs officials may discuss whether I am dressed properly or carrying excess baggage and help me to get these things sorted out. Immigration officials, in my dreams, play an even more interesting role. In one dream, for example, I noticed that the immigration official to whom I had to present myself at a foreign airport was reading a book on synchronicity. When I expressed interest, he led me into a back room, where several of his colleagues—dressed in blue, high-necked uniforms of a distinctively "French" design—discussed early research on the theme that had been conducted in France. This gave me useful and specific leads for my own research.

• *The hotel manager.* In another dream, I found myself in a hotel in a foreign country where a power problem was causing intermittent blackouts throughout a whole city. Then the hotel manager showed himself. He was an immensely charming, confident, even radiant, man who assured me that everything could be put right. He proceeded to demonstrate. He increased the voltage on a generator, raising the energy flow to several times the maximum level shown on the gauge. Nothing blew up, and the lights in the city came back on. After this dream, I noticed a marked increase in my energy level and was able to complete a book project at record speed.

The hotel manager often appears to me in dreams as the person responsible for the management and effective operation of the whole establishment—i.e., my whole psychophysical condition. Similarly, the *restaurant manager* figures as the person who oversees my social and eating habits.

• *The taxi driver.* I learn a lot from taxi drivers in dreams, where they are quite as unpredictable as in New York City. I have described the helpful role of the cabdriver who showed up in a splendid vintage car in a series of dreams.

• *The elevator operator.* This is someone who can help to transport you to higher levels. He may or may not hold the door open for you if you are running late or expect a tip. In one of my dreams, an elevator operator waited for me patiently while I carried a dead relative who was in a bad way, groggy and disoriented, inside an old-fashioned lift. When we had risen to a higher floor, the dead person vanished into a TV set inside the lift.

GUIDES UNDER FAMILIAR NAMES

Dream guides also appear under the names of people we know in waking life, if only by reputation. In dreams of this kind, you may be receiving a message from a specific person, whether or not that individual is conscious of sending it in waking life, or tuning in to your HSP faculties. But it is amusing to watch how dream messengers often seem to "dress up" in identities that are familiar to us to get their messages across. The mechanism is described in Homer's *Odyssey*. When the goddess Athena wants to get a message to Nausicaa, to make sure the princess will meet Odysseus when he washes up on the "ironbound coast" of Phaecia, she appears to Nausicaa in the guise of one of the girl's closest friends.

A deceased British novelist, John Braine, turned up in one of my dreams and told me his life story. He explained that as a young author he had published a best-seller, then spent a period in the doldrums, trying to repeat his own formula, before he decided to work on a book on dreams. He said he had masses of material and I was welcome to use it. I was excited to discover huge quantities of information, neatly arranged in aluminum filing boxes. Braine proceeded to give me some practical tips on his writing method, how he would "go at it night and day" writing at high speed without editing until he completed a first draft. This was useful advice, both on method and content. I also noticed the pun in the name of the dream visitor: Braine = brain.

Before I met Jeremy Taylor, one of the great contemporary teachers of dreamwork, he appeared to me in a dream and offered equally practical counsel on techniques I might use in my classes. Jeremy appeared in this dream as a lean, clean-shaven young man with longish brown hair. I was slightly thrown when I first encountered him in the flesh as a big, huggable teddy bear with a patriarchal beard, then realized that I had seen my dream teacher as I myself had looked in my early twenties.

I should note at this stage that dreams also serve to lead us beyond teachers in waking life whom we have outgrown. A woman in one of my groups was troubled by a dream in which she felt she had stolen a fire ritual from a shamanic teacher—I'll call him Luis—with whom she had studied for several years. Through dream reentry, she realized that the fire she thought she had stolen belonged to *her*, that the lopsided grin on her teacher's face (in the dream) reflected his possible guilt or embarrassment over various issues, not a judgment on her, and that other teachers were waiting to help her on the next stage of her journey.

— DREAMS AND THE HIGHER SELF

In all our dealings with inner teachers, there is a vital question that will never go away. How can we distinguish a genuinely transpersonal contact, who may or may not be a beneficent guide, from a split-off aspect of the dreamer's own personality?

"The experience of awe is a valid way of knowing" is the response of one Jungian analyst, possibly the best answer we are likely to come up with.

At levels beyond the ego, the distinction between what is transpersonal and what is an aspect of the dreamer's own identity may prove to be a false divide. What is truly transpersonal (i.e., beyond your ordinary personality) may in no way be alien to your larger Self. You will discover your own truths about this as you move closer toward the dream source, and your own Higher Self.[9]

JOURNEYING FOR GUIDES

*I*n Active Dreaming workshops, one of our principal goals is to establish direct personal communication with our spiritual guides. When a possible guide has revealed himself in dreams, we attempt to resume contact through the techniques of dream reentry and shamanic journeying explained in part one. In the absence of remembered dreams, we may try to open clear channels through meditation. We may also use shamanic drumming to make a conscious dream journey to the Upper World in search of the spiritual guides who wish to communicate with us *now*. The visual gateway for this journey is a place of ascent—a mountain, a tower, a tree.

I am thrilled by the richness and variety of the experiences reported by people who undertake this basic shamanic exercise, often for the first time. Some journeyers rise through many levels of dreaming, leaving their dreambodies and moving beyond familiar forms, to approach teachers on the higher levels. Some find themselves called back to earth. There are bound to be occasional mix-ups over flight paths. I used to suggest that journeyers might want to picture themselves traveling through the sun or the moon, into higher dimensions of reality where they might encounter spiritual guides. I stopped doing this when I discovered that a fair proportion of people in one group took this all too literally. They went shooting off through the moon or the sun, only to find themselves drifting out among the asteroids, still in the Middle World, only in outer space.

Here is a sampling of the waking dreams reported by members of a single workshop who journeyed for spiritual guides:

— CHRIST IN BUDDHIST MEDITATION

When I reached the summit of my journey, I saw Christ seated in a Buddhist meditation posture. I was reminded that Christ is my teacher and that I should use meditation to open clear channels for spiritual guidance. I found the image supremely beautiful. I am going to paint it.

— "YOUR CENTER IS THE SOLAR PLEXUS"

I pictured a literal mountain in Arizona I recently visited. I had a hard time getting airborne. Then geese came and stuck their necks under my armpits, trying to give me liftoff. I still seemed heavy and earthbound. I remembered the power of *intention*. Then I found myself zooming out into space. I saw lots of African elephants. Then I saw the huge, soft eyes of a native woman. She showed me my center is in the solar plexus, something I did not know before.

— ENCOUNTER WITH DECEASED PARENTS

I found my parents, who died when I was very small. They spoke to me in German, their native language. Beyond them, I saw religious images I associate with Christ. The dove descending into the chalice. I had strong feelings of being "homesick" when I heard the recall signal. I didn't want to come back, but I remembered my promise and I know I can make this journey again.

⟶ A FEATHER ON THE BREATH OF GOD

I turned into a feather and thought of Hildegard of Bingen's "A Feather on the Breath of God." I saw forms of the Goddess and asked, "Are you my highest guide?" The answer seemed to be no. Then I became an arrow and shot up through the roof of a temple. I encountered a radiant being that described itself as Uriel, a name I did not recognize until you later spoke about the archangel Uriel. I asked how I could maintain contact and I was given the image of a beautiful garden. I am going to do some spring plantings!

⟶ REENCOUNTER WITH A DREAM CHARACTER

I was sped upward by a host of winged beings. I had images of Yogananda, one of my early spiritual teachers. Then I met a young Indian who had visited me in several dreams. I had come to think of her as the embodiment of love, but she now appeared as a stern, demanding teacher. She gave me direct guidance on personal things I'm now going to have to work to get straight.

⟶ BACK TO WHERE I LIVE

I got airborne for a while, then I was pulled back to my apartment and especially my cat. My cat's name is Follower. I guess I was being told I have to bring all this back to where I live and go through a learning process before I'm ready to lead.

⟶ THE HANGING BAMBOO

I went up a peak in the Adirondacks where I go camping with my dogs. I found I had to leave the dogs behind. I had some loving reunions with people I know—mostly dead people. Then a guide I couldn't see clearly showed me an image I need to work with: a hollow bamboo, hanging in the air like a wind chime. I thought of that quote from Fools

Crow about how we need to become hollow bones for the spirits to work through.

— A GHOST FROM INSIDE MYSELF

I felt drawn a different way. I went to the cemetery where my brother is buried. We had a great reunion! He wanted to come with me but I realized I couldn't take him where I was going. Then something came out of my solar plexus. It looked like a misty ghost and took shape as a woman. I asked her name and she told me, "Athena."

I told her, "You can't be my guide. You're not supposed to come from within me. You have to be separate."

She corrected me, insisting, "I *can* come from within you." She told me to look down.

I looked down and saw my brother's tombstone. The inscription leaped out at me: *To thine own self be true.*

All these experiences, from the earthiest to the most ethereal, offered valuable life messages and validating personal symbols. I have offered them as a sampling of perceptions of the numinous among contemporary Americans with jobs and families and traditional upbringings whose only difference from other people, if indeed it *is* a difference, is that they have resolved to approach life as a spiritual journey, not merely a process of "getting through." These experiences, which often involved reestablishing contact with a guide who had previously appeared in dreams, illustrate the many masks of the messenger, as well as the way that, as we become a world society, we may finally be moving beyond tribalism to a point where we can honor and learn from all authentic spiritual traditions.

THE ARCHANGEL OF DREAMS

Gabriel is the archangel of dreams, also closely associated with the moon and all that it rules, and with the direction of the West.

Gabriel first appears in Scripture in the Book of Daniel, where he acts as a dream interpreter. Daniel is troubled by a vision he does not understand. The archangel comes to guide him, in the guise of a man. But "when he came, I was afraid and fell upon my face."

In the New Testament, Gabriel is the angel of the Annunciation. He appears to Mary to announce the divine nature of the child who will be born through her, as he had appeared to Zacharias to announce the coming of John the Baptist. Gabriel also visits Joseph in a dream to reveal the nature of the Christ—ensuring that Joseph did not divorce his wife for suspected infidelity. He returns in another dream to warn the family to flee from Herod's persecution.

In the third of the great monotheistic religions, Gabriel has a special relationship with the prophet Muhammad. In folk tradition, the prophet's dream initiation is as savage as any shaman's tale of being dismembered by spirits. As it is told, Muhammad is sleeping alone in an isolated cave when three angels descend on him, hack open his chest, and remove his heart, which is replaced only after it has been cleansed in pure water from a holy well in Mecca. Only now is Muhammad ready to meet the archangel.

Gabriel comes to him the following night, when the prophet lies between sleep and waking:

> Gabriel the archangel descended in his own form, of such beauty, of such sacred glory, that all my dwelling was illuminated. . . . He kissed me between the eyes and said, "O sleeper, how long wilt thou sleep? Arise!"

Gabriel now brings Muhammad a mystical steed, the Buraq, which is usually depicted as a mule with a woman's face. Like the mind, the steed is restive and must be calmed by the angel before Muhammad can ride it to the upper worlds. They fly to Jerusalem at the speed of thought. They journey to higher realms from the Dome of the Rock. They explore successive heavens—some say seven, others nine—where the prophet encounters Masters who once lived on earth, as well as angels who have never shared in the human condition. Gabriel parts company with Muhammad at the Lotus Tree of the Farthest Boundary of the ninth (or seventh) heaven. This marks the limit of the Realm of Images; beyond this Gabriel cannot go.

When Muhammad returns to his body, with the material for the Koran, he finds that water from the jug kicked over by Buraq at the start of their ascent is still trickling to the floor. His journeys through all the heavens have occupied less time than it takes to empty a jug of water.[10]

So Gabriel is honored by all three peoples of the Book, by Jews, Christians, and Muslims. The fact that he is both the angel of dreams and the angel of incarnation points to his special role as a mediator between human consciousness and the higher realms from which spirit descends into the body.

The name Gabriel is a composite of two Hebrew words, meaning "man" and "God." As Rabbi Joel Covitz comments, "Gabriel brings man to God and God to man, thus divinizing man and humanizing God."[11] He works, above all, through dreams, and he is no stranger in the dreams of modern Westerners, though we have been told through dusty centuries that the time of revelation is over.

I saw Gabriel, and still see her, as a woman.

She came to me in a season of storms, both inner and outer. I had been engaging in all kinds of psychic experimentation, fueled by contacts with Native American shamans and by my discovery of Robert Monroe's remarkable book, *Journeys out of the Body*. I had no difficulty getting out of my body, or making contact with all sorts of entities that were in a similar condition. My problem was that I had rushed into all of this without taking care to ground and protect myself. If you call up the spirits, they *will* come. But to call up the spirits without taking effective precautions to keep out unwanted intruders is like throwing open your doors in the middle of the night in the midst of a large city and inviting all comers to party. I know what I am talking about!

An amazing lightning storm in the midst of my foolishness seemed to mirror these inner disturbances. Around 3 A.M., my wife and I watched spears of lightning hurled down in a circle around the farm-house. It was a bit like watching an artillery gunner trying to get an exact bearing on his target. One of the lightning bolts struck the old tin roof of the red barn on the other side of the parking area. We watched it jump and streak, like a fiery serpent, from one end of the roof to the other. It touched a lightning rod and vanished. Then the storm was over.

We knew we had been lucky, because there were no lightning rods on the main house. I corrected that within the week, when a cheerful man called Dan Carroll turned up at my door out of the blue, offering to sell me lightning protection. I took him out to the barn and told him our story. When he inspected the lightning rods on the barn, his eyes widened. He said, "You must have a protector higher up." He showed me that most of the old cables had snapped and were dangling loose. The only lightning rod that was grounded was the one the lightning bolt had struck—I almost wrote *chosen,* since the lightning had had to run the whole length of the roof to reach that rod. If the lightning had settled anywhere else, the old wooden barn would have gone up like tinder, threatening the house.

I gave thanks for this minor miracle, in a nonspecific way.

The following day, I was reminded that our unseen helpers have more specific names.

She first appeared to me on a clear, sunny morning, near the old oak tree to the west of the house that I had come to love. I say "she" because the beauty of her face and form seemed more feminine than masculine. But there was no specific indication of sex. She first appeared as a radiant being of Light. I could see her clearly, with my eyes open. Her presence brought tears of joy. They welled up from deep within me. I felt cleansed. I experienced an overwhelming sense of grace that I tried to express in a poem:

Song for Gabriel

> My heart is a song that rises
> It is a rainbow bridge
> spanning abysses
> of place and time.

My heart is a song that rises
to walk in the One Light
to heal the wound
between earth and sky.

My heart is a song that rises
It is the crystal fire
that wakens the sleeper
into the dream.

My heart is a song that rises
It is the pure waterfall
that cleanses my path
with tears of joy.

The poem only hints of the oceanic quality of the initial contact. Few thoughts were exchanged that could easily be translated into words, though much specific guidance came later, in dreams of both the sleeping and the waking kind. I knew simply, in that moment, that the power that brings our world into being and maintains it daily is the power of LOVE, and that however far we stray from our paths, we will be guided back—and shielded and protected—if we invoke that power by one of its saving names. There are many such names. In a time of trial and testing, when our backs are up against the wall, we will recover the names we truly believe in. The name that came to me then was one I had almost forgotten, in my disappointment with organized religion and my wanderings among many traditions.

And who was the messenger? I knew her name. I wrote it down, at the time, the way it sounded: Gabrielle. I knew that she was a spiritual being, but it did not occur to me then that she might be related to the Archangel Gabriel, whose name is correctly pronounced Gah-bri-el. If the thought had occurred to me, I would have dismissed it as presumptuous. Who was I to merit the personal attentions of Gabriel? That, surely, could only be a delusion of the kind you hear babbled in mental wards. And I must admit that though I was moved to the core by the sense of grace that came with this encounter, I was still highly reluctant to get caught up in the conventional iconography of angels and archangels. All that seemed like cutesy, clichéd stuff, grist for the greeting-card industry and the peddlers of religious images.

So I simply remained open to further communication, from a being whose name I continued to record as Gabrielle. In dreams, she showed herself in various forms and settings. In one dream, I saw her in a desert landscape where violent winds whipped up storms of red sand. She showed me a vast stone temple, towering more than twenty stories high, with an equal-armed cross carved above the archway. I saw her again, dressed in blue and silver. She guided me on a journey in which I seemed to shrink to infinitesimal size and traveled through a galaxy inside the heart of an atom. She showed me the crescent moon, lying on her back, making the path of creation.

In the months when I was engaged in trying to clean up psychic clutter, for myself and others, she returned again and again with counsel and encouragement. She instructed me that the key to psychic self-defense, like all things that matter, is extremely simple: "Love, and go higher. You can go infinitely higher than any earthbound or malevolent entities." She reassured me, "You have always been for the Light. You have been shown the dark side many times in order to learn how to overcome it, for the benefit of others."

I knew these communications were a gift. I used them and honored them. But I still refused to make an association between my Gabrielle and the archangel of dreams. My ego had been out of line often enough in the past; I was determined not to allow it to puff itself up by claiming direct contact with an archangel!

Then in one of my workshops I listened to a retired fireman describe his experience in attempting to contact a spiritual guide. "I got a fellow called Gabriel," he reported. "Almost too pretty for a man. I was nervous about calling him Gabriel. He told me it was okay to call him Gabe. That made me more comfortable. He gave me to understand there are lots of little Gabriels people can talk to if they're open."

Maybe that's how it is.

SCREENING SPIRIT CONTACTS

Spirits on the lower planes can lie, cheat, and steal, just like ordinary people. A great deal of psychic clutter and confusion is caused by playing with Ouija boards and the kind of vulgar spiritualism that has people sitting round a table in a darkened room asking, "Is anyone there?" Still more serious problems may be caused by would-be magicians and dabblers in the occult who ritually invoke the spirits without guarding against intrusions by unclean or malevolent entities. I have witnessed a number of "pagan" ceremonies in which psychic energies were called up without being screened or released at the end of the rituals. In psychological terms, such exercises are an invitation to dissociation. In shamanic terms, they invite possession or psychic vampirism. At one such gathering, I was troubled to see an ersatz shaman allow her body to be occupied by a spirit guide I perceived as nothing loftier than a dead European sorcerer who had abused psychic powers. At a climactic point in the rituals, she collapsed and had to be carried from the circle, leaving her acolytes completely unprotected against whatever had been called to join the living.

No responsible spiritual practitioner invites contact with the spirits without a clear and sufficient purpose. He will always take care to *ground and protect* himself and those with whom he is working. He will be vigilant in screening contacts on the inner planes and in verifying any messages that come through.

It is likely that you have already had contact with spirit entities, in the dream world or in waking states. You may have been confused or troubled by some of these contacts. It is important to recognize that while spirit contacts may be entirely *real*, they are certainly not always what they seem—i.e., what the visiting entity would have us believe, or what we may wish to believe. You should not go by appearances. On the astral level, even more than on the physical, appearances can be quite deceptive. I have run into cases of earthbound entities and *criminal souls* borrowing the semblance of other people who have died for purposes of psychic fraud. They do this by hijacking the astral vehicle, or "subtle body," that is discarded when the spirit moves higher on the roads of Light. The work of impersonators manipulating these astral shells is the source of a good deal of psychic litter.

You may be convinced that spirit contacts are no delusion, that your visitors are real. But how do you know whom to trust? Here are a few rules of thumb I have come to apply in communicating with the spirit world:

1. Identify the entity. Ask for its name and other means of identification. Seek specific information previously unknown to you that you can later verify.

2. Avoid contact with an entity that communicates in the language of either domination or submission. Faustian deals are always likely to end badly! Dreaming or waking, you should avoid either bullying or allowing yourself to be bullied.

3. Watch your vibratory level. Like attracts like. An entity that is drawn to you at a time when you are toxic (due to alcohol or drug abuse) or have given yourself over to negative thoughts and feelings is unlikely to be a guide from one of the higher planes—unless it is attempting an emergency rescue operation. If you have been indulging in a sexual fantasy, you will draw a different kind of contact than if (say) you have been meditating on the Cabalistic Tree of Life—which is not a moral judgment, simply a practical observation.

4. Watch the point of contact. If you have been journeying outside your body, do *not* entertain contact with entities that approach you near your final point of return. This is a moment when you may be especially vulnerable to psychic attack.

5. Check your energy level after contact. If you feel drained and listless, this is often a sign that you have opened yourself to an "energy thief." Of course, there are energy thieves among our living acquaintances, too; we all know the kind of person who leaves you feeling your batteries have been sucked dry. Any relationship that takes your energy without returning it is unhealthy.

6. *Trust your feelings!* Do your encounters bring a sense of grace? Are you more open to love and healing? Do you wish to share your gifts with others, without exacting a price? Or are you left with murky obsessions and delusions of power? If you think having a "spirit guide" gives you anything to brag about, or the right to use or manipulate other people, you are definitely on the wrong track!

7. *Keep your sense of humor!* Humor, humanity, humility, and humus are related words. Keeping your sense of humor will keep you human, will remind you that you are not in control and will never have all the answers, and will bring you back to the good deep earth. As I get older, I get more and more certain that the most important distinction between people is between those who have a sense of humor and those who don't. If you don't see the point of that, you're not ready for this path.

OF GARFIELD AND GUARDIAN ANGELS

"*Y*ou shall yourselves choose your presiding spirit," Plato advises in Book X of *The Republic.*

I once conducted a dream workshop for the congregation of an Episcopalian church in New York. I cited the profound words of John Sanford, who is an Episcopal minister as well as a Jungian analyst: "Just because the churches have decided to pay no attention to their unconscious does not mean that God will stop trying to speak to men."[12]

During the break, I was approached by an older woman wearing a severe gray dress. Her face was kindly but careworn; she looked like a person who had given much of herself to serving others.

She asked earnestly, "Is it possible for me to meet my guardian angel in my dreams?"

"Certainly," I responded.

The woman frowned. I asked what was troubling her.

"It's like this. I have tried to incubate dreams in which I would meet my guardian angel. I wrote down my wish. I prayed and prayed. And I got Garfield the cat. He came twice."

Though it was hard for me to see Garfield as a guardian angel, I could see a way in which he might be a messenger for this dreamer. I tried an old trick: "Suppose I've just arrived from outer space. I've never heard of Garfield the cat. You have to describe him to me."

"Well, he's fat and greedy and he's always thinking about himself."

"What message do you suppose he might have for you?"

Her face suddenly brightened. She sneaked a look at the buffet table where dessert was waiting. "You mean it's okay for me to have a piece of chocolate cake?"

"Garfield thinks so."

This is a case of the working in dreams of what Jung described as *compensation*. Parts of the dreamer's psyche relegated to the sidelines by her focus personality in waking life return in dreams to insist on entirely natural needs she has tended to repress—in this case, the need to indulge herself occasionally and not always to be putting other people first.

If Garfield was not a guardian angel, he was at least a dream messenger. I got a character almost as outrageous as Garfield when I incubated a dream on the question "How can I write this book in a way that speaks to people in all walks of life?" Here is what I got:

That's Entertainment!

A brash, lively character in a loud suit jumped out. He reminded me of a crude Hollywood huckster, the kind of bit producer who spends much of his time cruising starlets and chomping on fat cigars. He also reminded me of Al, the somewhat unreliable, and far from ethereal, angel in Quantum Leap *on TV.*

He told me his name was Marty. He had come with a whole three-ring circus and began to show off his tricks. He turned handstands that carried him from one side of the big top to the other. He was literally bouncing off the ceiling. "It's about entertainment, kid!" he shrieked.

He went flying across the bleachers, grabbed a pretty blonde, and started kissing her passionately. He winked at me and said, "You can make love to anyone you like in your dreams and nobody's gonna file a divorce suit." Before he applied himself to the blonde again, he repeated, "It's about entertainment!"

Marty may not sound like a highly evolved spiritual personality, but he was reminding me about something important: Whatever else dreamwork may prove to be, it ought to be *fun!* Whether or not Marty is simply an aspect of myself, who is to say he is not an authentic guide? True guides speak to us where we live and adapt themselves to the condition of the country. There is a marvelous Buddhist teaching about that, titled (in the Thomas Cleary translation) "Entry into the Realm of Reality." A pilgrim on a spiritual quest is instructed by a long succession of teachers. When each is finished, he passes the wayfarer on to the next. The pilgrim is astonished to find that these spiritual masters appear in every conceivable guise: as king and pauper, ascetic and whore.[13]

The costumes of the guides who appear in dreams are inexhaustible and constantly being adapted to the prevailing myths of our culture. Here is a woman executive's description of a series of dreams:

Space Invaders

In several dreams, space aliens invade my home. They are trying to abduct me. I'm scared but also fascinated. I hide from them at first because I think they are going to perform an experiment on me. When I finally confront them, they show me they have all kinds of intellectual and psychic gifts. They can teletransport themselves across vast distances. They tell me I have powers equal to theirs if I am only ready to learn how to use them.

Listening to the reports of "alien abductions" and close encounters with "extraterrestrials" that have filled the popular media in recent years, I am often reminded of accounts among many indigenous peoples of the psychic storms that accompany shamanic initiation. There are many common themes: of being forcibly seized by beings from another world, of being transported to another location, of being operated on and having alien substances inserted into one's flesh. I am not going to explore this interesting theme in any depth here, except to observe that we will always get into trouble when we confuse what happens in one order of reality with another. And to note that in a society weened on *Star Trek* and the myths of science, it is entirely appropriate that dream guides should appear in space suits as often as in flowing robes.

Think again about the guides who may have appeared to you already in your dreams. Are you ready to resume contact? Remember you will need to clear a space where you can see and hear. I was reminded of that once by a dream in which I was wandering through an immense house when a friendly couple came running after me to tell me my father was on the phone. They said he had telephoned several times already. I realized that I had been unable to hear the phone from where I had been. I needed to go into a special room to take the call, which contained important counsel for me and my family.

One more tip, if you go sifting through your dreams for traces of possible communication from a spiritual guide: *Pay special attention to images of TV sets, especially when they involve switching channels*. The vocabulary of dreams is heavily influenced by our external environment, and the image of switching channels is a rather exact metaphor for another kind of "channeling." I have watched a succession of dream teachers, ranging from a deceased in-law to a Hasidic master, project themselves from a kind of TV set and vanish back into it after finishing their communications.

Whatever stage you are at in your personal journey, you can hope for guidance and healing from your inner teachers because, however unready we may be, they are always ready for us. "My opening and his entering were but a single moment," in the haunting words of Meister Eckehart. Your Life Teacher, your guardian angel, is never remote from you. As Plotinus says:

> There is in all of us a higher man . . . A man more entirely of the celestial rank, almost a god, reproducing God. When the soul begins to mount, it comes not to something alien, but to its very self.[14]

As you explore further, you may come to recognize that you are within this Higher Self, more than it is within you.

9

DREAMS OF HEALING

Something we were withholding made us
weak until we found it was ourselves.

Robert Frost

Listen, my dream!
This you told me should be done.
This you said should be the way.
You said it would cure the sick.
Help me now.
Do not lie to me.
Help me, Sun person.
Help me to cure this sick man.

Blackfoot healer's song

WORKING WITH YOUR DREAM DOCTOR

A Toronto mother told this heartrending story:

"When my son was two years old, I had a disturbing dream. I saw him quite a bit older, sitting in a rocking chair in what seemed to be a hospital room. He was just rocking back and forth. He was white as a sheet. All the juice seemed to have gone out of him.

"When he was seven, I saw that scene in waking life. He had been diagnosed two months earlier with leukemia. They couldn't stop the disease and he died that year. One of the crazy things was they had rebuilt that hospital. The room he was in didn't exist when I had the dream."

Still grief-stricken several years after her loss, the mother wanted to know if it was possible she could somehow have saved her son's life if she had recognized the warning in her dream and sought medical help before the symptoms of leukemia were detected. There is no way of answering that question; certainly there was no cause for a devoted mother to add feelings of guilt to the pain she already carried.

However, it is evident that on many occasions we receive dream warnings about possible health problems long before any physical symptoms are manifested. Such early diagnosis through dreams is entirely natural. Dreams are bodytalk as well as soultalk, and the physical symptoms of disease are not isolated events but are outward signs of a person's psychospiritual condition.

If our society were serious about cutting the costs of medical care, dreamwork would be taught and practiced in every school, community center, and clinic. Dreams supply nightly health reports that are as precise and objective, when accurately recorded, as any X ray or EEG and may be far more timely, since they reveal problems that could result in physical illness before we develop physical complaints. These dream checkups do not require copayments, Medicare, or even the cost of busfare to the doctor's office. They give us diagnostic and prescriptive information that may be helpful for others as well as ourselves.

I had a memorable personal experience of this when a woman who has participated in a number of my dream experiments called me before breakfast one weekday, sounding breathless and anxious. "Are you okay?" she demanded. She told me the following dream:

> We were together in a store that sold tribal artifacts and Native American stuff. You were examining the contents of a glass-fronted case. Then you staggered and slid down the side of the case and collapsed on the floor. You couldn't speak clearly. You seemed to be having some type of stroke. I made the store manager call an ambulance. When the paramedics arrived, you were chipper as usual. You seemed to have fixed yourself. But one of the paramedics read you the riot act. He said if only you'd been taking that pill you were supposed to take, this wouldn't have had to happen.

The dreamer did not know what to make of the bit about the pills. She knew that I do not take any kind of medication and keep as far away as possible from allopathic physicians. She had called me, in the first instance, because she feared something bad might have happened to me.

While I reassured her that I was fine, I recognized that her dream contained a possible warning to me. Unknown to the dreamer, I had gone to a hospital emergency room a couple of years earlier because I felt more than usually wired. When they asked me at the desk what was wrong, I told them, "I feel I might be about to blow up." This produced a doctor in what may have been record time! He discovered, after a brief and humorous examination, that I was experiencing the predictable effects of my then habit of gulping down several mugs of espresso during my predawn writing sprees. He suggested that I cut down hard on the caffeine, and also, since hypertension has been a problem for most of the men in previous generations of my family, that I consider taking a child-size aspirin daily, to lower the risk of developing high blood pressure. I took an aspirin a day for a week or so, then forgot all about it. The woman's dream gave me a tap on the shoulder. I remembered the doctor's advice and reverted to the aspirin routine, reminding myself that aspirin is derived from a natural remedy, the gift of the willow.

If it is possible for dreams to produce such timely and practical health suggestions for persons other than the dreamer, it is hardly surprising that dreams are constantly giving us advice on how to provide for our own wellness. We often neglect the warnings because we do not want to clean up our diet or lifestyle, or out of rank fear. But the dream source is highly inventive in rescripting messages in ways that make it harder and harder for us to ignore them. Here is a dream that came to a junk-food addict at a time when his three main food groups were french fries, barbecued ribs, and Kentucky fried chicken:

> I am in this kitchen where there are frying pans on all the hot plates. They are frying up human babies in the pans to make grease to cook the food. I wake up wanting to throw up.

After this dream, this fellow was actually known to order salads.

The vocabulary of dream health reports is rich in metaphors that give us fresh and personal ways of naming and visioning our condition and possible complaints—and thereby of working with the power of healing imagery.

In relation to healing, the great gifts of dreaming are these:

1. Dreams give us our own images. The power of guided imagery in healing work is immense, as evidenced by the work of Bernie Siegel, Jeanne Achterberg, and others. The body does not know that our images are not "real"; muscles and nerves and blood flow respond to mental and emotional events as if they were physical happenings.

You can test this for yourself by pausing to think of something that makes your heart beat faster. You might think of making love or climbing stairs or jogging round the park. Put your attention on that activity. Is your heart beating faster now? Maybe you need to slow it down. Think of something that makes your heart beat slower. Maybe you're floating on water or lolling by the ocean. Feel better now?

Several years ago, a horrific crime was committed in California. A psychotic raped and tortured a woman, ending his attack by chopping off her arms below the elbows and leaving her in the middle of the desert to die of blood loss and heat exposure. A few days later, she was found still alive. Somehow she had managed to stop the bleeding and survive the desert sun. When she was able to talk, she explained that the Bionic Woman (as played by Lindsay Wagner on TV) had always been her hero. She had willed herself to become Bionic Woman, to do the impossible, to stop the bleeding from the stumps of her arms. And her body had believed her.[1]

Authentic images, like that woman's, are full of power. They are our most effective tools for communicating with our immune systems, and even with specific organs. Follow your dreams and you will get far more than you can ever get from the guided visualizations you will find in books and tapes; you will find the images that belong to you and speak most clearly to your body.

2. Dreams tell us what is wrong with us in ways that help us get well. Dreams do not present problems without suggesting ways of dealing with them. They give us timely warnings of developing ailments, couched in language that may be humorous or shocking but is always personal and specific.

Dreams "name" our complaints in ways that are more original and more human than those of many medical practitioners, whose method of announcing a diagnosis of a major disease can resemble that of an Aboriginal sorcerer pointing the bone at an intended victim. Dreams give us names and images we can work with. Instead of inducing passive dependence on an authority figure, they offer us chances to work on our own healing.

I believe these comments hold true even if your dreams are showing you a terminal illness. Death is no defeat, not if you are going at the proper time, and if you are ready for the next life experience that awaits you. The dreams of dying people take them beyond the swinging door and prepare them to move through it with confidence and grace.

3. Dreams show us the meaning of illness. While doctors may treat physical symptoms in isolation, dreams rarely (if ever) do this. Dreams provide a context of meaning. They demonstrate how our ailments are related to our whole psychospiritual condition. They remind us that health and wholeness are matters of soul and suffer when we forsake the path of soul for our little agendas.

Dreams also recall the positive aspects of disease, the way that a health crisis can force someone to push a personal "reset button" (in Bernie Siegel's evocative phrase): to take time out from bad habits, negative attitudes, the rat race of getting the bonus or the promotion.

Dreams help us connect our ailments to our larger story. A patient who has a sense of living a larger story and can draw on the passion and creative energy that flows from that is a survivor. You can't kill that kind of spirit.

4. Dreams put us in contact with our Inner Healer. The source of dreams always seems to be interested in correcting imbalance and restoring harmony in our lives—and in our world. From the perspective of the Navajo *hataali*, or "healing singer," all illness stems fundamentally from imbalance. I think the *hataali* is right. The dream source is constantly sending us pictures and advisories to help us correct imbalance before it results in an external crisis.

Work with dreams and you will discover a healer in you. Take a moment to examine your present attitudes to that proposition. Ask yourself the following questions, which are inspired in part by John Selby's book *Conscious Healing:*[2]

— WHO IS THE HEALER?

1. Where do you think healing comes from?
2. Do you see any positive value in your current illness or difficulties?
3. Are you punishing yourself in some way?
4. Can you heal yourself?
5. Are you ready to heal yourself?
6. If you healed yourself, how would your friends respond?

BODYTALK

— 1. HOUSE CALLS

It has become hard to find a family doctor who makes house calls, but your dream doctor is willing to drop by anytime, not only to help you cope with symptoms of illness but to alert you to steps you should take to prevent illness from coming about.

Here is a dream reported by a middle-aged man:

How to Avoid a Heart Attack

I enter a large hospital, bundled up in a heavy overcoat on top of a suit and sweater, although the weather is mild. I am looking for some free brochures on "How to Avoid a Heart Attack." I notice a huge line of people, mostly men about my own age, waiting outside the cardiology department. A friendly security guard tells me where I can get the brochures. He asks if I am a smoker. When I tell him I am, he asks me to pick up some small cigars for him. He joins me later in a crowded diner where people are leaning on me. He clears a space for both of us. I remembered his stogies and offer them to him. He says he doesn't need them now; he's quit smoking. I notice he's slimmed down a lot and looks good.

The dreamer had borderline high blood pressure, and a family history of strokes and heart problems. He recognized he had received a gentle health advisory. He thought the fact that he was wearing heavy clothing in mild weather was a caution to lose some weight. He was impressed by the way the security guard looked fit after he gave up smoking. He especially liked the theme of "free advice."

This dream contained guidance on how to avoid a possible health problem before it produced serious symptoms. Your dream doctor is a holistic practitioner whose clinic is equipped to produce a *total readout* on your psychophysical condition, at no charge. This theme was underscored in one of my own dreams that also contained a lifestyle warning:

Speeding

I am speeding down the highway in a beautiful racing-green Jaguar. I am having a marvelous time, but I am driving incredibly recklessly. I make a right-hand turn from the fast lane, sheering across the road at about 100 mph. An avuncular character, protective but stern, tells me I need to be more careful: "If you smash up that vehicle, you won't find it easy to get another one like it." He tells me to open the trunk. I'm impressed to see it's full of high-tech medical monitoring equipment—scanners, blood-pressure gauges, ultrasound devices.

— 2. EARLY WARNING

When disease begins to develop, dreams often provide warnings of specific problems before physical symptoms have become manifest. Such dreams can enable you to take timely preventive measures. The intrusion of a virus is often depicted in dreams as something breaking into the dreamer's house. The growth of cancer cells is frequently perceived in dreams as an infestation of rooms in the house by spiders, bats, or other creepy-crawlies—or as the growth of something unwanted in the dreamer's body. Here is a dream that alerted a forty-year-old woman to a possible problem:

Unwanted Baby

I am pregnant with a child I don't want. The father is my ex-boyfriend, who abused me and my daughter. It is hateful to have this thing growing inside me. I feel it's deformed and could kill me. I decide to abort it. I put the misshapen fetus in a box and send it back to the father. In ordinary life, I have never had an abortion and can't imagine having one.

When dreams of this kind are reported to me, I usually advise the dreamer to have a conventional medical checkup.

However, it is important to observe that such dreams give us our own ways of *naming* and *imaging* possible health challenges. Whether or not the need for medical intervention is indicated, these can provide powerful tools for self-healing. If you can visualize a possible problem—as an infestation of bats, an alien fetus you need to evict, or a toxic dump that needs to be cleaned up—you may be able to work, through positive imaging, to change that scene for something better. If you work with authentic images (and dream images are always authentic) and lend the full force of your intention to revisioning them, this can be a profoundly healing process.

— 3. DREAM DIAGNOSIS

Dream doctors sometimes offer a diagnosis in conventional medical language, as well as in images. One bitter Northern winter, when I had been working day and night at my computer and had hardly seen the sun for many weeks, I developed a painful swelling under my right eye. In a dream, I called on an Australian doctor in 1930s London. He was a cheerful, robust fellow, the model of an old-fashioned general practitioner. He told me my problem was herpes. I was jolted by a word often associated with a sexually transmitted disease. "No, no," he reassured me. "It's just herpes zoster." To demonstrate the nature of the complaint, he pulled out of my face a long white thread, which was evidently connected to the nervous system.

A glance at a medical dictionary confirmed that herpes zoster ("creeping herpes") is nothing more exotic than shingles, a recrudescence in adults of juvenile chicken pox. Interestingly, my dream doctor's removal of the "white thread" had a marvelous effect on my waking condition. Within a few days, the shingles blisters had dried up and fallen away, leaving fresh, glowing skin.

— 4. DREAM PRESCRIPTIONS

Dreams quite frequently suggest specific courses of treatment for different complaints. These may involve lifestyle changes, conventional medical treatments, alternative remedies, or soulwork that addresses the hidden sources of disease.

Don Eligio Panti, a revered Mayan *h'men* ("one who knows") in Belize, prays for a guiding dream when he does not understand a patient's condition or familiar remedies fall short. His dream guidance often comes from a spirit guardian who demonstrates a specific treatment— for example, a small plant he describes only as "cancer herb" to treat a leg ulcer.[3]

As we also saw in my friend's "aspirin dream," we can receive dream prescriptions for the benefit of other people as well as ourselves. You must consult your conscience as to whether and how you should pass these on. You will want to follow two basic guidelines: (1) never set yourself up as an unlicensed medical practitioner; and (2) always advise the other person to check the information and seek a second opinion from a professional. I was once advised by a dream doctor to tell a woman who was consulting with me to add "crushed seashells" to her diet. I reported this with some trepidation and was reassured to learn that at one point in her life, she had been given the same counsel by a holistic practitioner and knew what product to buy at a health food store.

Dream remedies of this kind sometimes seem to well up from the whole history of trial and error of our species. Stanley Krippner tells the story of a woman who was suffering from a serious intestinal condition that modern medicine had been unable to cure. She dreamed she should eat papaya, a fruit she abhorred in waking life. She followed the dream prescription, and her intestinal problems vanished.[4]

SOULTALK

A nurse once complained to me that in the hospital where she worked, patients were often referred to by the names of their symptoms: "The cardiac case in the ER," "The Alzheimer's in geriatric." Unlike many hospital doctors, your dream doctor associates healing with wholeness and examines your total condition, physical, emotional, mental, and spiritual. Dream doctors, like shamans, recognize that physical symptoms may have their origin and meaning in areas that escape medical scanning devices.

If you are working with your dreams, you are already aware that your identity and consciousness are not confined to your body. You may already be aware that your physical body is enclosed by an energy field that sustains its vital processes and that the condition of this energy field determines your vulnerability to the sources of disease. If not, you should try this simple exercise, inspired in part by a marvelous tape by Lani Leary called *Healing Hands,* which should help to heighten your awareness of your energy field:[5]

EXERCISE: BECOMING CONSCIOUS OF YOUR ENERGY FIELD

1. Sit in a comfortable position and relax. Go with the flow of your breathing. See light streaming down through the crown of your head. Let yourself be filled by the light.

2. Now hold up your hands in front of you, palms outward, and spread your fingers until the skin is tight. Maintain the pressure.

3. When you relax the pressure, focus your attention on the palms of your hands. How do they feel? Warmer or colder? Do you feel any tingling sensations?

4. Pass your hands up and down, back and forth, across each other, with the palms facing, a foot or so apart. What do you feel now? Do you feel something different, perhaps a gentle tingling sensation, when your palms are facing each other?

5. Move your palms closer together, very slowly. Can you feel the ball of energy that is now shaping itself between your hands? How does it feel?

6. Now pull the energy that has taken form back into your heart center. This energy is always available to help you to heal yourself and others.

RECLAIMING LOST ENERGY

Shamans describe the hidden causes of disease in a language that is not taught in medical schools. The reasons why people become ill (and suffer other misfortunes) may be identified as *energy loss, soul loss, negative*

intrusion, psychic attack, or *"ghost sickness."* Though such descriptions are not in medical lexicons, they are embedded in everyday speech, as when we say, "Part of me was missing," "He wasn't himself last night," or "I'm having a low-energy day." Dreams often depict the sources of illness in similar ways. Such dreams are a gift, because to grasp the source and the deeper meaning of disease is the gateway to real healing. Dreams frequently reveal the ways in which we unwittingly allow other people to drain our energy.

After separating from a lover, a man had the following dream:

> I saw myself joined to my ex-girlfriend by a cord that somehow extended across the hundreds of miles between us. This cord was attached to my body at or near the navel. It looked like an umbilical cord. It was fleshy and seemed to be pumping blood and nutrients. I thought it wasn't healthy to be joined to my ex-girlfriend this way.

This dream coincided with a period of poor health when the dreamer seemed to have little resistance to illness and frequently experienced major energy dips. Every few days, he would wake from sleep feeling utterly drained. Normally hard-driving and outgoing, he seemed to have lost his ambition and his zest for life.

When he shared the dream with me, I said that if this were my dream, it might be telling me why I was losing energy. On one level, he had parted company with his girlfriend. On another, he was still attached to her, leaking energy through the psychic cord he had perceived in his dream. Maybe his former partner was in a similar situation. When we break off emotional relationships, we often leave part of ourselves behind; it can take years, sometimes a whole lifetime, to get this back. The result is energy loss, which may extend to soul-loss.

I asked the dreamer if he was ready to sever that psychic connection. He was not enthusiastic about severing the cord he had seen in the dream. The thing had seemed so physical he feared a scene of gouting blood and guts if he tried to cut it. Also, in a part of himself he was by no means sure he wanted to make final the separation from his lover. He compromised. He tried to reenvision the cord he had seen as an electric extension cable, one that could be neatly unplugged. This was cute, but it didn't work. He got to the point, after worsening illness and even scarier energy lows, when he resolved to cut the connection in earnest.

In a dreamlike state, he used a scalpel to sever the cord cleanly. He pictured the trailing ends drying up and falling away, like a baby's umbilical after birth.

This operation on the inner planes had an astonishly positive effect on the dreamer's health and energy level. He bounced back, throwing himself into work and play with revived gusto.

The story has an interesting sequel. When he met his former girlfriend some months later, she told him she had had a dream in which she saw the two of them joined by a cord at the heart (not the solar plexus, as in his dream). She had felt this was wrong and pictured herself cutting the cord with a pair of scissors.

Most interesting of all, far from parting as strangers, the couple were now able to come together as soul friends on a deep level. That had become possible only because they had both reclaimed what belonged to them.

Clairvoyant healers, working with the human energy fields, often perceive psychic cords of the type that appeared in these spontaneous dreams. Barbara Brennan has some useful insights on this in her book *Hands of Light.*[6] If we form a strong emotional attachment to someone, we form a link that can be perceived through HSP. Needless to say, this is by no means a negative phenomenon in general; if we were not linked to others, we would hardly be human. However, these psychic cords can become conduits through which we leak energy and become vulnerable to unwanted influences from another person's field.

Dreams provide other imagery for energy loss. The blood-sucking vampire who figures in many Western dreams is not only the product of the popularity of Anne Rice's fiction. The dream vampire is a powerful representation of the energy thief. On the psychic level, vampirism is a real phenomenon. Read Carlos Castaneda's strange book *The Art of Dreaming* and you will find yourself in the coils of a long-dead sorcerer who lives just beyond physical reality and sustains himself by feeding on the energy of the living—including Castaneda, if the author means what he appears to be saying. The blood-sucking creatures who turn up in dreams are often Halloween fright versions of entirely corporeal people. Such dreams can be highly instructive, tutoring us on how we give up our energy to others, and the need to reclaim it.[7]

For example, some years ago I was giving a great deal of my time and energy to a depressed community in the Northern rust belt. My efforts, with those of a few dedicated volunteers, ultimately succeeded in raising a large chunk of money for the local community college through a festival intended to build local pride and a greater sense of possibility. Though the result was immensely rewarding, during the many months of preparation I felt weighed down by constant bickering and negativity within the community. Driving back home one snowy afternoon, I was so fatigued I almost lost control of the wheel. That night, I had the following dream:

Opening My Wrists

I am in a public place, like a town square. I take a knife and deliberately open both of my wrists. I am not trying to kill myself. I am doing this so anyone who wants to drink my blood can come and drink. Hundreds of people are crowding around me to get a taste, as if my veins are a public drinking fountain.

I did not need to do extensive dreamwork to get that message! It inspired me to take long-overdue action to limit the time and energy I was giving up, under circumstances with no sufficient return. The universe works through an exchange of energies. The energy thieves in our lives are those who try to use our energy without a fair exchange. We have all met the kind of person who after an hour or two leaves you feeling, quite literally, that your batteries have been drained. Our dream source is clear-sighted about how we damage ourselves by tolerating such one-way transfers, as in my dream of slashing my wrists.

CALLING BACK LOST SOUL

*W*hen we are exposed to unbearable pain or trauma, we may lose a part of our vital essence, a part of soul. It may remain stuck in the Middle World, close to the place of trauma, or it may go to other worlds. This often seems to happen in cases of childhood abuse. It is evident in many other cases of what psychiatrists call post–traumatic stress syndrome, as with war veterans suffering from "shell shock." When we succumb to addictions, bad habits, and negative thoughts and feelings, part of our soul stuff also goes away. While therapists speak of the need to reclaim the "inner child" or to surface repressed memories, shamans see soul-loss as a quite literal phenomenon. Part of the victim is missing because a part of her soul, which may be perceived as an image of the victim at the time of the loss, has been lost or stolen. The shaman's task is to journey into the hidden dimensions of reality where that soul part has strayed and bring it back.

We need to be whole. But bringing back lost soul parts before we are ready to handle the painful memories they carry with them is risky. Dreams show us what we may have lost when we are ready to bring it back and deal with those memories. A woman's dream helped her bring back a part of herself that had been missing since early childhood:

Baby Beside the Flag

I saw my two-year-old self. She was crouched in a fetal position in a corner of a funeral parlor, next to a coffin draped with the American flag. I felt her grief at the loss of her father and the loneliness and abuse that followed. I knew she was ready to come back to me. I went back inside the dream, carrying a teddy bear. When she saw it, she came flying toward me in a shimmer of light. I guess we became one. I felt pain in my heart, as if a bullet of light had been shot into me. But it was a happy pain.

Another woman dreamed she watched herself robed in funereal colors, riding in a boat along the River of the Dead. She realized she was looking at a younger self, haggard and red-eyed with grief over the loss of the baby she had been forced to abort when she was just eighteen years old. This dream prompted her to consult a shamanic practitioner, who conducted a formal soul retrieval, during which she saw her teenage self reenter her, through the top of her head, in a radiant swirl of light. Reabsorbing the memories that came flooding back was not easy. For several days, she was prone to uncontrollable fits of weeping. She needed a lot of love and support. But when she came through this passage, she found she had abundant energy—all that teenage zest—and her friends told her she looked fifteen years younger.

In my own dream, I discovered a younger self who had gone missing during my boyhood crises of illness. I saw him as a cherubic young boy, complete with wings, perched on a cloudbank quite close to me. It seemed he was waiting for a signal to return. Becoming conscious inside the dream, I conjured up the image of a glowing crystal. The light brought him back to me at once. I asked why he had gone away. "You were always sick," he reminded me. "I wanted to run and play."

After this experience, I found myself wanting to run and sport in the woods for hours at a stretch. I even started kicking a ball around for the first time in decades.

If you want to know more about bringing back missing soul parts, one of the most basic shamanic operations, read *Soul Retrieval* and *Welcome Home,* two luminous books by Sandra Ingerman, a gifted and generous shamanic teacher.[8]

WARNINGS OF PSYCHIC ATTACK

*B*ecause thoughts and feelings are already actions, and because we are all connected, without realizing what we are doing we can cause each other real damage by giving vent to negative emotions. I learned something about this when I felt the need to conduct a complete cleanup of my affairs, on the psychic plane. Part of this cleansing was my personal version of what traditional Iroquois sometimes call a "confession on the road." You go to a private place and give voice to all the guilt and bad experiences you may be carrying. You ask forgiveness of anyone you may have hurt. If you reach deep enough, you may finally be able to forgive yourself.

After this experience, I dreamed I ran into a man who had been one of my worst enemies earlier in my life. Our encounter took place in a men's room. He was initially hostile, but I put my hands on his shoulders and said, "I love you," staring into his eyes. With a hissing sound, all the anger and bitterness came out of him and he became a smiling boy. Then, needing to throw up, I leaned over a sink. I was astonished to see myself spitting out *buckets* of rusty nails.

I woke up feeling on top of the world. The image of rusty nails stayed with me. I remembered how tribal shamans sometimes display a rusty nail (or another projectile, such as a splinter or small bone) as evidence that they have sucked out the roots of a patient's disease. In a spontaneous sleep dream, the same image described the possible cumulative effect of many years of hostility and "bad-mouthing." This dream made me determined to monitor how I speak, and even think, about others.

A full-fledged psychic attack, complete with ritual sorcery and focused projection of negative energy, is no trivial business. The attacker will seek to establish a psychic link between himself and his intended victim. He may attempt this by borrowing or stealing a personal item from the victim, or placing an object in his house. The use of a "voodoo doll," representing the intended victim, is common in many varieties of black magic. The sorcerer may try to direct earthbound spirits or created thought-forms—known in esoteric tradition as "elementals"—against his target. I wish I could report that this kind of thing is mere superstition, or is confined to "primitive" societies.

A Texas woman who had been involved in a bitter dispute with a former business partner shared the following dream sequence with me:

Night Calls

Over a period of more than a week, my sleep was broken every couple of hours by the sound of a phone ringing inside my head. I woke up feeling sick with fear. Then I dreamed of intruders in my house—a middle-aged Hispanic man who looked evil and crafty, and a blond woman who told me my cat belonged to her. Against my will, I handed my cat over to her.

I woke up feeling terrible that I'd given up something I love, something that belongs to me.

I guess my desperation made me brave. I went back into my dream. I found myself drawn to a house in another town. I entered a small room where a black cat with no eyes was sitting in a niche high up on the wall. At the far side of the room was an altar that seemed to be made of terra cotta. I saw a woman lying there. She had strange markings over her eyes.

I realized she was a doll. Then I heard someone chanting the number of my house over and over again.

Through her dream reentry, the Texas woman had gained an important clue to the nature and origin of a psychic attack that she now connected with trouble in her waking life as well as her disrupted nights. Subsequent investigation enabled her to confirm that the realtor with whom she had had a falling-out had hired a *mayombero*—a sorcerer who practiced a low version of Palo Mayombe, a tradition that has roots in Central Africa—to attack her in order to stop her pursuing her claim to her rightful share of the assets of the former partnership. The sorcerer lived in the town she had visited in her dream reentry.

I advised her to clean house, both literally and metaphorically, taking special care to remove items associated with her former partner. I suggested that she should walk the boundaries of her property (in a clockwise direction, starting in the east) and visualize herself constructing, with each step, a wall of light around her home. I told her to continue the visualization until she saw her home enclosed by a sphere of light that was fully real to her, and to make it her intention that this light should be a welcoming beacon to those who came in love but a consuming terror to those who came with unclean or hostile motives. I counseled her to reach deep inside herself and invoke the help of spiritual guardians by the names she *truly* believed in.

A determined and malevolent psychic attack may call for specialist help. However, spontaneous dreams may not only alert the intended victim to the problem, *but may themselves provide the antidote*. An Iroquois friend told me of a conscious dream in which he was warned of a psychic attack against him and was able to identify both his antagonist and the sorcerer hired to perform the deed. From that moment, the spell began to turn against its senders.

A man who was the target of Indian "love magic" tells of a similar dream:

Love Magic

I found myself inside a woman's body. She kept crooning crazy stuff, like "I am the most beautiful woman in the world" and "You will never want to touch another woman," as she stroked her breasts and her butt. I got a real creepy feeling. I felt I'd somehow been sucked out of my own body without my consent. I sensed something was wrong with her blood, and she wasn't all that good-looking. I started looking around for the source of what was going on. I saw a man in the corner, watching all of this closely as he worked some magic in a pot. He was missing part of an arm. He reminded me of a witch I once ran into on a reserve up in Canada.

When the dreamer consulted me, we were able to identify the characters in his dream—a former lover and the sorcerer she had hired—and the methods they were using in their attempt to manipulate him. A psychic link between the dreamer and his former lover had survived the end of their affair, as is often the case after the break-up of a relationship. This was the line that was being used in the effort to reel him back into the relationship (in a rather literal sense, to judge by his description of being "sucked out of his body" without his consent). The people who were seeking to control him had tried to strengthen the bond by using personal items that had been stolen from him.

The first step to be taken in defending this man was to sever the link between him and his former lover. He made a conscious resolution to do this, confirmed by personal rituals, including the careful removal from his apartment of various objects that had been left by his former lover. His home was cleansed, and he adopted certain other precautions, including a process of psychic shielding that incorporated visualizations similar to those used by the Texas woman. The success of these methods was suggested both by a notable rise in the man's energy and sense of well-being, and by the fact that a person connected with the attack returned the items that had been stolen from the dreamer without any discussion with him.

BASICS OF PSYCHIC SELF-DEFENSE

If we are vulnerable to psychic attack and other negative intrusions, it is because we have left ourselves open. We do that in many different ways: by failing to guard our energy, by mixing with the wrong people, by giving in to fear or anger or addiction. Some people actively invite problems, by taking their troubles to corrupt practitioners, by mouthing occult formulas they do not understand, or by summoning spirit entities they do not screen and do not know how to send away. An otherwise rational and successful woman I know—a Ph.D. in psychology, no less—wrote to a self-styled "shaman" in Brazil when she was going through a bad patch, and was persuaded to mail a pair of her husband's soiled undershorts to a man she had never met, for purposes that were never made clear to her. In place of getting rid of her old problems, she found she had invited in a battery of new ones. Dabblers in ceremonial magic are asking for similar trouble, as are people who fool around with Ouija boards and automatic writing without a clear understanding that if you call on the spirits, something *will* come— and you had better know how to deal with it if it is not what you wanted.

Psychic self-defense has three fronts, as Dion Fortune observes in her classic book on the subject.[9] It involves *strengthening and repairing the energy field; cleansing the environment;* and *breaking unhealthy contacts* (with people and entities who may or may not be living). None of these elements takes precedence over the others. But in practice, if a psychic link exists between a person and someone or something who is draining her energy or seeking to manipulate her, the first step will be to cut that connection. As we have seen, dreams can provide exact guidance on when, where, and how to accomplish this.

Here are a few basic techniques you can employ to strengthen your energy field and improve your general psychic health:

1. Keep your energy high. This means proper attention to diet, exercise, and personal habits as well as inner work. Breathing exercises are especially useful. So are White Light visualizations in which you see your body filled with and shielded by radiant energy. Here is one of my favorites:

Visualization: Sun in the Solar Plexus

Relax and follow your breathing. Close your eyes and see light flowing into you with your breath. Release any negative thoughts and feelings as you breathe out.

Soon you will see a blazing sun, rising from within your solar plexus. See its rays spreading through every cell of your body, from your toes to the top of your head. See the light flowing through you and radiating out beyond the limits of your body, forming a shining aura that shields you and surrounds you.

Repeat this until you feel your body responding to the imagery. Use it whenever you want to feel stronger and brighter.

2. Monitor your thoughts and feelings. You need to learn to discriminate which are your own, as opposed to thoughts and feelings you are picking up from other people. There is truth in the saying "You can't afford a negative thought." Pay attention to the thoughts and expectations you project onto other people and situations; you will encounter them again.

3. Be careful whom you invite "home" figuratively as well as literally. If you are a receptive person, as all active dreamers are, you may pick up many kinds of astral visitors. Remember to check their identity and motives.

4. Shield yourself and your environment against unwanted visitors. Shamans and other spiritual practitioners offer many methods for doing this, such as smudging and rituals of banishing and invoking spirit entities. The heart of the matter is your focused intention. You may visualize a sphere of light enclosing your home or your immediate environment. You may wish to invoke spiritual allies to stand guard at the four quarters, and the Above and Below. But it is sufficient to focus your will on creating a sphere of light that will be a welcoming beacon to those who come to you in love, and a fiery shield that will repel any who come with hostile or unclean intentions. If they have the force of your belief, such mental screens truly work.

On an earthier note, it is quite a good idea, especially in times of psychic disturbance, to try *sleeping with water*. All this involves is putting a glass of water close to your bed. You should remember not to drink it in the morning! (You should pour it into the ground or down the drain.) Water naturally absorbs lower energies.

5. Remember it's okay to ask for help. You have spiritual guardians, whether or not you remember them or honor them. If you feel you are under psychic attack, you should call on their help and protection by whatever names you truly believe in.

6. First and last, do no harm. Even if you become aware that you have been the target of a psychic attack, you should respond in the spirit of love, not revenge or hatred. What goes around comes around (really!), and those who abuse psychospiritual powers will reap the consequences.

THE HEALING DREAM

*T*he people who journeyed from all across the Greek world to seek healing dreams in the shrines of Asklepios left some interesting reports on the votive stelae they erected to honor the god. A woman blind in one eye dreamed that the god personally appeared to her, cut out the damaged eyeball, and poured a healing potion into the socket. She woke to find she had recovered her sight. A man with an ugly red brand mark on his forehead dreamed the god tied a bandage round his head. When he woke, he discovered that the brand mark had been transferred to a literal bandage, and his forehead was unblemished. A man who could not get rid of body lice dreamed the god brushed him clean and woke to find the vermin gone.[10]

In these cases, we are dealing with more than dream diagnosis and prescription. The dream itself is the healing experience.

I have often wondered what exactly went on in those shrines of Asklepios. The temples were home not only to gold-and-ivory statues of the god and his son (who also made dream appearances, as a radiant boy or a dwarflike being) but to swarms of whitish yellow snakes, sacred to Asklepios. My wife, Marcia, shared with me a dream that gave me a better feeling for some of this than anything I had found in libraries:

The Snake Dance

I am with Robert in a house filled with snakes. The rooms are vast and sparsely furnished, with snakes all around. I am uncomfortable, but Robert tells me not to worry. Then he goes out, telling me he'll fix things when he comes back.

I go through the house looking for a room that is uninhabited by snakes. I go into a sunroom that seems to be empty. Then I notice a whitish snake head peeping out from under a wicker settee. Snakes start slithering out from everywhere. They are all white or pale with faint patterns, some fattish, others pencil thin. They are getting more and more active. Robert has not come back, and I really want to get out of the dream. But I am now conscious I am dreaming, and I decide to stay with the dream, because I have often run away from dream snakes in the past and these don't seem dangerous.

Now one particularly athletic fellow has slithered through a pass-through in the wall and is hoisting a partner over the wall. The effect is of ballroom dancing, though the snakes don't have arms. The shape the snakes form together also reminds me of a caduceus. Their movements galvanize all the other snakes into more frenetic movement. They rear up and form a circle round me, rattling. They are not rattlesnakes, but they are making a loud, joined rattling as they dance all around me.

I am not enjoying this. But I find it fascinating, even mesmerizing. The snakes dance faster and faster. Then they become still and slither away.

Robert turns up when all the excitement is over. He has a package under his arm in a brown paper bag. Its shape reminds me of a half gallon of ice cream and I wonder if this is my reward. I feel I have been through a very specific and deliberate test.

This dream left Marcia feeling good, with a definite sense of accomplishment. She had stayed with the dream, though she dislikes snakes, and had been rewarded with two remarkable images: of the twined snakes forming the healer's staff, and of the circle dance in which the "rattlers" reminded me of participants in a shamanic circle. In a rather similar way, overcoming fear or aversion toward the snakes who inhabited the almost unfurnished shrines of Asklepios would have been one of the preliminary tests for a pilgrim in search of dream healing. I did not find this association at all far-fetched, since Marcia had recently presented me with a modern Greek statue of Asklepios with one of his snake mascots twined around his arm; it stands near me as I write, and I occasionally place it at the center of healing circles.

Healing dreams sometimes come as spontaneous gifts in the midst of modern life. An American physician reports the dream of a patient who saw a native shaman wave a blue rattle at her damaged organ—and woke up cured. I have had several dreams that I regarded as profound healing experiences. Here is one:

Releasing Dark Eagle

I am bent on separating myself from a powerful entity that is attached to me. It is half-bird, half-human and is batting around my head. It makes threatening passes. It is bent on punishing me for some offense.

I try to release this troubling presence at the edge of a bay or inlet in a flattish landscape. The Dark Eagle—as I now see it—will not leave me. It flaps and feints at my head, more menacing than before.

I move on to a clean, wooded area. A footbridge rises in a high arc over a stream. Caves or niches are in the rock wall below. I figure I might be able to leave Dark Eagle here. I walk up onto the bridge and carefully release him from a metal screen where I now have him pinned. He drops down to a recess in the rock wall. I am relieved to confirm he cannot rise to the level of the bridge I am now walking. I stroll away feeling on top of the world.

Before this dream, I had been suffering from a whole constellation of aches and pains for which I have no medical names, since I did not consult a medical doctor. I had developed persistent flulike symptoms, headaches, and a pervasive sense of oppression. I came back from this dream feeling wonderful, my vitality restored.

The half-bird, half-human quality of my "disease demon" made me think of the wind-borne spirits viewed by Iroquois traditionalists as the carriers of disease. It bore an even closer resemblance to the disease bearer the ancient Greeks called the "dark *ker*," a kind of personal Fury. You can read about that in the marvelous books of Jane Ellen Harrison, who revitalized our understanding of what mythology meant in the daily lives of the Greeks.[11]

I incubated this dream. I knew I was in bad shape and needed urgent help. I decided to apply to my dream source before I applied to a physician. To give all my associations with this dream would fill more than one chapter. It is enough to note that my dream had the desired effect; I woke to find that all my physical symptoms of illness, as well as my general malaise, had vanished along with my Dark Eagle.

If you wish to incubate a healing dream, pay close attention to how the ancients went about this. There were four key steps to be taken before asking for a healing dream from Asklepios: (1) the journey to a sacred place; (2) preparation through cleansing and initiatory tests; (3) invocation of a higher power; and (4) sacrifice. If you are asking for a big gift, the gift of healing, you may choose to find your own equivalents for each of these steps. Here are some suggestions, in which I have borrowed from Patricia Garfield's discussion of the theme in her seminal book *Creative Dreaming:*

— EXERCISE: INCUBATING A HEALING DREAM

1. Journey to a sacred place. You may find it impractical—or objectionable, in the light of your religious beliefs—to travel to a sacred site. But you may be able to sleep out at a special place in nature, or somewhere near the sea. At the least, you will want to assure that your sleeping place will be private and undisturbed, and that you can choose your own time to return from the dream.

2. Preparation. You need to remove impurities from your physical and psychic environment. Bathing in seawater, or with sea salt added to your bathwater, works well. You should abstain from drugs and alcohol and preferably from sex (sorry!) for at least twenty-four hours before you ask for a healing dream. Through breathing exercises and White Light visualization, try to release any negativity you are carrying.

A second aspect of this preparation is that you should now be accustomed to working with your dreams and that you should have learned the discipline of *staying with the dream*. Before pilgrims were admitted to the sacred dormitories of Asklepios, they were required to report initiatory dreams; there is an important lesson here, usually forgotten in accounts of this kind of dream incubation.

3. Invocation. Ask for help from a higher power in words or images that come from your heart, not some book. You may invoke a personal deity, your guardian angel, your Inner Healer, or a cosmic power. What matters is that your invocation be energized by genuine belief and genuine need. You may wish to reinforce your request by lighting a candle, burning incense, or writing it on a piece of paper you can place under your pillow.

Don't be afraid of asking too much, provided your request is life-affirming and will harm no one. Don't get hung up on symptoms. Ask something like this: "I ask to be healed and to live a full and creative life."

4. Sacrifice. This is your commitment to honor and return the gifts of the forces that support your life. What you are able to receive is intimately related to what you are willing to give. If you are asking for the gift of healing, maybe the most valuable sacrifice you can give is a self-offering. You might express it as a pledge along the following lines: "I promise to use this gift for the purpose of soul and spirit and the benefit of others." However expressed, your self-offering must come from the heart, and you will be required to honor it.

DREAMS OF FUSION

*D*reams not only show us different aspects of ourselves; they offer a path to wholeness and integration. Deirdre Barrett, a Harvard hypnotherapist who has worked with many cases of dissociative disorders, notes that sometimes "the lasting integration of two personalities seems to take place in a dream," although in clinical experience this phenomenon is quite rare. One patient dreamed of attending a wedding with a second self; at the end of the ceremony, only one person stood at the altar. Another patient dreamed she said good-bye to the person she had come to recognize as her "alter," who then moved toward her and "faded into me like mist."[12]

Dreams of fusion can be profound healing experiences. In the cases like those reported by Deirdre Barrett, the dreamer appears to have recovered a missing part of herself and made it fully her own. Maybe that part went away because of unbearable pain or abuse at some earlier stage in her life. Its homecoming may amount to a *soul retrieval,* which may be brought about by a healer or come spontaneously when the subject is ready. The way may be opened by a sensitive therapist or a shamanic practitioner or simply by positive life changes, but the true healing can be the gift of the dream in itself.

I have experienced dreams of fusion in several important passages of my life. One such dream followed a shamanic soul retrieval in which I recovered my "lost boys," parts of me that had left me in early childhood because of the pain and isolation inflicted by chronic illness. Other fusion dreams suggested integration on a different plane.

After my return to teaching, a guide who had often appeared to me in my childhood came back in a powerful dream as a radiant young man. He told me that he lived "in the time of Ammianus Marcellinus," a Roman historian of the third century. He spoke to me about the practices of a Mystery school to which he belonged. Then I saw his spirit fuse with mine in a blaze of light. This vivid dream had a transpersonal quality that was underscored by the synchronistic experiences of two people who were close to me. One of them heard the name Philemon repeated several times in her sleep. About the same time, a male friend living sixty miles away woke from his sleep with a start, hearing *my* name being called.

My personal experiences, and those shared by participants in my workshops, have led me to believe that fusion dreams offer not only the mending of the divided self, but the possibility of alignment with deeper spiritual energies.

I was privileged to work with a young woman called Elizabeth whose transformative experience of self-healing centered on dreams of this kind.

Elizabeth had an MA in psychology and had worked with abused children, which had helped her to deal with personal memories of childhood trauma. In dark passages in her life, she had sometimes felt the loving presence of a guide she perceived as a beautiful woman with rainbow lights in her hair. She thought of this presence as the Woman of Many Colors. She tried to paint the radiant face she had seen in dreams and meditative states.

But, as for all of us, for long periods Elizabeth felt out of touch with her guide and wretchedly alone and divided, inclined to distrust the validity of her inner experience. Like many psychically receptive people, she had boundary problems. She was constantly picking up negative thoughts and feelings from the people around her, and these affected her moods and her health. She was troubled by death dreams in which she saw herself stalked and murdered. She often felt at war with herself, even that she was several different people.

This was reflected in the remembered dream she chose to explore in a weekend workshop:

My Three Selves

I am three people, both male and female. We are moving through a vast forest, toward the edge of a clearing where a man is standing. He is holding a wand. A voice from above tells us that we are searching for "the proof of divine love."

One of my three selves—the one I will call "I"—asks the man if it is the right time to carry out this mission. He says, "Go ahead and good luck!" He seems to be the timekeeper, whose job is to make sure everything happens at the right time and the right place, with the necessary help.

My three selves run into the clearing like frisky puppies. One lags a bit behind the others. I hear beautiful singing in the forest beyond the far side of the clearing. I tell the others this must be what we have come to find. We race toward the singing. I try to remind myself that this is not a contest, but a quest we all share.

One of my other selves grabs me by the shoulder. "Look!" I realize that now it is both day and night. The moon and sun are together in the sky. White clouds are massing, taking living form. Immense energies are moving through the sky. It is beautiful to watch, but so powerful, so much bigger than me, that I have to scream. I scream and scream and wake up scared by my own cries. I know this goes beyond me.

With the help of the drum, Elizabeth reentered her dream to find out why she had been so scared. She quickly returned to the entrance to the forest clearing. Its guardian was waiting for her, as before, and gave her permission to enter.

Carried by My Guide

I walk into the clearing and I realize I am no longer three people. I am one. I hear the singing in the forest and I resolve to find out where it is coming from. Again, it is both day and night; sun and moon are together in the sky.

I enter the woods on the far side of the clearing and I am amazed to find that the singer is the woman of many colors who has guided and protected me before. I embrace her and ask her why I was so scared.

She tells me, "You were frightened because you did not go with me. You should not go alone. It is my task to carry you."

She picks me up and carries me to where the sun and moon are shining in the sky.

She explains, "This universe belongs to you, as you belong to it. The sun and moon belong to you, and you are part of the forces of nature you see in the sky. You need never be afraid, because you are part of it. You were scared because it seems so much bigger than you. You have to surrender to it in order to live your life as you should."

When the drum sounded the recall, Elizabeth returned by the path she had taken, thanking the timekeeper, who still stood guard at the entrance to the clearing.

Elizabeth was powerfully moved by this experience. She felt she had made an important discovery. "I learned that the many-colored woman is my Higher Self and that I should always be with her. I lost contact with her when I was trying to do too much 'by myself,' to live and act out of my little self, which was always divided."

But her explorations had just begun. Now that she had found her path beyond the dream doorway, she was able to journey much further.

When Elizabeth was invited to journey on the question "How can I heal myself?" she found the Woman of Many Colors waiting for her again, in the middle of a long path covered with white stones. The guide told Elizabeth she would take her to a "special place." This proved to be another magical spot in the forest, where a circle of gnomelike men in pointed caps offered her a bowl steaming with golden fluid.

"I feared it would burn my throat and larynx," Elizabeth recalled, "but I decided to drink it anyway. The fluid streamed through my body and crystallized in my blood as golden sparkles. The little men were very excited and kept congratulating me. I realized that some weakness in my blood had just been healed. The little men were very down-to-earth. One of them told me, 'You could do with a good back rub as well.' I felt I had been prepared for the next step."

The next step, later that day, was a journey to confirm her relationship with a spiritual guide. She expected, naturally, to encounter her Woman of Many Colors again. But she got rather more than she expected. If you are living the path of soul, you will get used to expecting the unexpected.

Elizabeth was fast becoming a seasoned traveler in nonordinary reality. When the drumming began, she sped back to the entrance to her forest clearing and was again given the nod by its timekeeper-guardian.

Fusion with the Guide

I find my many-colored woman under the sun and moon. She knows what to do. She cuts a circle in the grass and stands inside it, holding me up high. Suddenly a strong wind carries both of us up into the sky.

We swirl round and round. Then I am back in a nightmare from my childhood, from when I was seven or eight years old. In this nightmare I am drawn with tremendous force into a tunnel. I can see light at the end but I am unable to reach it. The tunnel is tremendously long and I have to battle with terrific energy forces spiraling round inside it. In childhood, I always woke from this full of terror, with a wet bed.

Now I am in that tunnel with my guide; we move straight toward the circle of light at the far end. We come out into a beautiful otherworldly scene. The sky is purple. We keep flying higher and higher, until I realize we are flying into the sun. It is getting hotter and hotter. I am melting. I am melting into the woman who carries me. My body shakes and shivers. The experience is overwhelming. Finally I have melted into the Woman of Many Colors, and she into me. We have become one.

Suddenly a bird appears. It flies into my throat and flaps its wings. Charcoal dust comes out.

I feel an emptiness around me. From this emptiness the face of a man takes form. It is like an amber-colored mask, vaguely Egyptian. It is clear to me this person can assume any form. He tells me, "Well done!" His voice is loving. He explains he has come to prepare me to meet new guides.

I do not want to go back. But he reminds me I have important tasks on earth, that there are people who love me and depend on me. He makes me eager to get on with my job on earth.

I fly back to the clearing. I feel sixty percent bigger than I was before. I look at myself and see the many colors of the woman from my visions. I walk to the forest gate and thank the timekeeper.

When the drumming stops, I feel many tears inside. I feel I received something that was never lost but was never fully part of me: my inner source, my connection with the divine spirit. When I cry, I know that pain and joy are equal. I have to laugh and cry at the same time. It frees me.

That night, after the workshop, Elizabeth took the advice of her little nature spirits and treated herself to a massage. The masseuse told her she could feel the drumming in Elizabeth's skin. The advice from the little men in the forest was not the least-valuable insight Elizabeth had received. After experiences of this depth, it is important to do something to ground yourself in ordinary reality—to eat some earthy foods, move your body, go dancing, share a few jokes.

The nightmare from childhood that erupted from Elizabeth's memory during her *big* journey is shared by others, perhaps by most of us. In another of my workshops, a woman found herself stuck inside a stone tower on a cold, dirty stairway that led on and on, up and up, toward a hopelessly distant sky, her path blocked by a horrible black bird. She felt she was about eight years old—and was, for a time, as repressed memories and traumas came back. When she finally broke through to the light in a later journey, immense vistas opened to her. In both cases, we can see the dreamer moving toward wholeness, bringing back a part of herself that had been lost or paralyzed.

To integrate experiences of this power and to emerge stronger, you need to be prepared—and protected. There is a right time and space for these things. Elizabeth's encounters with the timekeeper underscore the necessity of getting this right.

Elizabeth came through her encounter with the Higher Self with greater energy, heightened creativity, and a driving sense of purpose that propelled her into fresh experiments in teaching, writing, and personal relationships.

To me, the most beautiful element in her story, and the one that leads to deepest reflection, is her experience of *fusion* with her Woman of Many Colors. This prepared her for encounters with guides on higher levels. This is true initiation.

SHARED DREAMS AND HEALING

*W*e can seek dream healing for others as well as ourselves. This takes us into the area of *interactive dreaming*.

Tanya Wilkinson, a San Francisco psychologist, made a study of nine cases in which therapists and their clients reported overlapping dreams at about the same time. For example, Tanya dreamed she was looking into the water near the Golden Gate Bridge and saw a school of killer whales dancing around a submerged car. Shortly afterward, her client told her he had dreamed he drove his car into the bay at the same point and was alarmed to see killer whales swimming all around him.

Significantly, among the nine cases Tanya reported, only one involved therapy that was pronounced an unequivocal success. In this single case, client and therapist reported more than overlapping dreams; they appear to have experienced a shared dream in which the therapist took action that directly helped the client. The therapist dreamed that a rat was biting him between his thumb and his forefinger. He wanted to shake it off. But realizing that the rat was terrified, he stroked it to calm it down. Then the rat detached itself.

To his astonishment, the therapist's client reported that on the same night, he dreamed a rat was biting his hand, at the same spot. "Then a hand entered my dream, calmed the rat down, and detached it."

This was a turning point in the therapy. The client's confidence in his therapist was understandably boosted, and he proceeded to make rapid progress. Though the therapist's claims are more modest, it might be that, without being fully aware of what happened, he played a healing role inside an interactive dream.[13]

What may have occurred spontaneously in this case can be accomplished intentionally, through conscious dreaming, as in Wanda's story.

WANDA RENEGOTIATES HER CONTRACT

*O*ver a period of twenty years, Wanda Burch had a recurring dream:

> *I am moving, then dancing, along a narrow passage. I recognize friends and relatives who have died. They are urging me to keep moving forward. At the end of the passage, I see a wooden door. I know that when I pass through this door, I will die. I am told repeatedly that this will happen in the year I turn forty-three.*

Wanda first had this dream when she was at college in Memphis, Tennessee. Through many changes in her life—through marriage, childbirth, and her move to a job in New York—the dream kept coming back to her. The dream locale remained the same, but the cast of characters and other elements were continually evolving.

In the original dream, Wanda saw only a few dead people in the passage. In the last dream of the series, some twenty years later, the passage was crowded with scores of dead people. This time, Wanda was dressed in white lace, as if for a wedding, and carrying a bouquet of flowers. This dream came to her in the year she turned forty-three and was diagnosed with breast cancer.

The first news about the specific nature of her illness did not come from the doctors, or even from a physical self-examination. It came from her dreams. While Wanda's dreams of dancing among the dead seem to have been preparing her for the possibility of an early death, a second series of prodromal dreams alerted her to the presence of cancer in her body months before any physical symptoms could be detected. In one of these dreams, she was riding in a car when she noticed a globular compass on the dashboard. The compass turned dark. Inside it, she saw stars radiating out from a central mass.

Dreams of this kind led Wanda to check herself in for a mammogram. The results were negative. The first physician she consulted told her she had nothing to worry about. And when she examined herself, Wanda could find no trace of a lump.

But the threatening quality of her dreams led her to seek a second opinion. A specialist agreed to conduct a biopsy, which revealed a solid malignancy in Wanda's left breast. It was metastasizing fast. Individual cancer cells were invading other parts of her body, very much like the stars in the dream compass.

Wanda came home close to desperation. "I was hyperventilating," she recalled. "I threw myself on the sofa, panting and crying. I was praying for help. I kept asking, 'What can I do to be healed?' "

Exhausted, she finally dozed off. A dream came to her in which a radiant helper showed her a dark spot inside one of her breasts from which a dark, toxic fluid was seeping into her body. The helper took hold of her breast and it became a sponge. "Somehow he pulled all the poison back to the point from which it had come. Then he drained it into a bowl."

She woke reenergized. She took the images from her dream and worked with them, over and over, in waking visualizations. "I kept pulling the disease back to the dark point that was its source. I did this again and again until it seemed totally *real*."

Wanda's oncologist believed in the healing power of imagery. Even so, he was stunned by the improvement in her condition that he discovered at her next examination. The spread of the cancer cells from the primary tumor had been reversed. But the doctor felt that a modified radical mastectomy was unavoidable.

Wanda's dreams had prepared her for this ordeal, too.

The week of the biopsy, she dreamed she discovered a huge bat under a criblike bed:

> *I rushed at the bat. I picked it up by the head and broke its neck with my hands. I threw it down a flight of stairs and saw it impaled on a knifelike tool that was sticking out from the wall. The ceiling was covered with smaller bats. I asked my friend to help me. We started exterminating the bats with poison. We got the room clear. Then I curled up in the bed, inside the dream, and went to sleep.*

This dream also influenced Wanda's decision to submit to aggressive chemotherapy after her surgery.

She made a rapid recovery after the operation, but went through bouts of deep depression and violent mood swings during the chemotherapy. Her hair fell out. Her dreams turned darker. One of them spoke to her about the effect of the drugs; she saw her childhood home turned into a crack house.

In a terrifying dream visitation, Wanda struggled with a powerful being who told her that her time was up. He insisted, "You have to leave."

In this period, Wanda and I shared an interactive dream that she sees as a turning point in her recovery. I had become deeply worried about her. She had just heard the news that Jill Ireland had died after a six-year fight with breast cancer. Understandably, this had shaken Wanda's belief in her ability to heal. As she told me later, "The news of Jill's death hit me like a blast from a cannon. I would burst into tears and could not stop crying. I was sure I would die soon." She brooded on all those dreams of the dancehall of the dead, the dreams that seemed to have been telling her, since the start of her adult life, that she was fated to die this year.

In a conscious dream, I journeyed to check on Wanda. I found her in a night setting, in a cave that was also a temple. Robed women stood in a circle nearby, performing a ceremony. But Wanda was not part of this. She was frozen, paralyzed in terror of shadowy, snakelike forms that menaced her on all sides. I grabbed two of these snakelike things and wound them into a caduceus. Instantly, the healing staff came brilliantly alight in my hand. It radiated intense golden light. I touched Wanda with it, willing the transfer of healing energy.

Wanda promptly vanished.

I thought, "O Lord, what have I done this time?"

Then I saw Wanda flying about high in the air, frisky and mischievous, liberated from whatever had been sapping her vitality. I joined her and we flew off on various explorations. We investigated some parallel life experiences we may have shared, including one in Europe several centuries ago.

I wondered how much of this experience, so vivid and seemingly real to me, had been shared by Wanda, and whether the transfer of healing energy I had willed had actually taken place. I soon had my answer. Wanda called me early the next day. She told me she had dreamed I came to her and flooded her with light. She remembered dreaming in Latin, which related to those past-life explorations. She had awakened feeling buoyantly alive, released from the malaise of the previous weeks.

Wanda's sense of returning power prepared her for the *big* dream that followed, the night before she turned forty-four. She feels that this dream gave her a new lease on life, in the most literal sense:

> *I am climbing to the top of a mountain, where an awesome presence is waiting for me. I know that this is the divine power that sent the messenger who told me it is time for me to leave the earth. This entity moves like waves of light. It conveys its wishes and emotions by thought.*
>
> *I am terrified, but I never back away. The entity reminds me that I agreed before I came to this earth that I would leave when I was forty-three. I acknowledge this is true. I am shown the contract I signed.*
>
> *I agree that I signed this contract freely. But I argue passionately that there are good reasons why it should not be executed now. I tell the entity I didn't want to come here when I made the contract, but now I have people I love and people I believe I can help to heal, because of what I have gone through.*

I tell him, "You must know this, because you allowed me to discover my illness through dreams before my time was used up."

There is a time lapse. It seems like an eternity. Then I am presented with a new contract. I am given more time, to help others.

Wanda was trembling and sobbing when she woke from this dream, with the joy that clutches at the heart. "This was not like any dream I had before," she insists. "I was both awake and asleep, and I know the renegotiation was *real*. I was permitted to move beyond the messenger of my death to a spiritual authority who permitted me to alter the choice I made before I was born."

Wanda has kept her side of the bargain.

In active dreaming, she practices distant healing, working with colors and light energy. Her dream guides advise her on specific treatments. Among these guides, her deceased grandmother, who was an herbalist and "wise woman" in rural Alabama, and two Native Americans, one a Seneca who is also a healer in ordinary reality, have become especially important.

In one of her dream visitations, Wanda's grandmother took her into the woods and showed her a plant growing in a damp hollow. She made Wanda touch the ragged edges of the long green leaves, the spores underneath, and the furry stem, so she would be sure to know the plant again. She instructed Wanda on how to use this plant as a diuretic and to clear obstructions.

With a little research, Wanda was able to identify the plant as hart's-tongue fern, well-known in Europe but fairly rare in the United States. She found a supply and has used the plant successfully to treat various symptoms.

At the time of writing, Wanda's cancer had been in remission for over five years.

She believes she is living in a time of grace, called to love and serve. Her ability to distill *meaning* from the terror of her ordeals, and to build life-affirming purpose in others, are the gifts of dreaming. A gentle, unassuming person, she says simply, "I am alive because I dream."

I believe that is true of all of us.

THE CREATIVE POWER OF DREAMS

Whatever we build in the imagination will accomplish
itself in the circumstance of our lives.

W. B. Yeats

Sleepers are workers.

Heraclitus

I think continually of those who were truly great.
Who, from the womb, remembered the soul's history
Through corridors of light where the hours are suns,
Endless and singing. Whose lovely ambition
Was that their lips, still touched with fire,
Should tell of the spirit clothed from head to foot in song,
And who hoarded from spring branches
The desires falling across their bodies like blossoms.

Stephen Spender

GETTING THROUGH SCHOOL

*O*ne of the most common dream themes is of finding yourself back at school. You might be running late for a class or be in danger of failing an exam because you have not prepared. Maybe you fail to graduate. You may recognize one of your dreams in this version, contributed by the CEO of a chemicals manufacturing company:

Flunking My Finals

> *I'm back in college, taking my final exams. I haven't done my homework. I can't even make sense of some of the questions. I fail to get my degree and wake up so terrified I have to run downstairs to my den and check the certificates I have framed on my wall.*

At the time, the CEO was facing the challenge of introducing a new product to the market. His dream evidently held up a mirror to his situation, reminding him not only that he was being tested but that he needed to recognize that he was in a learning situation and might need to change his approach to his problems.

Such dreams are often lumped together, somewhat dismissively, as a classic "anxiety dream." In fact, when taken on their own merits, these dreams often prove to contain highly specific and helpful advice. For example, when I was pushing myself to work day and night to meet a December deadline I had set for a book, I had the following dream:

Summer Assignment

> *I'm back at university, in danger of losing my scholarship because of poor marks in one subject. My history professor tells me everything will be*

fine if I finish a paper to the best of my abilities over the summer vaca-
tion. He urges me to take my time and give this my best.

In Australia, where I went to university, December is high summer, so I did not miss the analogy between my dream professor's advice and the cruel deadline I had set for myself in waking time. The dream took me back to a literal episode from my undergraduate days, when I was allowed to make up for missed assignments by writing a long paper over the summer break. I got the message that I should stop worrying about deadlines and take the time needed to complete my book as a labor of love. My college paper had itself been a labor of love: my chosen theme was the paintings and personal mythology of Norman Lindsay, the Australian artist who shocked bourgeois sensibilities by filling his canvases with pagan myths and naked women. Lindsay is celebrated in a recent movie, *Sirens,* in which he is played by Sam Neill. Synchronistically, I wandered into a cinema where it was playing a week or so after my dream and was munching my popcorn before I realized that the film explores the same theme as my college paper.

In a woman's dream, the back-to-school theme takes a different twist:

Learning a Foreign Language

I am back in school, learning a foreign language. I am told that if I graduate, I will be given a higher degree in philosophy. The work is hard, but a teaching assistant gives me private coaching. He takes me to a place in the deep woods. He tells me I'll find it easier to study there.

The motto this dreamer formulated was "I need to express myself a different way and get back in touch with nature." She started making weekend trips to a state forest.

Maybe you have experienced an Ouspensky dream, like the one described in his *Strange Life of Ivan Osokin,* a dream in which you find yourself back in school, with all your present memories, and the whole thing seems thoroughly real.[1] I have recorded many dreams that are variations on this theme. In some of them, I want to light up a cigar or pipe in school and have to remind myself this isn't allowed. In others, I try to find crafty ways to make use of information or skills I gained twenty years after leaving school without exciting the suspicions of classmates or teachers. Though I can generally find messages for my waking life, such dreams often feel more like journeys through time than routine "anxiety dreams."

In the dreams of schoolchildren, the theme is "back to the future" rather than "back to school."

Evan was an athletic, hyperactive teenager who dropped out of high school before graduating. He was popular with girls and had a good time for a few months running around in an old pickup. But after a succession of dead-end jobs at a fast-food restaurant, a supermarket checkout, and a factory assembly line, it came home to him that his worried parents might be right: his job prospects were going to be grim so long as he lacked the most basic educational qualifications. He agreed to go back to school to work for his high school diploma. As before, he had a hard time knuckling down to his studies. By his own account, a series of dreams pulled him through:

The Room That Got a View

I am walking toward a dock, some kind of waterfront area. Two men are hanging around. One looks pretty sharp. He's wearing a white uniform. The other looks crapped out. He's a blue-collar type, in his work clothes. I get the feeling both of these men are me, and that this has something to do with my direction. We don't speak to each other. I walk on into a big narrow building.

This building is a place I keep going back to in my dreams.

In the first dream, when I saw the two guys on the dock, I really hated the feeling I got inside that building. I found myself in a bare room with no windows and no doors. I felt suffocated in there. I woke up gasping for air.

I didn't get everything this dream was telling me at the outset. I thought about the guy in the white uniform. He could have been Navy. Then my mom ran into a man who was in the Coast Guard, and he set up an interview. The Coast Guard said they would take me if I got my high school equivalency. That perked me up a bit in class because I've always loved the water.

When I started doing better in school, my dream building changed. The walls were no longer bare. There were windows, looking out over water and a big city in the distance. There was a lot more life and action, inside and out. The week I finally made the grade, the dream room had doors leading out to the sea. They were wide-open. Then the Coast Guard sent me down to Cape May and I found myself in a building a lot like the one in my dream.

Listening to this account, I felt at times that I was sharing a happier version of Ouspensky's story. Now the schoolboy remembers, through dreams, a future that he enjoys and is able to steer his life toward it.

If we are alive and growing, our lives will never cease to be learning experiences. Dreams not only take us back to school; they help us to get through the school of life.

DREAM REHEARSALS

*T*hrough dream radar, we are constantly tracking forward, exploring what lies around the corner. These scouting missions include rehearsing for challenges that lie ahead. As you become a conscious dreamer, you can make conscious use of this dream function to rehearse for future situations: a job interview, a speech at the board meeting, your appointment with your baby in the delivery room.

Recent research indicates that pregnant mothers who remember and work with dreams of childbirth may experience easier labor and fewer complications than the average. As Alan Siegel reports in *Dreams That Can Change Your Life,* fathers also rehearse for childbirth; pregnancy dreams are commonly reported by men as well as women. A common dream motif for pregnant fathers is "fetal identification," in which the dreamer may find himself emerging from a cave through a narrow passage, bursting from an underwater bubble or fighting his way to the end of a swimming pool. Such dreams are often accompanied by a deep sense of bonding with the unborn child.[2] In the age of Lamaze classes, it is not surprising that many male pregnancy dreams show the father as an active participant in childbirth. In a luminous, happy dream before the birth of my youngest daughter, I underwent an operation that seemingly enabled me to give birth at the same time as my wife; I ran through a sparkling creekbed to bring this news to my wife.

Dream rehearsal, both in spontaneous sleep dreams and through conscious dreaming, is especially helpful during major changes. These may be predictable life passages such as leaving home, finding a mate, starting a career or a family, changing jobs or partners, midlife transition, the loss of close friends or relatives, and preparation for the soul's journey after death. Or they may be sudden upheavals that overthrow stable patterns, shatter our illusions of control, and provide new opportunities for spiritual growth. At such turning points, as Alan Siegel observes, "we experience a bittersweet sense of the meaning of life. Our defenses are down and we feel a now-or-never sense of urgency. At these times we are more open to taking risks and making dramatic positive changes than we would be during more stable times."[3]

The dreams that accompany and follow such crises as job loss, sudden illness, or a family breakup can help us to grasp the opportunity for new growth and to find a new balance. More than likely, your dreams showed you these turning points long before you came to them and have already rehearsed you for dealing with them, whether or not you have been paying attention.

Dream rehearsal is especially helpful if you are considering changing jobs or need to find new employment. This was a major theme for a dream group I conducted in the winter of 1994–95 for New York State employees who were understandably concerned about job security in the wake of the cutbacks promised by the newly elected Republican administration.

One employee in that group reported a series of dreams in which she had pleasant encounters with acquaintances who had retired from state government. She found one of them living at an idyllic wooded location near the Canadian border. She had not seen this person in years. She was interested to find, in the dream, that her friend seemed to be leading a vigorous, active life, including canoeing and cross-country skiing. Work with this dream led the dreamer to formulate the following message: "Retirement can be a great opportunity for new growth." She proceeded to check out the early-retirement packages that were announced in conjunction with the cutbacks in state government.

Megan, another dreamer in the group, had already arranged to switch jobs. She was about to follow her supervisor, who had found a position with a private corporation. The week before she moved into her new office, she dreamed that this supervisor was rude and snappish toward her, though she had always found him charming and patient in waking life. He turned his back on her as he spoke. In her dream, Megan burst into tears and wondered if she should quit her job. Waking, she was troubled by the prospect that their relationship might deteriorate among the competitive stresses of a new environment. The only positive note she could find, as we worked with this dream, was that she felt her supervisor was not angry with her, but with other people in the company who were doing something behind the scenes. One week later, the scene from her dream was played out in waking life. The supervisor was cold and brusque and swiveled his chair during the conversation so he was looking out the window, with his back to Megan. She reminded herself of her dream insight: "He isn't mad at *me*." This helped her control her emotions. Instead of bursting into tears, she did some checking and learned that her supervisor had just discovered he was the target of some office intrigues.

Because dreams are wishes of the soul, dream rehearsals for job change take us beyond horizontal agendas—will I get the job, the money, the plaque on the wall—to the issue of whether a possible career move will bring a happier, more fulfilling, and creative life. A computer programmer who had just received a promotion that brought with it a big pay increase reported a dream in which her workspace was so cramped she felt she could hardly breathe. In the same dream, she found herself developing tunnel vision before going completely blind in one eye. This dream led her to make a more thorough exploration of the work conditions she could now look forward to, and to pay attention to a possible literal health warning about the effects of eyestrain associated with computer work, as well as the symbolic message she expressed as follows: "By pushing myself up the career ladder at the expense of my personal life, I'm in danger of developing tunnel vision."

One personal note: To make best use of dream rehearsal in waking situations, we need to get over the gee-whiz reaction we sometimes experience when we see a dream scenario being played out in ordinary reality. I once dreamed I visited a powerful executive in a curious office in a high-rise building. The office was shaped like an elongated triangle, tapering to a point behind the boss's desk. Another interesting detail in the dream was that when I arrived for this meeting, the boss came out of a men's room near the reception desk and greeted me before I had announced myself to the receptionist. Many months later, my agent set up an appointment for me with Tom McCormack, the president of St. Martin's Press, and I made my first visit, in waking life, to the Flatiron Building at 175 Fifth Avenue in New York City. I was bowled over when Tom walked out of a men's room near the reception desk and greeted me. My sense of wonder increased when he showed me into his office and I found myself inside the elongated triangle from my dream. I was so fascinated by the way my dream was being played out, step by step, that I found it quite difficult, in the conversation, to express myself freely and spontaneously—another learning experience.

— A DREAM ROOM OF YOUR OWN

Whatever your field of interest, you can benefit from dream rehearsal. I know a prominent hostess who insists she will not decide on a menu or finalize seating arrangements until she has pictured the whole evening in a "daydream." Stephen LaBerge reports the case of a surgeon who claims he halves the time his operations might normally take by rehearsing them in lucid dreams or half-dream states. As you develop your gifts as a conscious dreamer, you will find you are able to apply the techniques of dream rehearsal to any situation that is looming in your life. This is more effective and far more realistic than (say) trying out lines you might use on a new date or a prospective boss while you look at yourself in the bathroom mirror.

By this stage, you have probably discovered special places in the dreamworld to which you can return. Perhaps you have already guessed that you have the power to create (or at least cocreate) locales in nonordinary reality where you can do special things. Such created locales in the dreamscape can provide an ideal environment for researching, as well as rehearsing, new projects. They may be places where you can rendezvous with teachers in your field. Your selection of a dream workspace will be shaped by your interests. If you are a visual artist, you may choose to visit a dream studio where you can experiment with new styles and media, or a dream gallery where you can inspect finished works you might choose to reproduce. If you are a trial attorney, you might decide to go to a law library where you can look up obscure precedents quite painlessly, or to a forensic laboratory where evidence is evaluated.

If you are an active dreamer on a shamanic path, your possibilities are limitless. I return in dreaming to many stable locales in the dreamscape, some of them shared with dreamers of various traditions. One of my favorites is a way station I picture as the Gallery of Time, from which I make dream safaris into other historical periods, from the future as well as the past.

Don't foreshorten your experiences in this territory by telling yourself they are only "made up." The Persian visionary philosopher Sohrawardi speaks eloquently on this theme:

> When you learn that there exists a world with dimension and extension other than the world of the senses . . . a world of innumerable cities, do not hastily cry "lie," because the pilgrims of the spirit succeed in contemplating this world and they find there every object of their desire.[4]

CREATIVE INCUBATION

A man will not dream of something to which he has never given a moment's thought," suggested Artemidorus, the Greek dream interpreter.[5] There is truth in this statement, which might be expressed somewhat differently: What you are likely to remember from your dreams and be able to put to use is related to your level of knowledge and understanding in waking life. You could spend night after night in private dream tutorials with the Greek philosophers, but if they insist on communicating in Greek and you have no knowledge of that language (or willingness to learn it), their conversation will be "all Greek" to you. I have had a number of dream conversations with quantum physicists and microbiologists who explained their theories with elegant diagrams and formulas drawn on blackboards. I am embarrassed to report that I lost most of this information, since their vocabulary was more foreign to me than Greek, despite my efforts to learn from the work of David Bohm, Fred Alan Wolf, David Peat, Rupert Sheldrake, and others.

The upside of this discussion is that if you have been putting your waking energy into a certain area, you are likely to receive further guidance during your sleep. You can incubate a dream to solve problems or provide creative inspiration in an intentional way, as we have seen. Or you can practice *spontaneous* dream incubation, by focusing your waking attention and imagination on the issue you wish to explore, especially late at night, just before going to bed. Because energy flows where attention goes, the dreams that follow may help you to go more deeply into your subject, find solutions to problems that baffled you, or lead you to approach the whole theme in a new way.

Hermann Heimholtz, a nineteenth-century German scientist, analyzed the process that had led to his discoveries and concluded that there are three basic stages in a creative breakthrough. The first is *saturation:* immersing yourself in your field of research, reading, consulting, gathering your materials. The second is *incubation,* which for Heimholtz meant "doing nothing": you give up actively trying to solve your problem. You take a walk, go for a drive, or (best of all) take a nap. You open yourself to sources deeper than waking awareness. The third stage of creative discovery is defined by Heimholtz as *illumination:* it often comes in a flash, and it comes from the deep. It may still need to be tested, verified, and integrated into your waking project.[6]

"Eureka" dreams have been central to the work of many famous writers, composers, scientists, and discoverers. Here are some examples:

⟶ DREAM DISCOVERIES

• William Blake made several attempts to devise a cheaper way to engrave the illustrations for his poems. He was stumped until his deceased younger brother Robert appeared to him in a dream and demonstrated a method of copper engraving that Blake immediately checked and put to work.[7]

• The scientist Otto Loewi had a hunch early in his career that nerve impulses might be chemically transmitted. Unable to come up with an experiment to prove this, he forgot about his hypothesis for seventeen years. Then, in the middle of the night, he woke from a dream in which he glimpsed a way of testing his theory. He jotted down some notes and went back to sleep. In the morning, to his bitter frustration, he found he could not decipher his scrawl. His dream source was generous. Loewi dreamed the experiment again the following night. This time, he took no chances; he rushed to his laboratory at 3 A.M. and performed an experiment on a frog's heart, as indicated by the dream. This dream-directed experiment inspired the work for which Loewi was awarded the Nobel Prize.[8]

• Many composers have revealed that some of their best music was the gift of dreams. Beethoven composed a canon in his sleep. Tartini sat spellbound in a dream while "the devil" played a violin sonata of wild beauty; waking, he transcribed it to the best of his abilities. Wagner disclosed that *Tristan und Isolde* flowed straight from a dream. Songwriter Steve Allen dreamed the lyrics of his hit "This Could Be the Start of Something Big." Billy Joel has described how the music for many of his songs has been the gift of his dreams, and in the case of one song (appropriately, "River of Dreams"), some of the lyrics as well.[9]

• Even rationalist philosophers are the beneficiaries of dream breakthroughs. A series of disturbing dreams marked a watershed in the life and theories of René Descartes. Voltaire, a livelier spirit, reported friskier dreams, in which he composed poetry and satires.[10]

• One of my favorite examples is the case of Elias Howe, the inventor of the modern sewing machine. Howe was stumped by one detail: where to put the eye in the machine needle. Then he had a scary dream in which "savages" took him captive. They danced around him with upraised spears, threatening to kill him unless he completed his invention. Terrified, Howe noticed something odd about the jabbing spears. They had eye-shaped holes near their tips. Waking, he realized he had been given the solution to his problem; he needed to place the eye of the sewing-machine needle near the point. The modern sewing machine, and a new phase of the industrial revolution, were born.[11]

The twilight zone of reverie or conscious dreaming is especially fertile ground for creative breakthroughs. Robert Louis Stevenson held his interviews with the "brownies" who helped him weave the threads of his stories while he lay on his bed in a half-dream state, one arm raised to the vertical from the elbow so he would not fall into a deeper sleep.[12] Salvador Dalí profited from catnaps in which he might hold a coin or some other metal object in his hand so that its fall would pull him back from sleep, and the possible loss of the images that were flowing to him in this relaxed state. Einstein revealed that the theory of relativity came to him while he was in a similar twilight state of consciousness. Friedrich Kekulé had racked his brain for years, trying to crack a chemical mystery: the molecular structure of benzene. The answer came to him one evening when he dozed off in front of the fire. He dreamed of atoms forming long chains, twisting and turning like snakes. As he watched, one of the snakes seized its own tail like the mythical uroboros. Kekulé woke in high excitement. Thanks to his snake dream, he now recognized that the structure of benzene is a closed carbon ring. This dream insight revolutionized modern chemistry and won Kekulé a Nobel Prize.[13]

This chronicle of dream discovery could easily be expanded into other fields. The process at work here is relevant to any field of endeavor in which you are seeking to push your limits. Jack Nicklaus dreamed up a new golf grip that made a winning difference in his game. Sports psychologist Paul Tholey has described how he has employed lucid dreaming techniques to help world-class skiers train their reflexes, explore the terrain, and prepare for the snap decisions required on the slopes.[14]

The common factor, in all these examples, is that the people who found the keys to creative breakthroughs in their dreams came prepared. As Rollo May observed in *The Courage to Create*, "insight never comes hit or miss, but in accordance with a pattern of which one essential component is our own commitment."[15] Whether you are seeking creative guidance from dreams to improve your golf stroke, write the great American novel, or find a cure for AIDS, the first step is to immerse yourself in your chosen field. The next is to stop trying so hard: take a long walk, go swimming, mow the lawn. When you lie down, make it your intention simply to open yourself to the flow of images from your dream source. Be prepared to be surprised! Your dreams may give you the missing link—the new golf grip or the eye of the needle. Or they may push you to re-vision your problem in a completely fresh way, as in my dream of the master chef who refused to work with my menu.

You may enjoy experimenting with some more specific techniques for seeking creative guidance from dreams. Here is one I have found useful:

— EXERCISE: CALLING IN AN EXPERT

1. Think about someone you regard as a master in your chosen field, a person who was consummately gifted and successful in this area. It will help if you focus on someone for whom you feel a strong affinity. The character you choose may already have appeared in some of your dreams.

2. Ask for guidance on your current project. If you are a therapist, you may want to seek insight from Jung. If you are speaking in public, you may consider asking Laurence Olivier for tips. If you are a painter, you may want to ask Georgia O'Keeffe for advice.

3. Hold the image of your chosen teacher in your mind as you relax toward sleep. If you are able to sustain a conscious dream state, you may now be able to go to a dream locale where you can rendezvous with your teacher. If you fall asleep, catch whatever you can when you wake.

4. Write down, or sketch, whatever comes to you, as rapidly as possible, without editing.

5. Be prepared for your previous way of approaching your project to be given a distinct tilt!

WRITING FROM DREAMS

*A*s a writer, I have always found dreams a principal source of creative energy and inspiration. On the most basic level, keeping a dream journal gets me started each day; I am writing before it ever occurs to me to ask myself what I am going to write about. This brings into play the writing "muscles," which may later be applied to specific projects that are waiting. In her wonderful book, *The Artist's Way,* Julia Cameron advises would-be writers to fill three pages of longhand every morning with whatever thoughts and feelings come into their heads.[16] If you don't have dreams, this is fine. If you do have dreams, it's better: you have themes already waiting, and they can lead you in many promising directions.

Many scenes, characters, and plotlines in my books have come straight from my dreams, as have research tips, bibliographic references, and guidance on editors and agents. I frequently ask for dream help with a project or try to shift into a dreamlike state of consciousness to visualize a scene, consult with a character or inner teacher, or leaf through unpublished material in my dream library.

Turning dreams into stories is not necessarily straightforward. Like much of waking life, dreams often lack shape and resolution. To turn a dream report into a narrative that can be relished, for its own sake, by others requires craft and cunning and also an element of *distance* that is likely to be lacking at the outset. Turning a dream report into a story can be marvelous, spontaneous therapy because it requires you to look at your dream self (perhaps your many dream selves) with the detachment of an observer on a higher plane. As you now proceed to exercise the godlike powers of the narrator to solve the mystery and invent a satisfactory ending for the story, you may find you are resolving some of your deepest issues.

Exercise:

⟶ DREAM INTO STORY 1: BECOMING THE NARRATOR

1. Find the dream that is plucking at you now. You may wish to experiment with a dream that is mysterious, troubling, or unresolved.

2. Now create a fictional character. You are going to attribute your dream experience to this invented personage, preferably as a series of literal events in this character's life. You may write in the third person or the first person, but you should take care to distinguish your fictional character's identity from your own.

3. Write a short scene placing your character in the thick of the action. Be as graphic as possible, and don't forget to describe your character's feelings and sensations. Relate the elements you have borrowed from the dream to the rest of this person's life. Perhaps these elements reflect a recurring situation, like always getting involved with the wrong man or fleeing a challenge.

4. Expand this scene into a short story in which your character solves a mystery, makes better choices, or wins through her trials to a happy ending.

You will probably find it helpful to allow yourself only limited time for both writing phases of this exercise—say, fifteen minutes for step 3 and no more than one hour for step 4. By setting the clock running, you limit the scope for interference by your inner critic; you simply have no time to worry about the quality of your final product.

Through this exercise, you can develop the discipline of looking at your everyday personality, as well as your dream self, from a different perspective. As you exercise the powers of the narrator over your character's fortunes, you may become more aware of your ability to reshape your own thoughts and feelings and the situations that arise from them.

━ DREAM INTO STORY 2: BORROWED DREAMS

In workshops, I find that one of the fastest and most powerful ways to get people to overcome performance anxiety and doubts about whether they can write is to encourage them to borrow another person's experience and make that the basis for a story. I call this privateering—a form of licensed piracy. The game is best played within a small group, say six to eight people, but you can also play it with a single partner. Here's how it works:

1. Take turns sharing your dreams. Remember to give each dream a title and describe your feelings and sensations.

2. Listen to each dream as the raw material for a story. Which elements could you borrow to make a story of your own? Maybe all you would borrow is the title or a peripheral detail or the sense of fear or elation. Maybe you want to borrow the whole of a dream as the basis for a thriller or a fantasy tale. Maybe you are tempted to steal a dream, attribute it (as is) to a fictional character, and locate the dream in the midst of her life.

3. Choose the dream you will use as the springboard for your own storymaking. There are no rules from this point, but here are some examples of different approaches:

Example A: A woman recounts a dream whose central image is of trying to cut up writhing snakes with a butter knife. Borrowing only this single image, an Irishwoman improvises a stunning scene that conveys all the rage and frustration of a wife trapped in a miserable marriage, through her reactions to the bucket of live eels her husband has left her to gut and prepare for dinner. As she reads the scene, we can *hear* the obscene sucking and slithering of the eels in the bucket.

Example B: A man borrows only the title of a woman's dream, "Living for Oblivion," and its underlying theme of drug addiction and wasted lives. He roughs out a terrific science fantasy centered on a wonder drug of the future that is the answer to all known human disease but has an unfortunate side effect: it kills human emotion and desire, so that the species ceases to love and to procreate.

Example C: A man shares a recurring dream that has come to him since kindergarten—of seeing the house collapsing around him, "melting like ice cream," and seeking safety under his father's car. A woman from Florida borrows the whole dream and locates it in the life of a person who lives in hurricane country and takes shelter under the car when the fury of the storm is unleashed.

4. Share the profits from your literary privateering with your partner.

THE WAY OF THE BEGETTER

*T*he Romans never described a person as a genius. They might say, "Apollonius *has* a genius"—i.e., a special relationship with a tutelary spirit. The word *genius* is related to *gignere,* which means to engender or "beget." It implies reproductive energy, the power of inseminating new life. The Romans called the marriage bed *genialis lectus.* As observed by Jungian analyst and classicist Marie-Louise von Franz, "this referred not only to sexual potency but also to the qualities that today we would call psychic vitality, temperament, resourcefulness and a lively imagination.'[7] In a well-bred Roman household, a statuette representing the personal genius of the father of the family usually stood near the hearth in the kitchen. It might be the figure of a young man, holding a horn of plenty or a phallus or a snake. The woman of the house was believed to have her own guardian spirit, or "Juno," who embodied the power of giving birth. In the Roman conception, each of us is born with a personal relationship with a spiritual patron, or genius, who is the source of creative energy.

James Russell Lowell was close to this perception when he wrote: "Talent is that which is in a man's power; genius is that in whose power a man is."

To live and work creatively, we need to make room for this energy. The Romans were on to something. To bring something new into the world is to give birth. We see this in the pregnancy dreams that are not about physical childbirth but about something new that is borning inside us. We can feel it in our bodies in a period of creative gestation.

When one of my books is ready to be born, I feel pregnant. I mean that in a quite literal sense. My appetites change. I develop odd cravings at strange hours. I forget to eat or sleep for days at a time, then walk out of a dinner party to crash or feed my face with something I wouldn't normally touch. I develop morning sickness. When my new baby is ready to come out, I can't stop the contractions, even though sometimes, like a woman I once heard screaming in a maternity ward, I want to yell, "This has to stop!" There is no dope, no epidural, no C-section available to dull the experience or shortcut the labor; whatever is in me has to come out the old-fashioned way. There *is* an equivalent to birthing in water, the blessed gift of going into a state of flow, in which I relax into the rhythms of what is fighting its way into the world.

The act of creation is perhaps the closest a man may come to a woman's pain and joy in the hours of childbirth. I will modify that statement in one respect. I once grew a kidney stone, and on a frigid night in midwinter, I felt a dragon's egg was trying to hatch in my belly. Maybe that was the closest I have come, in this body, to sharing a new mother's pain in the delivery room.

As Erich Neumann remarked, "Every human being is by nature creative. Yet one of the gravest and most menacing problems in our Western civilization arises from the fact that this civilization cuts man off from his natural creativity."[18]

To choose and act creatively, we must be able to put our commonplace selves, with their reliance on structures and schedules, on one side and make room for the source energy of the begetter. Creative inspiration, as all artists and discoverers know, comes through spontaneous combustion between the waking mind and other levels of consciousness. "I know now," wrote Yeats, "that revelation is from the self, but from that age-old memoried self, that shares the elaborate shell of the mollusc and the child in the womb, that teaches the birds to make their nest; and that genius is a crisis that joins that buried self for certain moments to our daily trivial mind."[19]

You cannot program a creative breakthrough, but you can clear a space where it may come about. Dreamwork is a wonderful aid to the creative process, because the source of dream images and the source of creative inspiration are not separate. When you resolve to catch your dreams, you are telling your creative source, "I am available. I'm listening." When you record your dreams, you are developing the arts of storytelling. You will discover your gifts as a writer, and if you are already a writer, you will find you have done your "warm-up" exercises almost effortlessly and are ready to go the distance. Best of all, through dreamwork you are constantly learning to approach challenges from new angles, in a spirit of play. The Romans believed that a person's genius rejoiced in good living, in laughter, in healthy sex, in having fun. Forget to play, and you are not working with your genius, for whom play is the only thing in mortal affairs worth taking seriously.

NOTES

INTRODUCTION: SUMMONED BY DREAMS

1. The inscription Jung placed over the gate of his tower read *Philemonis Sacrum—Fausti Poenitentia* ("Shrine of Philemon—Repentance of Faust—"). C. G. Jung, *Memories, Dreams, Reflections,* ed. Aniela Jaffe, trans. Richard and Clara Winston (New York: Vintage Books, 1965), 235 n.

2. James Cowan, *Letters from a Wild State: An Aboriginal Perspective* (Shaftesbury, Dorset: Element Books, 1991).

3. The Kagwahiv describe their shamans as *ipají,* which means "possessed of power." This power is gained from dreams and exercised in the dream state, and it is often said that "anyone who dreams has a little *ipají.* Waud Kracke, "Myths in dreams, thought in images: an Amazonian contribution to the psychoanalytic theory of primary process," in Barbara Tedlock, ed., *Dreaming: Anthropological and Psychological Interpretations* (Santa Fe: School of American Research Press, 1992), 34. On the shaman as dreamer in other South American cultures, see Lawrence E. Sullivan, *Icanchu's Drum: An Orientation to Meaning in South American Religions* (New York: Macmillan, 1988).

4. Robert Moss, "Blackrobes and Dreamers: Jesuit Accounts of the Shamanic Dream Practices of the Northern Iroquoians," *Shaman's Drum* 28 (1992).

5. J. N. B. Hewitt, "The Iroquoian Concept of the Soul," *Journal of American Folk-Lore* 8 (1895), 107–16. On the conception of the "free soul" or dreambody in other American Indian traditions, see Ake Hultkrantz, *Conceptions of the Soul among North American Indians* (Stockholm: Ethnographical Museum of Sweden, 1953).

6. After his parting of the ways with Freud, Jung reported, "I avoided all theoretical points of view and simply helped the patients to understand the dreamimages by themselves, without application of rules and theories. . . . That is how dreams are intended. They are the facts from which we must proceed." *Memories, Dreams, Reflections,* 170–71.

7. Medicine Grizzlybear Lake, *Native Healer: Initiation into an Ancient Art* (Wheaton, Ill.: Quest Books, 1991), 28.

8. Marc de Civrieux, "Medatia, a Makiritare Shaman's Tale," in David M. Guss, ed., *The Language of the Birds* (San Francisco, North Point Press, 1985). In-

terestingly, the Makiritare word for a powerful dream is *adekato,* which means literally a "soul journey"—i.e., a journey by the *akato,* the dreambody or double: ibid., 74.

— CHAPTER 1: BECOMING A DREAM CATCHER

1. On Islamic dream traditions, see G. E. von Grünebaum and Roger Caillois, eds., *The Dream and Human Societies* (Berkeley and Los Angeles: University of California Press, 1966).

2. Roseanne Armitage, Aaron Rochlen, and Thomas Fitch, "Dream recall and major depression" (paper presented at the XI conference of the Association for the Study of Dreams, Leiden University, 1994).

3. This is an understanding widely shared among shamanic traditions; cf. my essay "Blackrobes and Dreamers" in *Shaman's Drum* 28 (Summer 1992). For another view of dreams and the early survival of the human species, see Christopher Evans, *Landscapes of the Night* (New York: Viking, 1983).

4. Hans Dieter Betz, ed., *The Greek Magical Papyri in Translation* (Chicago: University of Chicago Press, 1986), 1:137.

5. Henry Cornelius Agrippa, *Three Books of Occult Philosophy* (1531), trans. James Freake, ed. Donald Tyson (St. Paul, Minn.: Llewellyn, 1993), 403.

6. Jeremy Taylor, *Where People Fly and Water Runs Uphill: Using Dreams to Tap the Wisdom of the Unconscious* (New York: Warner Books, 1992), 202.

7. Richard Winstedt, *The Malay Magician* (Kuala Lumpur: Oxford University Press, 1982). Jeffrey A. McNeely and Paul Spencer Wachtel, *Soul of the Tiger* (New York: Doubleday, 1988), explores several variants of the "tiger shaman" in Southeast Asia.

8. The person who first introduced "Senoi dream theory" to the West was Kilton Stewart, an adventurous American anthropologist, who first learned about the tribe when he visited Malaya in 1934 and was taken under the wing of Pat Noone. Stewart's 1951 article in *Complex* magazine has been widely reprinted. Patricia Garfield and Ann Faraday later made personal studies of Senoi practice. The key principles in Senoi dreamwork, as presented by Stewart and Garfield, could be stated as follows:

1. You should always confront and overcome adversaries in dreams.

2. You should pursue pleasurable experiences in dreams all the way.

3. You should try to achieve a positive outcome inside your dreams and bring back a gift.

G. William Domhoff challenged whether the Senoi actually practice the dream theory attributed to them in *The Mystique of Dreams: A Search for Utopia through Senoi Dream Theory* (Berkeley, University of California Press, 1985), sparking a lively controversy that is still being waged. In an epistolary debate with Domhoff in 1995 issues of the ASD *Newsletter,* Jeremy Taylor makes the point that Senoi "dream theory" caught on in America because it *works.*

⎯ CHAPTER 2: NINE KEYS TO YOUR DREAMS

1. The gathering of first impressions is very different from the Freudian method of free association, which Jung criticized because it can produce a chain of irrelevancies leading further and further away from the dream and its meaning; Jung encouraged *direct* association, focusing on the dream itself. While free association played in an office may lead you away from the dream, your *first* associations, coming to you in a relaxed state at home, may help you get back into the dream.

2. W. Y. Evans-Wentz, *The Fairy Faith in Celtic Countries* (New York: Citadel Press, 1990), 288–89, 374–75.

3. Ann Faraday, *Dream Power* (New York: Coward, McCann and Geoghegan, 1972).

4. Cf. A. Irving Hallowell, "The Role of Dreams in Ojibwa Culture," in von Grünebaum and Caillois, eds., *The Dream and Human Societies.*

5. Cf. Roberta Louis, "An Evening of Dream Theatre with Jessica Allen," *Shaman's Drum* 28 (1992).

6. C. G. Jung et al., *Man and His Symbols* (London: Aldus Books, 1964); Barbara Walker, *The Women's Encyclopedia of Myths and Secrets* (San Francisco: Harper & Row, 1983); and J. E. Cirlot, *A Dictionary of Symbols,* trans. Jack Sage (New York: Philosophical Library, 1962) are good basic guides for symbol explorers. David Fontana's *The Secret Language of Dreams* (San Francisco: Chronicle Books, 1994) is a handsomely illustrated visual key to common dream motifs.

7. Artemidorus, *The Interpretation of Dreams: Oneirocritica,* trans. R. J. White (Park Ridge, N.J.: Noyes Press, 1975).

8. Cf. Frederick S. Perls, *Gestalt Therapy Verbatim* (Lafayette, Calif.: Real People Press, 1969).

—— CHAPTER 3: EXPLORING DREAMS WITH PARTNERS

1. See Montague Ullman and Nan Zimmerman, *Working with Dreams* (Los Angeles: Jeremy P. Tarcher, 1979) and Jeremy Taylor, *Where People Fly.*

—— CHAPTER 4: CONSCIOUS DREAMING

1. For a passionate critique of "control dreaming," see Strephon Kaplan-Williams, *The Elements of Dreamwork* (Shaftesbury, Dorset: Element Books, 1990).

2. Carlos Castaneda's mentor, Don Juan, instructs him to "set up dreaming" by reminding himself, each time he catches sight of his hands in waking life, that the next time he sees his hands in a dream he will remember that this is a dream. Your hands are supposed to become your *dreamsign;* as you start to make a habitual connection between seeing your hands and dreaming—the theory runs—you'll become lucid in more and more of your dreams. I have met few people who have had any consistent success with this method. A more promising variation on this technique is to ask yourself, "Am I dreaming?" whenever you look in a mirror. (Looking in mirrors in your dreams is always a worthwhile exercise in itself.)

I have heard similarly mixed reports about expensive devices like Nova-Dreamer and DreamLight that are supposed to help you become aware you are dreaming by beeping and flashing red lights during REM sleep. A *Life* magazine researcher tried one and woke to find she had flung the device across the room; she had no memory of any dreams, lucid or otherwise (*Life,* September 1995).

3. P. D. Ouspensky, *A New Model of the Universe* (New York: Vintage Books, 1971).

4. Tarthang Tulku, *Openness Mind* (Berkeley, Calif.: Dharma Publishing, 1978). On conscious dreaming as a core discipline in Tibetan dream yoga, see W. Y. Evans-Wentz, *Tibetan Yoga and Secret Doctrines* (New York: Oxford University Press, 1958) and Namkai Norbu, *Dream Yoga and the Practice of Natural Light,* ed. Michael Katz (Ithaca, N.Y.: Snow Lion, 1992). Here is a simplified version of a classic Tibetan incubation exercise for conscious dreaming:

Tibetan Method for Entering Conscious Dreams

1. Lie down and focus on your intention to remain aware that you are dreaming as you enter the dreamstate.

2. Lie on your side, with your knees slightly bent.

3. Hold your hands, palms together, under your chin, with your fingertips touching your left cheek.

4. Visualize a luminous blue lotus flower inside your throat. See the flower gently open until it is in full bloom.

5. While the flower is opening, visualize a glowing white light at its center. As you focus on the light, you will hear the "sound syllable" *aum* in your inner ear.

6. Continue to focus on the picture image, and the sound. Maintain your posture and your calm intention to remain fully conscious—until new images rise and you awaken to the fact that you are dreaming.

5. Robert A. Monroe, *Journeys out of the Body* (New York: Anchor Books, 1977), 195.

6. Arthur Avalon (Sir John Woodroffe), *The Serpent Power: The Secrets of Tantric and Shaktic Yoga* (New York: Dover, 1974).

7. Emanuel Swedenborg, *Heaven and Hell,* trans. George F. Dole (New York: Swedenborg Foundation, 1976).

8. Henry Corbin, *Avicenna and the Visionary Recital,* trans. Willard K. Trask (Princeton: Bolingen/Princeton University Press, 1990).

9. Johannes Wilbert, "Tobacco and Shamanistic Ecstasy among the Warao Indians of Venezuela," in Peter T. Furst, ed., *Flesh of the Gods* (New York: Praeger, 1972).

10. The princess Nausicaa, who finds Odysseus washed up on the Phaeacian shore because of a dream sent by a goddess, tells her attendants, "There is no man on earth, nor ever will be, who would dare to set hostile feet on Phaeacian soil. The gods are too fond of us for that." Homer, *The Odyssey,* trans E. V. Rieu (Harmondsworth: Penguin, 1963), 107.

11. The mother wrote the following account of her conversation with her son the evening after surgery: "He came into the room that evening and sat down on the side of the bed, very quiet, leaning close to me. He asked if I remembered my surgery. 'No,' I said. He said he had gone to the waiting room when I left for surgery. He had fallen into a deep sleep, waking almost the moment the surgery was over. Conscious he was dreaming, he had entered the operating theater with the intention of entering *my* dreams. But he felt uncomfortable because he realized that someone else was in the room, in a state similar to his own. He relaxed when he recognized the other person as my late father. He saw my father hovering over the operating table, making sure that all went well.

"Another presence was in the room. He described the presence as having no body but being filled with light.

"Then he decided to find out where I was. He found himself standing next to Robert and Marcia—we were close family friends—who were both telling me I must try to focus on something humorous. I was uncooperative and distracted, so Robert told me to think about the fun we had had at his fortieth birthday party. My son, who had not attended his party, now saw me standing in a doorway, laughing, with Robert behind me and a tall, very thin woman in a black dress in front of me. She was playing with a small diamond on a chain around my neck. When I asked him to describe the woman, he said she was black, with a large mouth and remarkably smooth skin, with no lines on her face. This was an exact description of a woman at Robert's party my son had never met. I had also been wearing the diamond pendant that night."

I can add one personal comment to this fascinating account. At the time of the surgery, I was focused on sending healing thoughts to the mother. Unaware of this, her son discovered me in his conscious dream.

12. I use the term *shared dreaming* to describe *intentional* dream encounters between two or more partners. There are many other varieties of dream overlap, or cross-dreaming. Sleep partners often report overlapping dream experiences. With or without the waking intention to do so, dreamers are constantly "dropping in" on each other. Someone else's dream memories may hold the key to your own dream, even if you do not remember encountering that other person in your dream. For example, I once had a powerful dream in which I had to undergo many tests and ordeals before I was permitted to take my place with a circle of warriors in winged helmets and ancient armor around an amethyst fire. A fellow dream explorer I had not noticed in my dream told me the next day that in *her* dream she saw me seated at a "purple fire" with a group of men that included a Native American shaman she named. I had not recognized him as one of the figures in my dream, but her insight led me to study with him for a time. Dreamworkers Linda Lane Magallon and Barbara Shor suggest *mutual dreaming* as a catchall term to cover all forms of synchronous or shared dreaming; see their essay "Shared Dreaming: Joining Together in the Dreamtime," in Stanley Krippner, ed., *Dreamtime and Dreamwork* (Los Angeles: Jeremy P. Tarcher, 1990). I prefer the phrase *interactive dreaming*.

13. W. Y. Evans-Wentz, ed., *The Tibetan Book of the Dead* (New York: Oxford University Press, 1960).

14. Morton T. Kelsey, *God, Dreams and Revelation* (Minneapolis: Augsburg Press, 1974), 264–65.

15. In the wake of Raymond Moody's *Life after Life* (Atlanta: Mockingbird Press, 1975), there have been a flock of accounts of visionary journeys reported during "near-death experience" (NDE). It is not necessary to suffer life-

threatening illness to make a conscious dream journey to explore the condition of the soul after death.

16. Malidoma Somé, *Of Water and the Spirit* (New York: Jeremy P. Tarcher/Putnam, 1994). On the Axis Mundi in world traditions, see Roger Cook, *The Tree of Life* (New York: Thames & Hudson, 1988); Nathaniel Altman, *Sacred Trees* (San Francisco: Sierra Club, 1994); and Moyra Caldecott, *Myths of the Sacred Tree* (Rochester, Vt.: Destiny Books, 1993).

➤ CHAPTER 5: SHAMANIC DREAMING

1. Bruce Carpenter and Stanley Krippner, "Spice Island Shaman: A Torajan Healer in Sulawesi," *Shaman's Drum* (midfall 1989).

2. Joan Halifax, *Shaman: The Wounded Healer* (New York: Crossroad, 1982), 72.

3. Adrian K. Boshier, "African Apprenticeship," in A. Agoff and D. Barth, eds., *Parapsychology and Anthropology* (New York: Parapsychology Foundation, 1974), 273–93.

4. Marius Barbeau, *Medicine Men of the Pacific Coast, Bulletin 152* (National Museum of Man, Ottawa) (1958).

5. A. P. Elkin, *Aboriginal Men of High Degree,* 2nd ed. (New York: St. Martin's Press, 1978), 77–78.

6. Ibid., 142–43.

7. C. G. Jung, *Memories, Dreams, Reflections,* ed. Aniela Jaffe, trans. Richard and Clara Winston (New York: Vintage Books, 1965), 183.

8. The fullest account of Jung's Ugandan experience is in Laurens van der Post, *Jung and the Story of Our Time* (New York: Vintage Books, 1977).

9. Mircea Eliade, *Shamanism: Archaic Techniques of Ecstasy,* trans. Willard R. Trask (Princeton: Bollingen Press, 1972), 4, 495.

10. Melinda C. Maxfield, "Effects of Rhythmic Drumming on EEG and Subjective Experience" (Ph.D. diss., Institute of Transpersonal Psychology, Menlo Park, Calif., 1990).

11. On traditional pathworking images and guided visualizations, see Dolores Ashcroft-Nowicki, *Highways of the Mind: The Art and History of Pathworking* (Wellingborough: Aquarian Press, 1987). Pathworking exercises based on the attribution of the major arcana of the tarot to the Cabalistic Tree of Life can be very powerful if your basic attunement is to the Western Mystery traditions, but I would not recommend combining these with shamanic drumming.

12. A. Leo Oppenheim, *The Interpretation of Dreams in the Ancient Near East* (Philadelphia: American Philosophical Society, 1956), 304.

13. Ibid., 218.

14. William N. Fenton, *The Iroquois Eagle Dance: An Offshoot of the Calumet Dance* (Washington, D.C.: Bureau of American Ethnology, 1953), 119.

15. Cf. Jesse J. Cornplanter, *Legends of the Longhouse* (Philadelphia and New York: Lippincott, 1938) and William N. Fenton, *The False Faces of the Iroquois* (Norman, Okla.: University of Oklahoma Press, 1987).

16. Reuben Gold Thwaites, ed., *The Jesuit Relations and Allied Documents* [*JR*], 73 vols. (Cleveland, Ohio: Burrows Bros., 1896–1901), 53:251–53.

17. The source is Father Jacques Frémin (1628–91), a Jesuit who traveled in Seneca country. *JR* 54:101.

18. *JR* 23:171–73.

19. C. G. Jung, *Synchronicity: An Acausal Connecting Principle,* trans. R. F. C. Hull, Bollingen Series (Princeton: Princeton University Press, 1971) and Jung's foreword to Richard Wilhelm's translation of *The I Ching or Book of Changes,* Bollingen Series (Princeton: Princeton University Press, 1990), are the great psychologist's clearest statements on the principle of synchronicity. Jean Shinoda Bolen, *The Tao of Psychology* (San Francisco: Harper & Row, 1979), is a delightful introduction to the theme. F. David Peat, *Synchronicity: The Bridge Between Matter and Mind* (New York: Bantam, 1988), shows how the observation of coincidence may give us experiential insight into the hypotheses of quantum physics.

20. Karl Kerenyi, *Hermes, Guide of Souls* (Dallas: Spring Publications, 1987), honors the god in his many guises.

21. My account of the oracle at Pharai is based on a tantalizing paragraph in Pausanias, *Description of Greece,* 2 vols., trans. Arthur Shilleto (London: Bohn's Classical Library, 1886), 2:46.

━ CHAPTER 6: USING DREAM RADAR

1. Philip H. King, "Healing the Healer: The Functions and Uses of Nurses' Dreams" (paper presented at the XI conference of the Association for the Study of Dreams, Leiden University, Netherlands, 1994).

2. The term *ESP* came into wide circulation through the pioneer work of J. B. Rhine and his wife, Louisa E. Rhine, at their Parapsychological Laboratory at Duke University; see Louise E. Rhine, *ESP in Life and Lab: Tracing Hidden Channels* (New York: Collier Books, 1969). I prefer to use the term *hypersensory perception* for several reasons: (1) Some of the phenomena attributed to ESP may be the product of sensory functioning beyond the normal human spectrum. (2) Some ESP sightings may actually be the result of journeying in the dreambody, as in Marion Zimmer Bradley's novel *The House Between the Worlds* (New York: Ballantine, 1981), in which the subject of a telepathy experiment is

able to perform flawlessly because he is able to slip out of his physical body and look at the cards inside the sender's booth. Though woven of much finer stuff than the physical body, the dreambody does have substance and sensory faculties. (3) We have inner senses as well as outer senses. The old Scots name for the power of clairvoyance is not the *second sight* but simply, *the Sight*.

3. Mrs. Atlay wrote an account of her experiences that Horace G. Hutchinson published in *Dreams and Their Meanings* (London: Longmans, 1901). Cf. Edmund Gurney, F. W. H. Myers, and Frank Podmore, *Phantasms of the Living*, ed. Mrs. Henry Sidgwick (New York: Dutton, 1918). Myers coined the term *telepathy*, which literally means "fellow-feeling at a distance."

4. Ward Hill Lamon's account, the primary source on Abraham Lincoln's famous dream, is reprinted in Stephen Brook, ed., *The Oxford Book of Dreams* (London, 1992), 143–44. Lincoln is said to have "attributed a prophetic quality to all his dreams"; W. H. Sabine, *Second Sight in Daily Life* (London: Allen & Unwin, 1951), 83 n. For further accounts of dream precognition in history, see Brian Inglis, *The Power of Dreams* (London: Paladin, 1988); Loyd Auerbach, *Psychic Dreaming* (New York: Warner, 1991); and Martin Ebon, *Prophecy in Our Time* (New York: New American Library, 1968).

5. J. W. Dunne, *An Experiment with Time* (London: Macmillan, 1927). Dunne made the important observation that dreams of future events are quite often dreams in which we read or receive news about those events. This bears thinking about. If you have a gift for dream recall, you may have a clear memory of the newspaper story or TV report you saw in your dream; but the reporter may or may not have gotten *his* story right. The "future" event may be reading the paper's account of an event that has already taken place, as in Dunne's dream of the volcanic eruption in Martinique.

6. Montague Ullman and Stanley Krippner, *Dream Studies and Telepathy: An Experimental Approach* (New York: Parapsychology Foundation, 1970). See also the authors' subsequent book (with Alan Vaughan), *Dream Telepathy* (London: Turnstone Books, 1973).

7. My version of Cambyses' dream is based on Book III of Herodotus, *The Histories,* trans. Aubrey de Selincourt (Harmondsworth: Penguin Books, 1983).

8. J. B. Priestley, *Man and Time* (London: Aldus Books, 1964), 258.

9. Fred Alan Wolf, a quantum physicist who had studied with shamans, explores some of these themes in *The Dreaming Universe* (New York: Simon & Schuster, 1994).

10. Sir Laurens van der Post, *The Lost World of the Kalahari* (Harmondsworth: Penguin, 1962).

⟶ CHAPTER 7: DREAMS OF THE DEPARTED

1. John Lame Deer and Richard Erdoes, *Lame Deer, Seeker of Visions* (New York: Pocket Books, 1976).

2. Cf. Raymond Moody, *The Light Beyond* (New York: Bantam, 1988) and Betty J. Eadie, *Embraced by the Light* (Placerville, Calif.: Gold Leaf, 1992).

3. Patricia Garfield, "Dream Messages from the Dead" (paper delivered at XI conference of the Association for the Study of Dreams, Leiden University, 1994).

4. My account of the dialogue between the shaman and the priest is based on a report from Father Buteux, a seventeenth-century missionary at Tadoussac; cf. *Jesuit Relations* 26:123–27. To convince the Indians of the pains of hell, Buteux's colleague at Onondaga, Father Millet, liked to sound the fire alarm and display slave fetters; *JR* 52:261–63.

5. Elisabeth Kübler-Ross, *On Death and Dying* (New York: Macmillan, 1969).

6. For different perceptions of the second body, or dreambody, see David V. Tansley, *Subtle Body* (London: Thames & Hudson, 1992); Lawrence J. Bendit and Phoebe D. Bendit, *The Etheric Body of Man* (Wheaton, Ill.: Theosophical Publishing House, 1989); and Arnold Mindell, *The Shaman's Body* (Harper San Francisco, 1993).

7. Edith Fiore's *The Unquiet Dead* (New York: Ballantine, 1987) is an important and courageous book and also one of the most *practical* discussions of how to deal with unwanted influences of the dead that I have found in the modern literature.

8. Gregory the Great, *Dialogues* 4:38. This Pope Gregory was a keen collector of out-of-body experiences. Asked to explain the fact that dying people sometimes perceived a ship coming to take them to the Otherworld, Gregory made this astute observation: "The soul needs no vehicle, but it is not surprising that, to a man still placed within his body, there should appear that which he is used to seeing by means of his body, so that he might in this way comprehend where his soul might be taken spiritually." (Quoted in Jacques LeGoff, *The Birth of Purgatory*, trans. Arthur Goldhammer [Chicago: University of Chicago Press, 1984], 206.) There is a rather close analogy with contemporary dreams of boarding an airplane or spacecraft to go to another dimension.

9. Carol Zaleski, *Otherworld Journeys: Accounts of Near-Death Experience in Medieval and Modern Times* (New York: Oxford University Press, 1987). See also I. P. Couliano, *Out of This World: Otherworldly Journeys from Gilgamesh to Albert Einstein* (Boston: Shambhala, 1991).

10. "A person who is involved in what is evil is in contact with hell—is actually there as far as his spirit is concerned. And after death, his greatest craving is to be where his own evil is. Consequently, after death the person himself, not the Lord, casts himself into hell." Emanuel Swedenborg, *Heaven and Hell,* 383–84.

11. Holger Kalweit, *Dreamtime & Inner Space,* trans. Werner Wünsche (Boston: Shambhala, 1988), 67.

12. Tom Cowan, *Fire in the Head: Shamanism and the Celtic Spirit* (Harper San Francisco, 1993).

13. Robert Moss, "Blackrobes and Dreamers," *Shaman's Drum* 28 (1992). See also my paper "Missionaries and Magicians: The Jesuit Encounter with Native American Shamans on New England's Colonial Frontier," in Peter Benes, ed., *Wonders of the Invisible World: 1600–1900* (Boston: Dublin Seminar for New England Folklife, Boston University, 1995).

➤ CHAPTER 8: DREAM GUIDES AND GUARDIAN ANGELS

1. Plotinus (205–70) taught that each of us is an "intellectual cosmos": that every human soul is a spectrum of possible levels of experience, and we choose the level on which we live. Our tutelary spirit, "the daimon allotted to us," exists on the level above the one we have chosen. As we rise to higher levels of spiritual evolution, perhaps through many incarnations (but also through spiritual emergence in this one), the level of personal guardian, or oversoul, also rises. "Our guardian is the next higher faculty of our being. . . . Our guardian is both related to us and independent of us. . . . Our guardian helps us to carry out the destiny we have chosen": *Enneads* III:4. Trans. Kenneth Sylvan Guthrie in Poltinus, *Complete Works,* 4 vols. (London: George Bell and Sons, 1918), 1:235–39.

2. Gary Zukav, *The Seat of the Soul* (New York: Simon & Schuster, 1989).

3. Yaya Diallo, *The Healing Drum: African Wisdom Teachings* (Rochester, Vt.: Destiny Books, 1989), 116–17.

4. Carmen Blacker, "Japan," in Michael Loewe and Carmen Blacker, eds., *Oracles and Divination* (Boulder, Colo.: Shambhala, 1981).

5. Dionysius the Areopagite, *Mystical Theology and the Celestial Hierarchies* (Fintry, Surrey: Shrine of Wisdom, 1965). These mystical works are the foundation of conventional Western angelology. For a larger view, see Maria Parisen, ed., *Angels & Mortals: Their Co-Creative Power* (Wheaton, Ill.: Quest Books, 1990), and Sophy Burnham's beautiful *A Book of Angels* (New York: Ballantine, 1990).

6. Cf. Anne Ross and Don Robins, *The Life and Death of a Druid Prince* (New York: Summit Books, 1989).

7. "Contrary to what the living may think, according to Cayce, not a few of the dreams where the living meet the dead are for the sake of the dead": Harmon H. Bro, *Edgar Cayce on Dreams* (New York: Warner, 1988), 180. Jung reported experiences of instructing "spirits of the departed" and his impression that these entities knew "only what they knew at the moment of death and nothing beyond that. Hence their endeavor to penetrate into life in order to share in the knowledge of men": *Memories, Dreams, Reflections,* 306–8. I have had a number of memorable experiences similar to these.

8. Cf. Edward C. Whitmont and Sylvia Brinton Perera, *Dreams, a Portal to the Source* (London and New York: Routledge, 1990). My favorite book by James Hillman, and a good introduction to his work with archetypal themes, is *The Dream and the Underworld* (New York: Harper & Row, 1979). Jung's seminal work in this area is *The Archetypes and the Collective Unconscious* (Princeton: Bollingen/Princeton University Press, 1980). Rudolf Otto, who coined the word, asserted that the *numinous* is experienced as "objective and outside the self," and that this experience is confirmed by feelings of awe, majesty, and heightened energy or vitality. See Rudolf Otto, *The Idea of the Holy,* trans. John W. Harvey (London: Oxford University Press, 1952), 11, 12–24.

9. The experience of communion with the Higher Self is beautifully conveyed by George Russell (A.E.), one of the leading figures in the Celtic revival:

> Some self of me, higher in the tower of being which reaches up to the heavens, made objective manifestation of its thought; but there were moments when it seemed itself to descend, wrapping its memories of heaven about it like a cloth, and to enter the body, and I knew it more truly myself than that which began in my mother's womb, and that it was antecedent to anything which had my body in the world. [A.E., *The Candle of Vision* (Dorset: Prism Press, 1990).]

"I could not so desire what was not my own" (ibid., #1); this is true soul-remembering. It is also true initiation. In the words of the founder of a modern Mystery school, "When the Higher Self and the lower self become united through the complete absorption of the lower by the higher, true adepthood is gained; this is the Great Initiation, the lesser Divine Union. It is the supreme experience of the incarnate soul." Dion Fortune, *The Mystical Qabalah* (York Beach, Maine: Samuel Weiser, 1984), 291.

10. Raymond de Becker, *The Understanding of Dreams,* trans. Michael Heron (New York: Bell, 1968), 45–47.

11. Joel Covitz, *Visions of the Night: A Study of Jewish Dream Interpretation* (Boston: Shambhala, 1991), 58. "As a messenger of God," Rabbi Covitz notes, "Gabriel has much in common with the Greek god Hermes, who also plays the role of mediating between the conscious and unconscious and hence is associated with dreams": ibid., 59.

12. John A. Sanford, *Dreams: God's Forgotten Language* (New York: Cross-road, 1984).

13. The way the form of the guide is adapted to individual levels of perception is reflected in a telling statement in the gnostic *Acts of Peter*. In this text, the apostle Peter evokes the mystery of the transfiguration, an event that was visible only to some and, even so, not to their ordinary sight. Of this event, Peter can say only, *"Talem eum vidi qualem capere potui"* ("I saw him as I was able to receive him"). His tone now becomes urgent. He tells the people who have gathered, "Perceive in your mind that which ye see not with your eyes." As the people pray, they perceive a brilliant light, visible to the blind as well as to others. The light assumes form. One person sees a child, another a youth, a third sees an elderly man. Everyone present can say, "I saw him as I was able to receive him." Montague Rhodes James, trans., *The Apocryphal New Testament* (New York: Oxford University Press, 1985), 321–23.

14. *Enneads* III:4.

— CHAPTER 9: DREAMS OF HEALING

1. Jeanne Achterberg discussed this case in a 1991 healing-imagery workshop; audiotapes are available from Sounds True Recordings, 735 Walnut Street, Boulder, CO 80302. See also Jeanne Achterberg's splendid book *Imagery in Healing: Shamanism and Modern Medicine* (Boston: Shambhala, 1985).

2. John Selby with Manfred von Lühmann, *Conscious Healing: Visualizations to Boost Your Immune System* (New York: Bantam, 1991).

3. Rosita Arvigo, *Sastun: My Apprenticeship with a Maya Healer* (Harper San Francisco, 1994).

4. Remarks by Stanley Krippner at a "personal mythology" workshop during the X conference of the Association for the Study of Dreams, Santa Fe, 1993. See Stanley Krippner and Alberto Villoldo, *The Realms of Healing* (Millbrae, Calif.: Celestial Arts, 1976); also David Feinstein and Stanley Krippner, *Personal Mythology* (Los Angeles: Jeremy P. Tarcher/Perigee, 1988).

5. Lani Leary, *Healing Hands: Three Meditations for Healing through the Human Energy Field* (1990). Audiocassette available from Sounds True Recordings, 735 Walnut Street, Boulder, CO 80302.

6. Barbara Ann Brennan, *Hands of Light: A Guide to Healing through the Human Energy Field* (New York: Bantam, 1988).

7. Carlos Castaneda, *The Art of Dreaming* (New York: Harper Collins, 1993).

8. Sandra Ingerman, *Soul Retrieval: Mending the Fragmented Self* (Harper San Francisco, 1991) and *Welcome Home: Life after Healing* (Harper San Francisco, 1994).

9. Dion Fortune, *Psychic Self-Defence* (Wellingborough: Aquarian Press, 1957).

10. C. A. Meier, *Healing Dream and Ritual* (Zurich: Daimon Verlag, 1989).

11. Jane Ellen Harrison, *Prolegomena to the Study of Greek Religion* (London: Merlin Press, 1980), 165–83.

12. Deirdre Barrett, "Dreams in Multiple Personality," in her forthcoming *Trauma and Dreams* (Cambridge, Mass.: Harvard University Press, in press). Barrett notes of these cases: "It is hard to say whether the integration truly occurred in the dream or was merely reflected by it."

13. Tanya Wilkinson, "Synchronous Dreaming in Dyadic Relationships" (paper presented at X conference of the Association for the Study of Dreams, Santa Fe, 1993).

⟶ CHAPTER 10: THE CREATIVE POWER OF DREAMS

1. P. D. Ouspensky, *Strange Life of Ivan Osokin* (London: Arkana, 1987), is a marvelous fictional introduction to the possibility that dreams may be "memories of the future."

2. Alan Siegel, *Dreams That Can Change Your Life* (New York: Berkeley, 1992), 85–94.

3. Ibid., 16.

4. Henry Corbin, "The Visionary Dream in Islamic Spirituality," in von Grünebaum and Caillois, eds., *The Dream and Human Societies,* 408.

5. Artemidorus, *The Interpretation of Dreams,* 17.

6. Heimholtz, a physicist, based his analysis of the creative process on his observation of how his own discoveries had emerged. Just as dreaming is a natural environment for creative synthesis, dreamwork reinforces the personal characteristics associated with high creativity, which Carl Rogers identified as (1) openness to experience, including tolerance of ambiguity and the willingness to suspend judgment and prior beliefs; (2) the possession of an internal source of valuation—i.e., not leaving it up to other people to decide what something is worth; and (3) the ability to play. See Rogers, *On Becoming a Person* (Boston: Houghton Mifflin, 1961). To borrow a phrase from Mihaly Csikszentmihalyi, dreamwork encourages the emergence of the "autotelic personality" who is also

the artist and creator in each of us; *Flow: The Psychology of Optimal Experience* (New York: Harper & Row, 1990), 83–89. For some fun creativity games, see Jill Morris, *Creative Breakthroughs: Tap the Power of Your Unconscious Mind* (New York: Warner, 1992).

7. *Oxford Book of Dreams*, 134–35.

8. Otto Loewi, "An Autobiographical Sketch," *Perspectives in Biology and Medicine* 4 (1960).

9. The most reliable account of the dream that led Giuseppe Tartini to compose his "Devil's Sonata" is probably that in Havelock Ellis, *The World of Dreams* (London: Constable, 1911). Billy Joel discussed the role of dreams in his musical compositions in a recent American TV special.

10. Marie-Louise von Franz, "The Dream of Descartes," in her collection *Dreams* (Boston: Shambhala, 1991).

11. Robert L. Van de Castle, *Our Dreaming Mind* (New York: Ballantine, 1994), 37.

12. Robert Louis Stevenson described the role of dreams and dreamlike states in the gestation of his stories in "A Chapter on Dreams" in his *Memories and Portraits* (New York: Scribner, 1925). He gave the "little people," his dream friends, credit for his best ideas.

13. Kekulé's breakthrough, which has been described as "the most brilliant piece of prediction to be found in the whole range of organic chemistry," came in a twilight state of consciousness, while he was dozing by the fire. He reported the circumstances to the German Chemical Society in 1890. Andreas Mavromatis observes that "it was under the special conditions prevailing in hypnagogia that a number of perceptual experiences came together and became relevant within a particular framework"; see his *Hypnagogia: The Unique State of Consciousness between Wakefulness and Sleep* (London and New York: Routledge, 1987), 193.

14. Paul Tholey, "Techniques for Inducing and Maintaining Lucid Dreams," *Perceptual and Motor Skills* 57 (1983). Tholey's work with athletes, especially skiers, is discussed in LaBerge, *Exploring the World of Lucid Dreaming*.

15. Rollo May, *The Courage to Create* (New York: Norton, 1975), 61–62.

16. Julia Cameron with Mark Bryan, *The Artist's Way* (New York: Jeremy P. Tarcher/Putnam, 1992).

17. Marie-Louise von Franz, *Projection and Re-Collection in Jungian Psychology*, trans. W. H. Kennedy (La Salle, Ill.: Open Court, 1985), 145.

18. Erich Neumann, *The Place of Creation* (Princeton: Bollingen/Princeton University Press, 1989), 137.

19. Yeats's account of the "crisis" of genius is quoted in George Mills Harper, ed., *Yeats and the Occult* (Toronto: Macmillan, 1975), 102. Arthur Koestler observed that the key to creative action is association between different levels of

consciousness: "In problem-solving pre- and extra-conscious guidance makes itself felt increasingly as the difficulty increases. But in the truly creative act both in science and art, underground levels of the hierarchy which are normally inhibited in the waking state play a decisive part"; see Koestler, *The Act of Creation* (London: Arkana, 1989), 658. Dreaming opens a direct channel to those "underground levels"; the ability to shift to a state of conscious dreaming is also the ability to switch into creative flow.

FURTHER READING

⟶ GENERAL

This is a general list of books I have found helpful that are mostly available in recent editions. In later sections I discuss works that are especially relevant to the practice of conscious and shamanic dreaming.

A.E. (George Russell). *The Candle of Vision.* Bridport, Dorset: Prism Press, 1990.

Achterberg, Jeanne. *Imagery in Healing.* Boston: Shambhala, 1985.

Achterberg, Jeanne, with Barbara Dossey and Leslie Kolkmeier. *Rituals of Healing.* New York: Bantam, 1994.

Artemidorus. *The Interpretation of Dreams: Oneirocritica.* Trans. R. J. White. Park Ridge, N.J.: Noyes Press, 1975.

Ashcroft-Nowicki, Dolores. *Highways of the Mind.* Wellingborough: Aquarian Press, 1987.

Assagioli, Roberto. *Psychosynthesis.* New York: Arkana, 1993.

Auerbach, Loyd. *Psychic Dreaming.* New York: Warner, 1991.

Becker, Raymond de, *The Understanding of Dreams.* Trans. Michael Heron. New York: Bell, 1968.

Bolen, Jean Shinoda. *The Tao of Psychology.* San Francisco: Harper & Row, 1979.

Borysenko, Joan. *Fire in the Soul.* New York: Warner, 1993.

Bosnak, Robert. *A Little Course in Dreams.* Boston: Shambhala, 1988.

Brennan, Barbara Ann. *Hands of Light: A Guide to Healing through the Human Energy Field.* New York: Bantam, 1988.

Bro, Harmon H. *Edgar Cayce on Dreams.* New York: Warner, 1988.

Brook, Stephen, ed. *The Oxford Book of Dreams.* Oxford and New York: Oxford University Press, 1992.

Browne, Sir Thomas. *Religio Medici* (1635). London: Dent, 1937.

Bryant, Dorothy. *The Kin of Ata Are Waiting for You.* New York and Berkeley: Random House/Moon Books, 1971.

Bulkeley, Kelly. *The Wilderness of Dreams.* Albany: State University of New York Press, 1994.

Burnham, Sophy. *A Book of Angels.* New York: Ballantine, 1990.

Cameron, Julia, with Mark Bryan. *The Artist's Way.* New York: Jeremy P. Tarcher/Putnam, 1992.

Chaney, Earlyne. *The Mystery of Death and Dying.* York Beach, Maine: Samuel Weiser, 1988.

Couliano, I. P. *Out of This World: Otherworldly Journeys from Gilgamesh to Albert Einstein.* Boston: Shambhala, 1991.

Covitz, Joel. *Visions of the Night: A Study of Jewish Dream Interpretation.* Boston: Shambhala, 1990.

Delaney, Gail. *Living Your Dreams.* New York: Harper & Row, 1979.

————. *Sexual Dreams.* New York: Fawcett Columbine, 1994.

Dodds, E. R. *The Greeks and the Irrational.* Berkeley: University of California Press, 1951.

Doore, Gary, ed. *What Survives? Contemporary Explorations of Life after Death.* Los Angeles: Jeremy P. Tarcher, 1990.

Dossey, Larry. *Recovering the Soul.* New York: Bantam, 1989.

————. *Meaning and Medicine.* New York: Bantam, 1991.

Duerr, Hans Peter. *Dreamtime.* Trans. Felicitas Goodman. Oxford and New York: Basil Blackwell, 1985.

Dunne, J. W. *An Experiment with Time.* New York: Macmillan, 1927.

Edgar, Iain R. *Dreamwork, Anthropology and the Caring Professions.* Aldershot: Avebury, 1995.

Epel, Naomi. *Writers Dreaming.* New York: Carol Southern Books, 1993.

Estés, Clarissa Pinkola. *Women Who Run with the Wolves.* New York: Ballantine, 1992.

Evans, Christopher. *Landscapes of the Night.* New York: Viking, 1984.

Faraday, Ann. *Dream Power.* New York: Coward McCann, 1972.

————. *The Dream Game.* New York: Harper Perennial, 1976.

Feinstein, David, and Stanley Krippner. *Personal Mythology.* Los Angeles: Jeremy P. Tarcher, 1988.

Fiore, Edith. *The Unquiet Dead.* New York: Ballantine, 1987.

Fontana, David. *The Secret Language of Dreams.* San Francisco: Chronicle Books, 1994.

Fortune, Dion. *Psychic Self-Defence.* Wellingborough: Aquarian Press, 1957.

————. *Moon Magic.* York Beach, Maine: Samuel Weiser, 1990.

Freud, Sigmund. *The Interpretation of Dreams.* Trans. John Strachey. New York: Avon, 1965.

Garfield, Patricia. *Creative Dreaming.* New York: Ballantine, 1976.

————. *Pathway to Ecstasy.* New York: Prentice Hall, 1989.

————. *The Healing Power of Dreams.* New York: Fireside, 1992.

Gawain, Shakti. *Creative Visualization.* New York: Bantam, 1982.

Gendlin, Eugene T. *Let Your Body Interpret Your Dreams.* La Salle, Ill.: Chiron/Open Court, 1986.

Gibo, Aiko. *Finding Your Guardian Spirit.* Tokyo: Kodansha, 1992.

Greene, Graham. *A World of My Own: A Dream Diary.* London: Reinhardt/Viking, 1992.

Grof, Stanislav, and Christina Stanislav, eds. *Spiritual Emergency.* Los Angeles: Jeremy P. Tarcher, 1989.

Guss, David M., ed. *The Language of the Birds.* San Francisco: North Point Press, 1985.

Hall, James A. *Patterns of Dreaming.* Boston: Shambhala, 1991.

Hartmann, Ernest. *The Nightmare.* New York: Basic Books, 1984.

Hillman, James. *The Dream and the Underworld.* New York: Harper & Row, 1979.

Houston, Jean. *The Possible Human.* Los Angeles: Jeremy P. Tarcher, 1982.

———. *The Hero and the Goddess.* New York: Ballantine, 1992.

Hunt, Harry T. *The Multiplicity of Dreams.* New Haven: Yale University Press, 1989.

Inglis, Brian. *The Power of Dreams.* London: Paladin, 1988.

Jaffe, Aniela. *Apparitions and Precognition.* New York: University Books, 1963.

James, William. *The Varieties of Religious Experience.* London: Longmans, 1952.

Joy, W. Brugh. *Joy's Way.* Los Angeles: Jeremy P. Tarcher, 1979.

Jung, C. G. *Memories, Dreams, Reflections.* Ed. Aniela Jaffe. Trans. Richard Winston and Clara Winston. New York: Vintage, 1965.

———. *Synchronicity, an Acausal Connecting Principle.* Trans. R. F. C. Hull. Princeton: Bollingen/Princeton University Press, 1973.

———. *Dreams.* Trans. R. F. C. Hull. Princeton: Bollingen/Princeton University Press, 1974.

———. *The Archetypes and the Collective Unconscious.* Trans. R. F. C. Hull. Princeton: Bollingen/Princeton University Press, 1980.

Jung, C. G. et al. *Man and His Symbols.* London: Aldus Books, 1964.

Jussek, Eugene G. *Reaching for the Oversoul.* York Beach, Maine: Nicolas-Hays, 1994.

Kaplan-Williams, Strephon. *The Elements of Dreamwork.* Rockport, Mass.: Element, 1991.

———. *Dreamworking.* Oslo, Norway: Journey Press, 1992.

Kast, Verena. *The Creative Leap.* Wilmette, Ill.: Chiron, 1992.

Kelsey, Morton. *Dreams: A Way to Listen to God.* New York/Mahwah, N.J.: Paulist Press, 1988.

Kerenyi, Karl. *Hermes, Guide of Souls.* Dallas: Spring Publications, 1987.

Koestler, Arthur. *The Act of Creation.* London: Arkana, 1989.

Kramer, Kenneth P. *Death Dreams.* Mahwah, N.J.: Paulist Press, 1993.

Krippner, Stanley, ed. *Dreamtime and Dreamwork: Decoding the Language of the Night Dream.* Los Angeles: Jeremy P. Tarcher, 1990.

Krippner, Stanley, and Joseph Dillard. *Dreamworking.* Buffalo, N.Y.: Bearly Limited, 1987.

Kübler-Ross, Elisabeth. *On Death and Dying.* New York: Macmillan, 1969.

———. *Death. The Final Stage of Growth.* New York: Touchstone, 1986.

Kurtz, Ernest, and Katherine Ketcham. *The Spirituality of Imperfection.* New York: Bantam, 1992.

Laski, Marghanita. *Ecstasy in Secular and Religious Experiences.* Los Angeles: Jeremy P. Tarcher, 1990.

Layard, John. *The Lady and the Hare: A Study in the Healing Power of Dreams.* Boston: Shambhala, 1988.

Luke, Helen M. *Dark Wood to White Rose: Journey and Transformation in Dante's Divine Comedy.* New York: Parabola, 1989.

MacDonald, George. *The Portent: A Story of the Inner Vision of the Highlanders Commonly Called the Second Sight.* Harper San Francisco, 1979.

MacKenzie, Norman. *Dreams and Dreaming.* London: Bloomsbury Books, 1989.

Matthews, Caitlin, and John Matthews. *The Western Way,* 2 vols. London: Arkana, 1985–86.

Mavromatis, Andreas. *Hypnagogia.* London: Routledge, 1987.

May, Rollo. *The Courage to Create.* New York: Norton, 1975.

Mead, G. R. S. *Thrice Greatest Hermes: Studies in Hellenistic Theosophy and Gnosis.* York Beach, Maine: Samuel Weiser, 1992.

Meier, C. A. *Healing Dream and Ritual.* Zurich: Daimon Verlag, 1989.

Mindell, Arnold. *Dreambody.* Boston: Sigo Press, 1982.

Moore, Robin. *Awakening the Hidden Storyteller.* Boston: Shambhala, 1991.

Moore, Thomas. *Care of the Soul.* New York: Harper Collins, 1992.

Morris, Jill. *Creative Breakthroughs.* New York: Warner, 1992.

Naparstek, Belleruth. *Staying Well with Guided Imagery.* New York: Warner, 1994.

O'Flaherty, Wendy Doniger. *Dreams, Illusion and Other Realities.* Chicago and Leiden: University of Chicago Press, 1984.

Oppenheim, A. Leo. *The Interpretation of Dreams in the Ancient Near East.* Philadelphia: American Philosophical Society, 1956.

Ouspensky, P. D. *A New Model of the Universe.* New York: Vintage, 1971.

———. *Strange Life of Ivan Osokin.* London: Arkana, 1987.

Parisen, Maria, ed., *Angels & Mortals: Their Co-Creative Power.* Wheaton, Ill.: Quest Books, 1990.

Peat, F. David. *Synchronicity: The Bridge between Matter and Mind.* New York: Bantam, 1987.

Plotinus. *Collected Works,* 4 vols. Trans. Kenneth Sylvan Guthrie. London: George Bell, 1918.

Priestley, J. B. *Man and Time.* London: Aldus Books, 1964.

Roberts, Jane. *Dreams, "Evolution" and Value Fulfillment.* New York: Prentice Hall, 1986.

———. *Dreams and Projection of Consciousness.* Walpole, N.H.: Stillpoint, 1986.

———. *Seth Speaks.* New York: Prentice Hall, 1987.

Sanford, John A. *Dreams: God's Forgotten Language.* New York: Crossroad, 1984.

Selby, John, with Manfred von Lühmann. *Conscious Healing.* New York: Bantam, 1991.

Siegel, Alan B. *Dreams That Can Change Your Life.* New York: Berkley, 1992.

Swedenborg, Emanuel. *Heaven and Hell.* Trans. George F. Dole. New York: Swedenborg Foundation, 1976.

Taylor, Jeremy. *Where People Fly and Water Runs Uphill.* New York: Warner, 1993.

Tedlock, Barbara, ed. *Dreaming: Anthropological and Psychological Perspectives.* Santa Fe: School of American Research Press, 1992.

Ullman, Montague, and Stanley Krippner. *Dream Studies and Telepathy.* New York: Parapsychology Foundation, 1970.

Ullman, Montague, with Stanley Krippner and Alan Vaughan. *Dream Telepathy.* London: Turnstone, 1973.

Ullman, Montague, and Nan Zimmerman. *Working with Dreams.* Los Angeles: Jeremy P. Tarcher, 1985.

Van de Castle, Robert L. *Our Dreaming Mind.* New York: Ballantine, 1994.

van der Post, Sir Laurens. *The Lost World of the Kalahari.* London: Penguin, 1962.

———. *Jung and the Story of Our Time.* New York: Vintage, 1977.

van Ouwerkerk, Aad. *The Four Elements of the Dream.* Wageningen, Netherlands: Four Elements, 1993.

Vaughan, Frances E. *Awakening Intuition.* New York: Anchor, 1979.

Vaughan-Lee. *The Lover & the Serpent: Dreamwork within a Sufi Tradition.* Shaftesbury and Rockport: Element, 1991.

von Franz, Marie-Louise. *On Divination and Synchronicity.* Toronto: Inner City Books, 1980.

———. *On Dreams and Death.* Boston: Shambhala, 1987.

———. *Projection and Re-Collection in Jungian Psychology.* La Salle, Ill.: Open Court, 1990.

————. *Dreams.* Boston: Shambhala, 1991.

von Grünebaum, G. E., and Roger Caillois, eds. *The Dream and Human Societies.* Berkeley: University of California Press, 1966.

Whitmont, Edward C., and Sylvia Brinton Perera. *Dreams, a Portal to the Source.* London and New York: Routledge, 1989.

Wilber, Ken. *No Boundary.* Boston: Shambhala, 1985.

————, ed. *Quantum Questions.* Boston: Shambhala, 1985.

Wiseman, Anne Sayre. *Nightmare Help.* Berkeley: Ten Speed Press, 1989.

Wolf, Fred Alan. *The Dreaming Universe.* New York: Simon and Schuster, 1994.

Zaleski, Carol. *Otherworld Journeys: Accounts of Near-Death Experience in Medieval and Modern Times.* New York: Oxford University Press, 1987.

Zukav, Gary. *The Seat of the Soul.* New York: Simon and Schuster, 1989.

⟶ ON CONSCIOUS DREAMING

Interesting studies of "lucid" dreaming include Celia Green, *Lucid Dreams* (London: Hamish Hamilton, 1968); Stephen LaBerge, *Lucid Dreaming: The Power of Being Awake and Aware in Your Dreams* (Los Angeles, Jeremy P. Tarcher, 1985), and its sequel (written with Howard Rheingold), *Exploring the World of Lucid Dreaming* (New York: Ballantine, 1992); and Kenneth Kelzer's personal report, *The Sun and the Shadow: My Experiment with Lucid Dreaming* (Virginia Beach, A.R.E. Press, 1987).

For a pointed critique of "control dreaming," see Strephon Kaplan-Williams, *Elements of Dreamwork* (Shaftesbury, Dorset: Element Books, 1990).

Of the many books by Carlos Castaneda that touch on the possibilities of conscious dreaming, the best for beginners may be *Journey to Ixtlan: The Lessons of Don Juan* (New York: Simon and Schuster, 1972). Florinda Donner's *Being-in-Dreaming* (Harper San Francisco, 1991) is a personal account by one of Castaneda's circle and rings truer than Castaneda's curious recent book, *The Art of Dreaming* (New York: Harper Collins, 1993).

On conscious dreaming as a discipline in Tibetan dream yoga, see W. Y. Evans-Wentz, *Tibetan Yoga and Secret Doctrines* (New York: Oxford University Press, 1958), and Namkai Norbu, *Dream Yoga and the Practice of Natural Light* (Ithaca, N.Y.: Snow Lion, 1992).

On out-of-body experience, by far the sanest, most practical, and most convincing book is Robert Monroe's *Journey out of the Body,* originally published in 1971; see also his *Far Journeys* (New York: Doubleday, 1985) and *Ultimate Journey* (New York: Doubleday, 1994). Earlier personal accounts include Oliver Fox, *Astral Projection: A Record of Out-of-the-Body Experiences* (1920) (Secaucus, N.J.: Citadel Press, 1962); Sylvan Muldoon and Hereward Carrington, *The Projection of the Astral Body* (1929) (York Beach, Maine: Samuel

Weiser, 1987); and Peter Richelieu, *A Soul's Journey* (1953) (Wellingborough: Aquarian Press, 1987), which is notable for its ascent to higher spiritual levels. J. H. Brennan, *The Astral Projection Workbook* (New York: Sterling, 1990), explains a number of Western esoteric techniques, including the "body of light" method, which involves visualizing a second self and transferring consciousness to it. David V. Tansley, *Subtle Body: Essence and Shadow* (London: Thames and Hudson, 1992), includes interesting reflections on the nature of the dreambody, as does Alice Bailey, *Telepathy and the Etheric Vehicle* (New York: Lucis, 1971).

The "near-death" experience is the type of out-of-body experience most widely recognized in Western society, thanks in part to the work of Dr. Raymond Moody; see his *Life After Life* (Atlanta: Mockingbird Press, 1975) and *The Light Beyond* (New York: Bantam, 1988). Betty J. Eadie describes her personal experience in *Embraced by the Light* (Placerville, Calif.: Gold Leaf Press, 1992). Such accounts have an ancient pedigree, as described in Carol Zaleski, *Otherworld Journeys: Accounts of Near-Death Experiences in Medieval and Modern Times* (New York: Oxford University Press, 1987). Sir William Barrett's *Death-Bed Visions: The Psychical Experiences of the Dying* (Wellingborough: Aquarian Press, 1986) was first published in 1926.

━ ON SHAMANIC DREAMING

One of the best introductions to shamanism I have read is by a psychologist, Roger N. Walsh, *The Spirit of Shamanism* (New York: Jeremy P. Tarcher/ Perigee, 1990). Mircea Eliade's *Shamanism: Archaic Techniques of Ecstasy,* first published in French in 1951, remains an indispensable guide. Other good introductory surveys include Joan Halifax, *Shaman: The Wounded Healer* (New York: Crossroad, 1982); Gary Doore, ed., *Shaman's Path: Healing, Personal Growth and Empowerment* (Boston: Shambhala, 1988), Shirley Nicholson, ed., *Shamanism: An Expanded View of Reality* (Wheaton, Ill.: Theosophical Publishing House, 1987); and Holger Kalweit, *Dreamtime & Inner Space: The World of the Shaman,* trans. Werner Wunsche (Boston: Shambhala, 1988). Joan Halifax's anthology *Shamanic Voices* (New York: Dutton, 1979) contains firsthand accounts of shamanic dream callings and initiations from many indigenous cultures, Nevill Drury, *The Shaman and the Magician* (London: Arkana, 1987), compares shamanic journeying techniques with those of Western esoteric orders.

Michael Harner describes his basic approach to journeywork in *The Way of the Shaman,* first published in 1980, and his prior experiences among the Indians of eastern Ecuador in *The Jivaro: People of the Sacred Waterfalls* (Berkeley: University of California Press, 1984). Other valuable guides to shamanic techniques include Sandra Ingerman, *Soul Retrieval* (Harper San Francisco, 1991); Serge Kahili King, *Urban Shaman* (New York: Fireside, 1990); and Felicitas D. Goodman, *Where the Spirits Ride the Wind: Trance Journeys and Other Ecstatic Experiences* (Bloomington: University of Indiana Press, 1990). Hank Wesselman, *Spiritwalker* (New York: Bantam, 1995), is a fascinating personal account of visionary experiences highly relevant to the shaman's way of "folding time."

The literature on tribal shamanism is immense. Books I found especially helpful in understanding Native American traditions include Roger A. Grim, *The Shaman: Patterns of Religious Healing among the Ojibway Indians* (Norman and London: University of Oklahoma Press, 1987); Thomas E. Mails, *Fools Crow: Wisdom and Power* (Tulsa, Okla.: Council Oak Books, 1991); Medicine Grizzlybear Lake, *Native Healer* (Wheaton, Ill.: Quest Books, 1991); Peggy V. Beck, Anna Lee Walters, and Nia Francisco, *The Sacred: Ways of Knowledge, Sources of Life* (Tsaile, Ariz.: Navajo Community College Press, 1992); and the justly celebrated John G. Neihardt, *Black Elk Speaks* (New York: Pocket Books, 1972). On the shamanic dream practices of the Iroquois, see my novel *The Firekeeper* (New York: Forge, 1995) and my essays "Black Robes and Dreamers: Jesuit Reports on the Shamanic Dream Practices of the Northern Iroquoians" in *Shaman's Drum* 28 (summer 1992) and "Missionaries and Magicians" in Peter Benes, ed., *Wonders of the Invisible World* (Boston: Boston University, 1995). My favorite source in this area is a 1724 work by a Jesuit missionary that should probably be recognized as the first "modern" work of anthropology: Father Joseph-François Lafitau, *Customs of the American Indians Compared with the Customs of Primitive Times,* ed. and trans. William N. Fenton and Elizabeth L. Moore (Toronto: Champlain Society, 1974).

Lawrence E. Sullivan, *Icanchu's Drum: An Orientation to Meaning in South American Traditions* (New York: Macmillan, 1988), is an adventurous cross-cultural study that contains an extensive guide to the literature on South American traditions. John Perkins, *The World Is As You Dream It* (Rochester, Vt.: Destiny Books, 1994), reflects a personal odyssey among the shamans of the Amazon and the Andes. Rosita Arvigo, *Sastun: My Apprenticeship with a Maya Healer* (Harper San Francisco, 1994), is a beautiful account of the practice of a Maya *h'men*. F. Bruce Lamb, *Wizard of the Upper Amazon: The Story of Manuel Cordova-Rios* (Boston: Houghton Mifflin, 1974), is one of the better accounts of a shamanic apprenticeship assisted by drugs (in this case, ayahuasca). Other interesting accounts from Central and South America include Heather Valencia and Rolly Kent, *Queen of Dreams: The Story of a Yaqui Dreaming Woman* (New York: Fireside, 1993); Gerardo Reichel-Dolmatoff, *Amazonian Cosmos: The Sexual and Religious Symbolism of the*

Tukano Indians (Chicago: University of Chicago Press, 1974); Barbara Ted-lock, "Zuni and Quiché Dream Sharing and Interpreting," in Tedlock, ed., *Dreaming: Anthropological and Psychological Interpretations* (Santa Fe: School of American Research Press, 1992); and Jon Christopher Crocker, *Vital Souls: Bororo Cosmology, Natural Symbolism and Shamanism* (Tucson: University of Arizona Press, 1985).

The indispensable book on Australian shamanism remains A. P. Elkin, *Aboriginal Men of High Degree* (New York: St. Martin's Press, 1977). In several recent books, including *Messengers of the Gods* (New York: Bell Tower, 1993) and *The Aborigine Tradition* (Shaftesbury and Rockport: Element, 1992), James G. Cowan celebrates tribal teachings. Jennifer Isaacs, ed., *Australian Dreaming* (Sydney: Lansdowne Press, 1987), contains accounts from native elders. Ronald Rose, *Living Magic* (London: Chatto & Windus, 1957), is an inquiry into hypersensory perception among the Aborigines by a hard-nosed investigator. See also Baldwin Spencer and F. J. Gillen, "Aboriginal Medicine Men," in *Shaman's Drum* 14 (1988).

On African traditions, see Malidoma Patrice Somé, *Of Water and Spirit* (New York: Jeremy P. Tarcher/Putnam, 1994); Yaya Diallo and Mitchell Hall, *The Healing Drum: African Wisdom Teachings* (Rochester, Vt.: Destiny Books, 1989); Marcel Griaule, *Conversations with Ogotemmeli: An Introduction to Dogon Religious Ideas* (London and New York: Oxford University Press, 1970); Judith Gleason, *Oya: In Praise of the Goddess* (Boston: Shambhala, 1987); Philip John Neimark, *The Way of the Orisa* (Harper San Francisco, 1993); Awo Fa'lokun Fatunmbi, *Iwapele: Ifa Quest* (New York: Original Publications, 1991) and *Awo: Ifa and the Theology of Orisha Divination* (New York: Original Publications, 1992); and Philip M. Peek, ed., *African Divination System* (Bloomington: Indiana University Press, 1991).

For introductory reading on shamanic practice in Asia, I recommend Carmen Blacker, *The Catalpa Bow: A Study of Shamanistic Practices in Japan* (London: Mandala, 1986); Sudhir Kakar, *Shamans, Mystics and Doctors: A Psychological Inquiry into India and Its Healing Traditions* (Boston: Beacon Press, 1982); Johan Engblom, "Bridge to Heaven: The Korean Mudang as Psychopomp," in *Shaman's Drum* 26 (1992); Edward R. Canda, "Gripped by the Drum: The Korean Tradition of Nongak," in *Shaman's Drum* 33 (1993); Robin Lim, "The Shamanic Healing Practices of Mangku Pohoh," in *Shaman's Drum* 37 (1995); Richard Noone, *In Search of the Dream People* (New York: Morrow, 1972); and Alexandra David-Neel, *Magic and Mystery in Tibet* (New York: University Books, 1965).

For the teachings of a shaman of the West, see Kyriacos C. Markides's remarkable *The Magus of Strovolos* (London and Boston: Arkana, 1985), and its sequel, *Homage to the Sun: The Wisdom of the Magus of Strovolos* (New York and London: Arkana, 1987).

Shamanic dreaming opens a door into ways of being and seeing that were common to all our ancestors. Recent attempts to reconnect with the shamanic elements in Celtic tradition include Tom Cowan, *Fire in the Head: Shamanism and the Celtic Spirit* (Harper San Francisco, 1993); John Matthews, *The Celtic Shaman* (Shaftesbury and Rockport: Element, 1990); and Nikolai Tolstoy, *The Quest for Merlin* (Boston: Little, Brown, 1985). Brian Bates, *The Way of Wyrd: Tales of an Anglo-Saxon Sorcerer* (London: Century Publishing, 1983), performs the same service for Anglo-Saxon tradition, under the mask of fiction. The firsthand account of a seventeenth-century minister's encounters in the spirit worlds of the Scottish highlands confirms that the current interest in these areas may be a return to the source; see R. J. Stewart, ed., *Robert Kirk: Walker Between Worlds* (Shaftesbury, Dorset: Element Books, 1990).

For an excellent overview of shamanic healing techniques, see Stanley Krippner, "The Shaman and Healer and Psychotherapist," in *Voices* (spring 1992). Also Holger Kalweit, *Shamans, Healers and Medicine Men* (Boston: Shambhala, 1992); and Draja Mickaharic, *Spiritual Cleansing* (York Beach, Maine: Samuel Weiser, 1988).

Fred Alan Wolf, *The Eagle's Quest* (New York: Summit Books, 1991), is a physicist's attempt to gain experiential insight into the world of quantum mechanics through shamanic practice.

For the shamanic odysseys of modern Americans, see Tom Brown Jr., *The Vision* (New York: Berkley Books, 1988); Joan Halifax, *The Fruitful Darkness* (Harper San Francisco, 1994); and Kay Cordell Whitaker, *The Reluctant Shaman* (Harper San Francisco, 1991). Perhaps the most important and inspiriting account by a modern Westerner of shamanic calling and initiation inside the dream world is the chapter entitled "Confrontation with the Unconscious" in Jung's *Memories, Dreams, Reflections,* though Jung was guarded in the language he chose to explain his experiences.

RESOURCES

The Association for the Study of Dreams is a lively international gathering of dream explorers whose members range from psychiatrists and anthropologists to artists and shamans. ASD publishes a newsletter and a research quarterly, hosts an annual world conference, and can supply you with further tips on setting up your own dream group. Contact:

> ASD
> PO Box 1600
> Vienna, VA 22183
> Phone: (703) 242-8888

Dream Network is a quarterly that publishes personal contributions from dreamers and a guide to ongoing dream groups in different parts of the United States. Contact:

> Dream Network
> 1337 Powerhouse Lane, Suite 22
> PO Box 1026
> Moab, UT 84532-3031

The Foundation for Shamanic Studies, founded by Michael Harner, sponsors workshops and advanced training programs in shamanism, including Sandra Ingerman's workshops on soul retrieval. FSS also produces drumming tapes. Contact:

> FSS
> PO Box 1939
> Mill Valley, CA 94942
> Fax: (415) 380-8416

Shaman's Drum is an adventurous quarterly magazine with firsthand accounts of shamanic practice, mostly among indigenous peoples. Contact:

> Shaman's Drum
> PO Box 430
> Willits, CA 95490

For information on my own Active Dreaming workshops and training programs, and on future publications, please write to:

> Robert Moss
> Way of the Dreamer
> PO Box 215
> Troy, NY 12181
> Fax: (518) 274-0506

I would welcome your account of any personal experiences you wish to share.

INDEX

ABOUT THE AUTHOR

Robert Moss is a lifelong dream explorer, a shamanic counselor, a bestselling novelist, and a student of the Western Mystery traditions. He has also been a professor of ancient history and philosophy, a foreign correspondent, a magazine editor, and an actor. His fascination with the dreamworlds springs from his early childhood in Australia, where he survived a series of near-death experiences and first encountered the ways of a dreaming people through his friendship with Aborigines. He has worked with his personal dream journals for more than thirty years. For many years, he has taught and practiced Active Dreaming, an original synthesis of modern dreamwork and ancient shamanic practice. Moss introduced these techniques to an international audience of psychologists, healers, and dream explorers at the world conferences of the Association for the Study of Dreams at Leiden University in 1994 and in New York City in 1995. His workshops are popular both nationally and internationally. His twelve books include *The Firekeeper,* which describes the practice of dream prophecy and psychic healing by Native American shamans. He was guided by dreams to his present home in Troy, New York, where he lives with his wife and daughters.